LITHIC DEBITAGE

Lithic Debitage

CONTEXT, FORM, MEANING

Edited by

WILLIAM ANDREFSKY JR.

THE UNIVERSITY OF UTAH PRESS

Salt Lake City

13 12 11 10 09   5 6 7 8 9

LIBRARY OF CONGRESS CATALOGING-IN-PUBLICATION DATA

Lithic debitage : context, form, meaning / edited by William Andrefsky
Jr.
    p.   cm.
Includes bibliographical references (p.   ) and index.
   ISBN 0-87480-679-8 (hardcover : alk. paper)   ISBN 978-0-87480-768-4 (pbk.)
   1. Tools, Prehistoric.   2. Stone implements.   3. Flintknapping.   I.
Andrefsky, William, 1955–   II. Title
   GN799.T6 L56 2001
   930.1'028—dc21   00-012561

Contents

Figures

Tables

Preface and Acknowledgments

In stone tool production technology literature, a detached piece is defined as a portion of rock removed from an objective piece by percussion or pressure. Debitage is defined as a detached piece that is discarded during the reduction process. Until fairly recently these discarded pieces have also been ignored in the analytical literature related to prehistoric stone technology. One of the purposes of this book is to assemble a collection of papers on lithic debitage that: (1) provides a historic perspective on debitage, (2) explores the sources and origins of debitage variation, (3) presents examples of contemporary debitage analysis, and (4) includes alternative opinions about debitage interpretations. In addressing these issues, the collection of papers as a whole shows that some of our basic beliefs about debitage are not necessarily correct and that debitage variability is extremely complex. However, the complexity of debitage is what makes it such an important tool in helping us understand the technological and social processes that account for this complexity.

This volume originally grew from a group of papers presented at the Society for American Archaeology meetings in Chicago in 1999. Since that time the collection of papers has changed with some new additions and with some of the original papers not being included for various reasons. I thank all of those who participated in the 1999 symposium.

I also thank the editorial staff and team of peer reviewers representing the University of Utah Press. They have made my job of editing less of a chore. In particular I would like to thank Jeff Grathwohl for his support, encouragement, and advice. Peter Bleed was very helpful with suggestions and insights—thanks Peter. Mike Shott, who seems to review everything, made valuable contributions with a lengthy report on an earlier version of the manuscript. His advice makes this a better volume. I also thank Robin Gould for her excellent copy-editing skills.

Two other people helped compile and process this document. Without their help I could not have completed this project in a timely manner. I appreciate the help of Ed Knell for working with the computer translations and table preparations along with reference checks and general trouble-shooting. Marilyn Bender also worked with tables, figures, references, and general editing—thanks again.

I

HISTORICAL PERSPECTIVES
ON DEBITAGE ANALYSIS

1

Emerging Directions in Debitage Analysis

WILLIAM ANDREFSKY JR.

Debitage, arguably the most common artifact type found on archaeological sites worldwide, has recently become one of the most controversial and apparently least understood artifact types. After being neglected by researchers for decades as prehistoric trash or debris, debitage has gradually gained importance as an artifact that can help interpret aspects of prehistoric human technology, economy, and organization. With the emergent importance of debitage as an interpretive tool, researchers have begun to systematically examine the variability among debitage specimens and between debitage populations. More importantly, methods have been developed to explore the sources and circumstances associated with debitage variability. As with most emergent areas of inquiry, recent debitage investigations have shown that we know even less than we thought about debitage and that some of the things we believed were true about debitage are wrong or misleading. For these reasons, the following papers have been assembled in an effort to show how natural and cultural conditions affect debitage variability and to show how methodological and theoretical applications can influence the interpretation of debitage variability.

In my opinion, the single most important paper written on debitage analysis in the past 15 years was the Sullivan and Rozen (1985) article calling for verification and replicability. This paper was important, not so much as a new technique of debitage analysis, but as a challenge to researchers. One of the things that made the Sullivan and Rozen paper so important in debitage studies was the immediate, fervent, and continuing response that their challenge has received. Debitage researchers promptly rose to the challenge, first by criticizing some aspects of the paper (Amick and Mauldin 1989; Ensor and Roemer 1989; Prentiss and Romanski 1989) and then by conducting detailed investigations pointed at some of the targets identified by Sullivan and Rozen (Bradbury and Carr 1995; Kuijt et al. 1995; Mauldin 1993). To this day, debitage studies are still organized around some of the techniques, assumptions, and conclusions made in that 1985 paper (Amick and Mauldin 1997; Prentiss 1998; Morrow 1997). As a result of the Sullivan and Rozen challenge, debitage variability is much better understood and debitage analysis has increased in sophistication.

With the increase in attention given to debitage analysis the field has expanded in many different directions and at many different levels of observation. Researchers are able to link certain kinds of debitage characteristics and certain kinds of analysis to behavioral parameters associated with artifact function, production, and use. At the same time, researchers are finding that some of the original assumptions about various kinds of debitage analysis and behavioral correspondence are not always correct. This has not only led to some confusion with regard to the proper or appropriate kinds of analysis to perform, but it has propagated and perpetuated erroneous interpretations about artifact function, production, and use on some sites. With these issues in mind, a brief review of debitage analytical techniques is provided below as a background to the assembled papers. Since there are so many different techniques of debitage analysis available and since debitage has been analyzed at multiple levels, the review is organized on three different scales of observation. Debitage analysis is reviewed first as an aggregate or population level, secondly as individual types, and finally at the attribute level. This review is not a complete coverage of debitage analysis but instead is provided as a technique to conceptualize the range of analytical methods often used and secondly to identify some of the emerging directions in debitage analysis and interpretation.

AGGREGATE ANALYSIS OF DEBITAGE

One of the most popular types of debitage analysis being used today is what has been referred to as aggregate or mass analysis (Ahler and Van Ness 1985; Ammerman and Andrefsky 1982; Stahle and Dunn 1982). Debitage aggregate analysis is usually conducted by stratifying the entire assemblage of debitage by some uniform criteria and then comparing the relative proportions of debitage in each stratum. The proportions are often measured by count and/or mean weight of debitage in each stratum. When different assemblages are stratified using the same criteria, differences and similarities in the populations can be used to make interpretations about the population.

Almost all forms of aggregate analysis incorporate some aspect of debitage size into the analytical formula. There are some exceptions, such as minimal nodule analysis (Larson and Kornfeld 1997) and flake index score analysis (Cowan 1999). Size is most often used because it is generally believed that the size of debitage is directly related to the size of the objective piece, and therefore can provide a good indication of the size of the objective piece. Since artifact production is a reductive or subtractive process, the size of debitage produced from the process generally becomes progressively smaller as the artifact nears completion. As the stone tool decreases in size it necessarily follows that the debitage removed from the tool during production also grows progressively smaller. It is not possible to remove a flake that has a larger linear dimension or mass than the largest dimension of the objective piece or tool being made. As such, the change in flake sizes during removal will follow a general pattern of decreasing size. This is true for core reduction to produce usable flakes and for tool production to obtain a finished product such as a projectile point.

Probably the most popular technique to stratify debitage into size groups is by sifting the debitage through a series of nested screens (Andrefsky et al. 1994; Kalin 1981; Patterson 1990). Segregating debitage through a series of nested sieves or screens is also one of the first types of aggregate analysis to appear in the literature (Henry et al. 1976). Using application load experiments, hard-hammer, soft-hammer, and pressure flaking loads were evaluated by frequency counts of six different debitage sizes (Henry et al. 1976). Maximum thickness and weights of individual specimens were also taken. The results of the analysis demonstrated significant differences in flake size between percussion and pressure techniques— pressure flakes were generally smaller than percussion flakes.

Stahle and Dunn (1982) also using nested screens to segregate debitage size grades attempted to discriminate different stages of projectile point production. Nine different size grades were used from inch to 1½-inch mesh size in ⅛-inch increments. Their results were plotted on a cumulative frequency curve and showed good segregation between early and late reduction stages in point manufacture. Their results also showed that the majority of debitage produced (70 percent) was less than ⅛ inch in size and that over 90 percent of all debitage was less than ⅜ inch in size. In addition to testing for different stages of reduction, they also explored assemblages with debitage mixed from several different stages and discovered that size grade aggregate analysis was not as effective when applied to mixed assemblages.

In another debitage aggregate study, Ahler (1989b) used nested screens made of sieve cloth in increments of ¹⁄₁₆, ⅛, ¼, and ½ inch. He minimized examination of individual specimens and relied almost totally upon size grades and their aggregate weights and counts, a technique quite different from some others. According to Ahler (1989b), one of the problems with doing an individual flake analysis is the amount of time needed to examine each piece within a population. He also noted that individual flake analysis was prone to error because of the large number of observations needed for most collections of debitage. Conversely, Ahler indicates that screen-graded or sized analysis allows the researcher to process large populations of debitage in a relatively short amount of time. Also since size grades are standardized by screen mesh size the analysis is replicable. Unlike some other kinds of debitage analysis, screen-sized aggregate analysis uses the entire assemblage as a data set. Broken flakes and shatter are not selected out of the analytical assemblage, decreasing the amount of time needed to process the debitage population (Ahler 1989b:87). By contrast, Henry et al. (1976)

weighed each specimen and measured maximum thickness, a process that required each piece to be handled separately and could take a great deal of time and effort if the number of specimens in a study were great. Like some of the other screen-sized studies, Ahler's research obtained reliable results when assemblages were not mixed (Ahler 1989b:102, 105). However, when excavated assemblages contained debitage mixed from several different kinds of reduction activity, the size-grade signatures could not correctly discriminate activities. Root's (1997) technique of debitage sorting using least squares regression shows some promise when dealing with mixed debitage assemblages.

Notwithstanding the mixed assemblage problem, aggregate analysis seems to be a good technique to determine various production stages. In other words, it appears that screen-sized aggregate analysis is useful for determining early and final stages of production based upon debitage. In a series of replication experiments, Morrow (1997:56) was able to use screen size grades calculating proportions based upon weight to recognize early and late stage production of a various objective pieces. He found that early stages of reduction produced higher relative proportions of debitage weight in the larger size groups than did the later stages of reduction. The later stages of reduction produced relatively higher proportions of debitage weight in the smaller size groups. Again, this makes sense because screen-sized aggregate analysis is organized around debitage size and debitage size is related to the size of the tool being made or reduced. However, debitage from mixed reduction stages were not easily discriminated when using screen-sized aggregate analysis.

Another discovery from Morrow's (1997) research was the fact that debitage produced from different kinds of tools could not be discriminated when using screen-sized aggregate analysis. Morrow's experimental data included production debitage from a bifacial core, blade core, bipolar core, and Clovis point. The relative proportions of debitage by count or weight for the various size grades were not significantly different for any of the debitage populations. In other words, regardless of the type of tool being made, screen-sized aggregate analysis produced the same pattern of size class distributions.

It is important to remember that screen-sized aggregate analysis is only one way to conduct an aggregate analysis. There is any number of techniques available to stratify debitage populations into different size groups. Weight is believed by many researchers to be one of the most reliable indicators of debitage size (Amick et al. 1988; Magne and Pokotylo 1981; Odell 1989; Shott 1994). Debitage size groups have been developed based upon the weight of individual specimens. For instance, Ammerman (1979) used weight groups of progressively larger sizes to segregate a debitage population for analysis. Some researchers have used length of the specimen to separate the population into different size groups. Raab et al. (1979) segregated debitage into size groups based upon 1-cm-length increments.

Another technique of size sorting is to place debitage pieces over different diameter circles (Andrefsky 1998). Each of these techniques requires handling individual specimens to obtain weight, length, or relative diameter. This is somewhat different than screen-sized analysis, which is reported to minimize handling of artifacts to conserve on time. However, even Ahler's (1989b:105) screen-sized analysis requires recording cortex amount for individual specimens. This necessarily requires handling individual specimens to record dorsal cortex values.

DEBITAGE TYPOLOGICAL ANALYSIS

Typological analysis of debitage deals with individual debitage specimens. In this kind of analysis individual artifacts are classified into types that have some kind of technological or functional meaning. For instance, debitage typologies have been developed to distinguish the kind of hammer used (Bradley 1978; Crabtree 1967), the stage of reduction (MacDonald 1994; Morrison and Andrefsky 1996), the type of artifact produced or worked (Frison 1968; Neuman and Johnson 1979), and the technology used (Parry 1987; Shott 1993). One advantage of using a typological analysis is the immediate behavioral inference gained from recognition of a single piece of debitage. For instance, if a notching flake (Titmus 1985) were identified in an assemblage it could be inferred that notched points were made at the site even if none were found. Similarly, if a bifacial thinning flake (Hofman and Morrow 1985) or a channel flake (Wilmsen and Roberts 1978) was discovered it would indicate that a biface was thinned or a Folsom point was fluted at the site. The realization that an individual flake contains significant behavioral information is a powerful argument for using debitage typological analysis.

The previous section noted that one of the drawbacks of using aggregate analysis was the inability to correctly identify different kinds of tools or cores from the debitage assemblage. This is one of the advantages of a typological analysis over an aggregate analysis. Debitage types are often linked to particular kinds of tools and reduction techniques. There are numerous kinds of debitage typologies available for researchers. Andrefsky (1998) recognizes four different genera of debitage typologies: application load typologies, technological typologies, cortex typologies, and free-standing typologies. Application load typologies are sensitive to the kind of hammer used or kind of force used to detach a flake from an objective piece. Researchers using this scheme typically classify flakes as derived from either hard-hammer percussion, soft-hammer percussion, or pressure flaked (Cotterell and Kamminga 1987, 1990; Crabtree 1972). Technological typologies separate debitage into groups based upon the kind of reduction technology employed to detach the flake from an objective piece. Some of the more popular debitage types found in this kind of typology are bifacial thinning flakes

(Shott 1993:29), retouch scraper flakes (Frison 1968), bipolar flakes (Flenniken 1981), retouch flakes (Nassaney 1996:206), and notching flakes (Titmus 1985). Cortex typologies use the amount of dorsal cortex found on debitage as a proxy for reduction stages or sequences of reduction. Such typologies often recognize primary, secondary, and tertiary flakes (Morrow 1984; Sanders 1992; Stafford 1980). Free-standing debitage typologies are usually not linked to the technology or function of tools produced, but instead use objective replicable criteria to build the typology. These types are then used as independent observations while making technological and functional inferences (Sullivan and Rozen 1985).

Although typological analysis of debitage has been shown to be effective for recognizing the kind of technology used or the kind of tool produced at some sites it does have some problems worthy of further discussion. The lack of consistent and replicable definitions for debitage typologies is well documented by Sullivan and Rozen (1985). Indeed, all good typologies must use mutually exclusive definitions for types and they must be replicable. It is important to reemphasize this point because so many typologies use nebulous terms to define types. For instance, Redman (1998) gives considerable attention to the fact that characteristics such as pronounced lipping and pronounced bulbs of force are not defined. At what point does a flake lip become pronounced? When is a bulb of force diffuse as opposed to pronounced? Without precise definitions for such terms it is impossible to replicate typologies.

A pressure flake is a good example of the problem(s) researchers often encounter when using typological analysis of debitage. Pressure flakes are those detached pieces resulting from the use of pressure forces as opposed to percussion forces. The advantage of using pressure flaking over percussion flakes is the increase in precision a toolmaker gains. Instead of attempting to strike a particular location on an objective piece and potentially missing that location and ruining the tool, pressure flaking allows the tool maker to place the hammer directly on the intended location of impact and then apply force by exerting pressure. The disadvantage of using pressure over percussion flaking is the loss in load application amounts. At any rate, it is theoretically apparent how pressure flakes are produced, but what are the criteria and characteristics that define a pressure flake?

Defining pressure flakes is important because they have been tabulated in many lithic studies as a specific type of detached piece, which are apparently discriminated from soft-hammer and hard-hammer percussion pieces (Daugherty et al. 1987:92–104; Draper and Lothson 1990:70–79; Sappington 1991:70). Unfortunately most of these studies do not provide good mutually exclusive definitions of a pressure flake. According to some researchers who do identify pressure flakes in their assemblage of debitage, pressure flakes are generally smaller, thinner, and weigh less than flakes detached by percussion (Ahler 1989b:91; Root 1992:87). Unfortunately smaller, thinner, and lighter flakes have been produced by percussion flaking as well as pressure flaking in experiments with bifacial production and with core reduction (Ammerman and Andrefsky 1982; Andrefsky 1986, 1998). In fact, the majority of debitage produced from almost any kind of lithic reduction activity produces small debitage (Baumler and Downum 1989; Henry et al. 1976; Kalin 1981; Patterson 1982, 1990; Stahle and Dunn 1982). Accordingly, it can be very difficult to reliably segregate a detached piece produced by pressure techniques from those produced by percussion techniques based solely upon the criteria of size.

It can be argued that debitage typologies are inductive techniques whereby the adequacy of the types can only be measured by their appropriateness for specific research questions (Dunnell 1971:190). In this regard there is no measure of substantive significance for debitage typologies outside of a research context. In other words, the meaning of types and typologies is therefore given by the theoretical assumptions, research methods, and questions that underlie a particular study (Voorrips 1982:95–98). Stated another way, all typologies that are based upon replicable characteristics and rules to administer characteristics are good typologies. However, the meaning of typologies is only as good as the theoretical assumptions and linkages that tie the typologies to interpretations. This is why a debitage typology that defines a type as being small and thin is adequate. But once that debitage type is interpreted as a pressure flake the typology loses its utility because it is well known that percussion flakes may also be small and thin.

The same argument can be made against many free-standing debitage typologies. Although free-standing typologies often use objective replicable criteria, the criteria are not always linked to aspects of prehistoric behavior. This can make the use of free-standing debitage typologies problematic when they are used as the basis for prehistoric behavioral interpretations (Amick and Mauldin 1989; Kuijt et al. 1995). For instance it is possible that a free standing debitage typology based upon two attributes (raw material type and size) may produce four types: (1) small, local raw material debitage, (2) large, local raw material debitage, (3) small, nonlocal raw material debitage, and (4) large, nonlocal raw material debitage. It is not clear how such a debitage typology should relate to interpretations about artifact types and production sequences, even though the typology is simple, replicable, and produces mutually exclusive types. However, if this debitage typology were linked to a context associating artifact production with distance to raw material source locations it would be relatively easy to justify predictions regarding the relative proportion of such debitage types. For debitage typologies to be useful they not only must meet the criteria for establishing mutually exclusive definitions of types, but they must also have justifiable assumptions related to the kind of interpretations they are being used for.

Typological analysis of debitage is often equated with individual flake analysis. This is because individual debitage specimens are examined and classified into types. Such analysis may not use the entire debitage assemblage because not all specimens in an assemblage may have recognizable characteristics to adequately classify the specimen. However, this may be one of the advantages of using a typological analysis. Recent studies have confirmed the point that some typological analysis of debitage can be an effective technique for making technological or functional interpretations based upon the occurrence of a single debitage specimen (Andrefsky 1998:120; Root 1992:83; Titmus 1985). In this regard individual flake analysis may be less time consuming than aggregate analysis because the entire debitage assemblage may not be included in the study.

One of the most serious critiques of typological analysis that has emerged from recent investigations is the lack of verification between the debitage type and the functional or technological interpretation. All too often debitage specimens are identified as a specific type with a specific meaning, yet it is not clear how such an interpretation was established. Along these same lines, recent studies have shown that some debitage types are not well enough defined to be identified. So even if a debitage type is well established as being associated with a certain function or technology it may be impossible to make that interpretation because that particular type is not defined with a mutually exclusive definition.

ATTRIBUTE ANALYSIS

Debitage attribute analysis begins with the selection and recording of debitage characteristics. Unlike debitage typological analysis, debitage attribute analysis examines the distribution of an attribute(s) over an entire population or assemblage. In contrast, debitage typological analysis examines debitage attributes on an individual specimen. In many regards debitage attribute analysis is similar to debitage aggregate analysis. However, debitage aggregate analysis is usually always linked to size classes and often examines relative proportions of size classes based upon count or weight or both. Debitage attribute analysis is not confined to size classes. There have been a variety of debitage attributes used to make inferences about technology, artifact type, and reduction stages. For instance, dorsal cortex amount has been used to determine stage of reduction and the type of tool produced (Gilreath 1984:3; Johnson 1987a:193; Magne 1985). Sassaman (1994a) has used debitage size based on square centimeter measurements to link sites to raw material source locations. Debitage size based upon weight has been used to determine differences between multidirectional and unidirectional cores (Andrefsky 1998:132). Striking platform types have been used to identify bifacial core production versus platformed core reduction (Parry and Kelly 1987) and Hayden and Hutchings (1989) have used striking platform morphology to determine the kind of hammer used for reduction.

Striking platform characteristics are among of the most commonly recorded in debitage attribute analysis. Striking platforms found on debitage are essentially the remnant of the point of applied load administered to the objective piece. Since the shape of the point of applied load is extremely important for determining the shape and size of the detached piece (Callahan 1979; Dibble 1997; Whittaker 1994), it can be an important indicator of the kind of technology used. As such, platform morphology is one of the most effective characteristics of flake debitage for addressing issues associated with the kind of technology used for chipped stone tool production and maintenance (Morrow 1984:21; Odell 1989: 185; Raab et al. 1979; Shott 1994:80).

Recent research has shown that a great deal of the variability found in debitage produced from different kinds of technological practices correlates to variability found in the striking platform morphology. For instance, variability in striking platforms has been used to determine the type of hammer used (Cotterell and Kamminga 1987; Frison 1968; Hayden and Hutchings 1989), type of objective piece being modified (Andrefsky 1995; Magne and Pokotylo 1981; Tomka 1989), and stage of biface production (Dibble and Pelcin 1995; Dibble and Whittaker 1981; Johnson 1989; Katz 1976). Unfortunately, striking platform characteristics are among the most difficult to consistently measure with accuracy, making them hard to replicate and measure reliably. Reliable and replicable measurement is one of the biggest problems facing debitage attribute analysis.

Measuring striking platform angles is typical of the kind of problem researchers face when attempting to conduct debitage attribute analysis. Striking platforms are usually small, and sometimes are difficult to even recognize. They are also found in many different shapes and sizes. Some striking platforms are rounded, others are flat, and others may have two, three, four, or more sides or facets. Because of the great amount of morphological variability in platforms it is almost impossible to define the striking platform angle. An angle is formed by the intersection of two lines or two planes. The surfaces of striking platforms are usually curved or rounded, and do not intersect to form an angle. How does one measure the angle on a rounded surface? A common definition for striking platform angle is the angle formed by the intersection of the striking platform surface and the ventral face (Dibble and Whittaker 1981; Shott 1993). Unfortunately, the striking platform surface is usually curved or contains many facets and it is often the case that the ventral face is also curved. This results in the possibility that many striking platform angle measurements can be derived from the intersection of the curved surfaces depending upon where the lines forming the angle are selected.

Given the possibility that a researcher can consistently select lines to derive striking platform angles, the angle has to be accurately measured. This is not often a replicable task. Not only do different people consistently record different values for the same specimen, the same person consistently records different values when asked to measure the specimen multiple times. In a series of measurement experiments conducted at Washington State University multiple values for the same striking platforms measured by different individuals and by the same individual a second time were tabulated over a period of several years. Even with trained recorders striking platform angle measurements were never consistently measured. Other researchers have noted the same kind of problems associated with replicability of striking platform attributes (Odell 1989).

Another popular kind of debitage attribute analysis involves measuring the amount of dorsal cortex (Johnson 1989; Magne and Pokotylo 1981; Mauldin and Amick 1989; Sassaman 1994a). Attribute analysis of dorsal cortex attempts to gain information about the reduction stages of tool production or reduction. It is typically assumed that the weathered exterior of lithic raw materials—the cortex—will be the first area removed in either tool production or core reduction. As flakes are removed, the exterior must be detached before the interior can be detached. This is a reasonable assumption, but it has been shown that such an assumption may not necessarily be correct in all cases. It has been shown that the kind of tool produced or reduced will produce flakes with differential amounts of dorsal cortex (Andrefsky 1998:112–114; Tomka 1989). Also it has not been clearly demonstrated that flakes with more cortex are necessarily removed earlier in the reduction sequence than flakes with less cortex (Mauldin and Amick 1989; Odell 1989). Cortex amount will vary depending upon the amount of cortex present on the objective piece, the technique of reduction, and the kind of artifact being produced. Tomka (1989:141) has shown, for instance, that dart point manufacture produces a relatively greater number of flakes without cortex than does biface production or multidirectional core reduction. This is apparently related to the fact that a dart point is initially made from a flake blank that has a dorsal surface with or without cortex, and a ventral surface without cortex. As such, the initial objective piece used for dart point production has less cortex present than the initial objective piece for either biface or multidirectional core production when a cortical nodule is used.

Other studies have shown that the size of an objective piece has a great influence on the amount of cortex the debitage assemblage will contain. Bradbury and Carr (1995) recorded dorsal cortex amounts on debitage from the reduction of a small nodule (90.7 g) and a large nodule (1,373.2 g). Both nodules were completely covered with cortex prior to reduction. Sixty-six percent of the debitage from the large nodule contained no dorsal cortex. This was in contrast to the small nodule, which produced only about 35 percent debitage with no cortex. Such studies indicate that the basic tenant of cortex attribute analysis (greater dorsal cortex means earlier reduction stage) may not be accurate in all cases.

There are an infinite number of attributes that can be recorded on debitage that range from nominal through ratio in scale. These attributes are often analyzed by researchers for trends within a population. In other words, attribute analysis is often conducted at the assemblage population level and seldom at the individual artifact level. Recent studies have shown that many debitage attributes co-vary with two primary characteristics of the objective piece size and shape. In this regard debitage attribute analysis should be helpful for addressing issues of production sequences (linked to size) and artifact types (linked to shape).

SUMMARY

Recent investigations have clearly shown that some techniques of debitage analysis are better suited for making certain kinds of interpretations than are other techniques of debitage analysis. Even though some researchers have questioned the concept of reduction stages (Shott 1996a), aggregate analysis has been shown to be effective for determining stages of reduction or production. Since aggregate analysis is linked to debitage size and tool or core reduction is also linked to debitage size, it stands to reason that aggregate analysis would be useful for making interpretations related to reduction stages or sequences. Similarly it would be expected that attribute analysis that examines size (such as flake length, width, weight, or area) would also be a good technique to determine reduction stages. In fact, complementary results should be obtained when both aggregate and attribute size analyses are conducted (Bradbury and Carr 1995; Morrow 1997).

It is also apparent that aggregate analysis is not particularly effective for determining the kind of tool produced or the kind of core reduced. Studies have shown that typological analysis is a more reliable method to obtain information related to the kind of objective piece being worked. At the same time, other studies have shown that debitage typologies are subject to problems if individual types are not well defined. Well-defined types often require meticulous measurement of attribute states. As such, it has often been found that one or two attributes are the discriminating characteristics of a particular debitage type. For example, in many cases the shape of a striking platform is the discriminating factor determining the difference between platformed core debitage from bifacial debitage. In such cases it may be as effective to simply measure striking platforms as opposed to developing debitage types.

On the other hand, debitage attribute measurement may be prone to error for a variety of reasons related to the small size of attributes and the number of observations. Recent studies have also shown that some debitage attributes are not simply correlated with a single production process but may vary depending upon a number of different contexts and situations. For example, debitage dorsal cortex has been shown to be influenced by the kind of tool produced and by the size of the original objective piece. This necessarily means that dorsal cortex amount does not always correlate negatively with progressive reduction sequences.

Controlled experiments have given researchers comparative samples to help determine how different contexts and production of different tools can pattern debitage. These experimentally derived assemblages have shown that one of the more difficult problems to overcome in debitage analysis is interpretation of mixed assemblages. To address this problem some researchers suggest that debitage assemblages should be stratified before analysis in an effort to obtain minimal episodes of production, reduction, and/or use. This suggests that aggregate analysis or attribute analysis of an entire debitage assemblage is not fruitful unless it can be established that the entire assemblage is associated with a single production episode. In other words, without stratification, debitage assemblages are prone to mixing problems.

One of the conclusions that can be reached from this review is that there is no ultimate kind or level of debitage analysis. There is no magic technique that will provide some final statement on the state of a debitage assemblage. Instead, it is apparent that different techniques will provide different kinds of information about the overall site assemblage. Various levels of debitage analysis as well as various techniques of debitage analysis within the same level can and probably should be used in concert with one another to maximize the amount and reliability of information gained. Instead of viewing different techniques of debitage analysis as competing strategies for handling debitage assemblages, researchers should adopt multiple analytical strategies suited to the contexts of each assemblage.

The following papers provide a glimpse of contemporary debitage analysis that marks some of the emerging methodological and theoretical directions in the field. The volume begins with two papers (Johnson; Magne) that put debitage studies into a historical perspective. These papers also review key topics in the upcoming chapters. All of the papers are drawn together at several different levels related to the kind of methods used, the kind of interpretations attempted, and the kind(s) of associations being made. For instance, half of the papers use some assemblage data drawn from controlled experiments (Carr and Bradbury; Pecora; Prentiss; Rasic and Andrefsky) to explore the parameters associated with debitage morphological variability. Some of these same papers are linked to other papers that attempt to correlate tool type production and reduction to debitage shape characteristics (Carr and Bradbury; Prentiss; Sievert and Wise; Whittaker and Kaldahl). Several papers emphasize the need to understand unique episodes of human site use and attempt to tackle this issue through a number of different analytical techniques (Pecora; Wenzel and Shelley; Whittaker and Kaldahl). One of these papers uses debitage analysis to gain information about the contribution of individuals in the production of assemblages (Whittaker and Kaldahl). Several other papers link debitage assemblages to human organization studies (Pecora; Rasic and Andrefsky; Tomka; Wenzel and

Shelley). These studies show how debitage is associated with prehistoric scheduling, mobility, and tool functions. Still other papers deal explicitly with linking
analytical methods to theoretical interpretations (Sullivan; Tomka). Both of
these papers use case studies derived from excavated assemblages to emphasize
their points. In some way, all of the papers show a strong concern for and com-
mitment to reliability of data and verification of results.

2

Some Reflections on Debitage Analysis

Jay K. Johnson

My first real job in archaeology began in 1976 when I was hired to direct the lithic analysis of a large collection of mostly Middle and Late Archaic quarry site material from the location of the proposed Yellow Creek nuclear power plant in northeast Mississippi. I got the job because I knew somebody who knew somebody who assumed that because I'd written a dissertation on stone tools, I knew everything there was to know about rocks. My dissertation was based on a collection of 1,307 artifacts from Chiapas, almost all of which were obsidian blades or blade core debris. So, when I showed up in Oxford and was confronted with literally tons of debitage, I had a strong incentive to immerse myself in the literature on debitage analysis. We ultimately counted, weighed, or otherwise recorded 3.47 tons of flakes and angular shatter (Johnson 1981).

I was lucky. The existing literature on debitage analysis was not that large. Archaeologists were just beginning to appreciate the potential of this category of artifacts in answering questions about the past. So, there were a lot of other young and enthusiastic people working with debitage, many of whom were recent graduates of Crabtree's summer lithic workshop and confirmed new archaeologists. In retrospect, I can recognize three major influences on the Yellow Creek analysis, only one of which deals specifically with lithic analysis. I met Stan Ahler just after I'd taken the job and he gave me a manuscript version of an early mass analysis paper (Ahler 1976). I made good use of the technique. Bob Thorne, the director of the Yellow Creek project, had been a student of Richard Krause who was a student of Irving Rouse. Thorne was teaching an archaeological theory course when I showed up and using Dunnell's (1971) *Systematics in Prehistory* as a text. I figured I'd better read it. I've never been sorry. Finally, one of the first courses that I taught at Ole Miss was statistics and I used the first edition of Thomas's (1976) *Figuring Anthropology*. That led me to read an important early statement on the need to objectify typologies in archaeology (Thomas 1970). The influence of these three people shows clearly in the Yellow Creek report and my subsequent work in lithic analysis.

I have come to realize that Yellow Creek was an ideal location in which to learn debitage analysis. Many of the problems that are addressed by the authors in this volume, lack of clear-cut staging (Sullivan) or mixed assemblages (Andrefsky, Carr and Bradbury), for example, were not a consideration. Because it was a chert-rich area in which biface production was staged at different locales relative to the outcrops, it was relatively easy to relate flakes to tool rejects to production stage to settlement pattern. And the whole thing changed through time. It was a fool's paradise.

Things became a little more interesting once I started doing work in the rest of the state. Most of Mississippi is located in the coastal plane with two major, relatively restricted chert resources, both of which are gravels. My first graduate student, Carol Morrow, wrote her thesis on a site located near one of the chert sources and we developed a production trajectory model (Johnson and Raspet 1980; Morrow 1984) that works pretty well for most of the state (Johnson 1989). As I write, there is a graduate student in our lab sorting rock according to the types Carol and I developed.

The point of all of the above is that it is about time that I review the literature on debitage analysis. I can think of no better place to begin than this collection. The challenge will be to add to what has already been said in the several chapters that follow. The following comments clearly grow from my trial by fire in the Yellow Creek analysis. There are, I think, some universal lessons that I learned which are reflected in this collection.

Since debitage is often the most numerous category in any site collection, a little thought at the beginning while setting up the analysis can save a lot of time later on. Perhaps the most important lesson Dunnell gave me was the necessity of keeping track of the scale of the analysis while designing the research. Some artifacts need to be recorded at the scale of individual artifact while others can just as easily be recorded at the assemblage scale, saving a great deal of work. The key to determining the recording scale is the recording unit. If each case is an individual artifact and the data that are recorded are observations on those artifacts (e.g., raw material, edge angle, length, removal sequence number), then the analysis is beginning at the artifact scale. If the cases are provenience units or replication assemblages and the data that are being recorded are counts per category (e.g., weight class, cortex type, platform type), the data are being recorded at the assemblage scale.

One of the things that almost everyone agrees on in this collection is that there are relatively few absolutely diagnostic debitage types. Andrefsky mentions notching flakes and channel flakes to which I'd like to add platform rejuvenation and ridge starter flakes for polyhedral core technologies. Ultimately, relating a group of flakes to a production stage or specific technology will rely on general characteristics of the overall assemblage. This means that while the analysis may begin at the artifact scale, it will most likely be conducted at the assemblage scale, using the attributes to create classes into which the artifacts are sorted or characterizing the assemblage directly in terms of the attributes (e.g., average edge angle).

Multivariate statistics have allowed lithic analysts to take full advantage of the second alternative, measuring assemblages in terms of attributes rather than types. In particular, replicators have come to rely on multivariate analytical techniques. However, the statistic of choice has usually been some form of factor analysis. I find this peculiar given the goals of the debitage analyses. Factor analysis assumes that you know little about the assemblage and designs the factor loadings so that they maximize the variation in the data. Those variables that have strong loadings on the first factors are those which show the most variation, not the ones that best answer the questions that are being asked. It may be that the major dimensions of variation measure nothing but noise.

Since most replicative experiments are designed to determine which variables best distinguish between different stages or techniques or technologies, they usually start with two or more contrast sets (e.g., debitage produced by hard hammer versus debitage produced by soft hammer). The ideal statistic would be discriminant function analysis that uses the original partitions of the data in order to extract eigenvalues that best replicate those divisions. It is, of course, still inductive, but the technique maximizes the interpretive potential of the results.

And how can the results of debitage replication best be used? Should the principal components or discriminant function formula be applied directly to archaeological assemblages? Few people would try that. As Prentiss, Pecora, Carr and Bradbury, Wenzel and Shelly, and Sullivan point out, the factors that influence debitage production variables are too numerous to control. These include idiosyncratic behavior, raw material characteristics, raw material availability, staging, and mixed assemblages to mention just a few. This suggests that the indeterminacy that Sullivan notes is an insurmountable problem if the goal is universal types at any scale of analysis.

The primary use of multivariate statistics in replicative experiments should be to identify those attributes that best measure specific assemblage characteristics. So, for example, if core debitage assemblages can be distinguished from biface debitage assemblages on the basis of flake facets, scars, and size (Carr and Bradbury), and I suspect, on the basis of the distribution of biface production rejects or exhausted cores, then my archaeological assemblages can be partitioned according to these two technologies, and my study of the debitage will be sure to include these three variables and exclude, say, flake width if that is not a discriminant variable for these technologies. In this way, there will be a productive feedback between the analysis of archaeological assemblages and replicative assemblages. The result will be refined strategies of analysis with context specific, polythetic assemblage classes.

Rasic and Andrefsky's chapter illustrates the second major contribution that replicative experiments can make in understanding prehistoric technology. Their experiments with blade cores and bifacial cores indicate that, among other things, blades can be produced more rapidly than biface flakes but, countering Sheets and Muto's (1972) pioneering experimental results, bifaces may be a more productive technology in terms of cutting edge if you count both the flakes and the biface. These results contribute directly to our ability to model the organization of prehistoric technologies. Their conclusion that blades appear and disappear in the archaeological sequence in response to a difference in "situational constraints" and the ability to predict future tasks and consequent cutting edge demands is similar to the argument that Tomka presents to explain the occurrence of formal tools in the late prehistoric and early historic record of portions of the western United States. Large numbers of bifaces and end scrapers appear to be a response to intensive hide processing, either deer for the skin trade or bison. This runs counter to the expectations that sedentary societies would be able to stockpile raw material and utilize expedient technologies (Parry and Kelly 1987). I found these arguments particularly compelling because similar patterning is evident in the distribution of end scrapers in the Southeast on an early historic time level. However, in the Chickasaw case, at least, it is coincident with an expedient core technology, appearing for the first time in this nonsource area of Mississippi (Johnson 1997). In fact, the blanks for the bifaces and scrapers from these sites were selected from large numbers of flakes driven from amorphous cores. Most of the unmodified flakes show evidence of use. It is clearly possible to mix formalized and expedient technologies.

In his introduction, Andrefsky cites Sullivan and Rozen's 1985 paper as one of the most influential articles on debitage analysis in the past 15 years. I would like to conclude by considering why that should be. In part, it is what might be called the *American Antiquity* effect. There have been few articles on debitage published before and since in that journal. A lot of people read it and a lot of people reacted to it. The paper also makes some very important methodological points. Many of the standard debitage typologies are poorly constructed. They are not operationalized to use Thomas's (1970) terminology. That is, the necessary and sufficient criteria for class inclusion are not defined in a way that anyone with a reasonable background in lithic analysis can duplicate the classification. Sullivan and Rozen (1985) use as an example the primary, secondary, and tertiary flake classification but almost any of the familiar flake typologies also illustrate the point. Part of the problem has been the attempt to relate flake types to specific activities. Bifacial thinning flakes are a prime example, where the definition will need to rest on general characteristics measured on an interval or ratio scale rather than the presence or absence of attributes.

However, the main reason that the Sullivan and Rozen typology "can incite great passion among debitage analysts" (Whittaker and Kaldahl, this volume) is their call for a "meaning free" typology (see also Sullivan, this volume). By this they mean that the typology is based on criteria that are not directly linked to a specific technology or production stage. Of course, immediately after it is applied, it becomes meaningful; whole flakes are more common in core/biface technologies (Sullivan and Rozen 1985). It is telling that Prentiss's (1998; this volume) refinement of the typology relies on size grades, one of the basic meaningful variables in debitage analysis. But the more fundamental problem with the Sullivan-Rozen typology is that we want our typologies to do more than predict, we want them to explain. This task becomes particularly troublesome with multivariate analyses if we begin with "free-standing" classifications (Andrefsky, this volume). It is as if you could predict what the stock market was going to do on any given day on the basis of what Alan Greenspan had for breakfast. It might be tremendously useful but not very satisfying.

Still, Sullivan and Rozen have done debitage analysis a tremendous service. The controversy that they inspired has forced us all to examine our own analyses more closely. I am pleased to be able to report that a good deal of progress has been made since I first started counting Yellow Creek flakes. For one thing, the literature on debitage analysis has grown exponentially. Recent summaries and anthologies (Amick and Mauldin 1989; Andrefsky 1998; Carr 1994; Shott 1994; Whittaker 1994) provide ready access to this growing body of data. Twenty-five years ago there were only a few archaeologists who could replicate stone tools and were interested in conducting systematic experiments. Today, particularly in debitage analysis, the situation is almost reversed. Most of the contributors to this volume have spent many hours making large rocks small. The benefits to us all are obvious.

However, it is also obvious that replication alone will not be sufficient. While general expectations about the shape of a debitage assemblage can be refined by the kinds of well-designed experiments that have become more and more common in recent years, as Rozen and Sullivan (1989a) pointed out in a reply to responses to their original article, the real test of experimental results is how they apply to the archaeological record. What can they tell us about tool production and use?

The primary lesson of the past 20 years of debitage analysis is something we always suspected but didn't want to admit: that many if not most of our flake typologies were based on false assumptions about the relationship between behavior and by-product. Or, if the assumptions were not absolutely wrong, they had to be qualified by so many conditions that they were practically wrong. In fact, and this is the most important message that the current literature holds for debitage analysis, it is unlikely that analyses that begin by counting flake types rather than measuring flake attributes will tell us what we want to know about the prehistoric past. And, these attributes would best be used in defining context-sensitive assemblage types rather that artifact types. Once again, it is all a matter of scale.

3

Debitage Analysis as a Scientific Tool for Archaeological Knowledge

Martin P. R. Magne

The papers presented in this volume cover a wide range of approaches to lithic debitage: basics in variability, real-world contexts of variability, and innovative ways of approaching the subject as a whole. One would think that this most basic of archaeological materials would by now be approached in largely consistent ways, that the types of answers derived would be well known, and that the principal contributions to the field would have been made by looking at debitage as a category of material culture with a unique yet far-reaching ability to inform the field. In many cases the papers herein reveal that kind of thinking is accurate, in others we can see there is still much progress to be made. The art and science of using lithic technological remains to understand how humans lived and how humans changed has progressed significantly over, say, the past 30 years, but when examining the papers contained in this volume, I want to know that it has also progressed in the past 10 years, using as my measure the Amick and Mauldin (1989) volume that focused on experimentation in lithic technology.

Organized at the SAA meetings 10 years before the one that gave rise to the present set of papers, the Amick and Mauldin session and subsequent volume had a strongly experimental bent (but not exclusively so) towards exhibiting the status of debitage studies at the time. Its strength was in the degree to which it showed the robustness that had developed in reduction experiments. There was then, as there is now, evaluation of the Sullivan and Rozen (1985) technique, and a few showings of very similar yet independently derived conclusions about the directional variability of certain debitage attributes as related to reduction stages. The volume was a landmark in showing that consistent results were beginning to be achieved. My own contribution to that session was to model ways that debitage characteristics at the assemblage level might help elucidate settlement occupation spans (Magne 1989), or at least keep us thinking beyond the flake. That and my own leanings (Magne 1985; Magne and Pokotylo 1981) in methodology are probably why I was kindly asked to contribute this piece. I therefore focus attention here on the subject of lithic technological analytical methodology, for understanding what different methods reveal about particular problems, and for learning what different problems require in the way of different methods. Given the explicit structure of the volume's content, I will address the three main areas of discussion: to attempt clarification of principal issues, to highlight the outstanding contributions, and to point out the areas where I believe we need to sort out some particularly troublesome problems.

In my view, our best insights into debitage variability—how variable it is and why—have come from experimentation. Without the hundreds, if not thousands, of individual studies, both formal and informal, into making different kinds of stone tools from different kinds of stone, and analysis of the resulting debitage, we would be left with purely inferential models of deriving meaning from debitage assemblages. There have been, and still are, many problems with experimentation—the strong focus on bifaces, the problem of low sample sizes of tools made, the low numbers of knappers, the problem of actual versus intended replication, the problem of what to measure and for what reasons, and so forth. I cannot dispute Andrefsky's (this volume) observation that the Sullivan and Rozen (1985) paper has been the lightning rod for debitage analysis over the past 15 years. Sure, there are some big issues with it (e.g., Mauldin and Amick 1989; Ensor and Roemer 1989; Shott 1994), but it stimulated the field. As Andrefsky says, there is no one single method that will ever be *the* way to analyze debitage. Still, there are serious outstanding methodological and philosophical issues with the Sullivan and Rosen Technique (SRT), some of which I will address later.

Prentiss offers an outstanding study that extends the utility of the SRT, uses well-designed experimental methods, and clearly applied multivariate statistical methods, building on his earlier work (Prentiss 1998). By adding flake size to the equation, Prentiss does something that some of us have thought needed doing but didn't really know how. That is, he combined the purely formal SRT with the long-held logical view of size-reduction correspondence with experimental replicability. The most substantive result is the increase that is apparent in reliability and validity in the SRT when size is an added criterion, in recognizing "core" versus "tool" production. As a bonus, the "Modified SRT" (MSRT) has the ability to recognize effects of percussor types, platform preparation, and degree of applied force. Nonetheless, I have the nagging feeling that we could do better by finding a basic typology that is more reliable to begin with than the SRT. The SRT, my methodology, and others, act to "break up" reduction into typologies or discrete classes, when in fact reduction processes are likely more or less "continuous." Classification exercises help make analysis easier but they distort reality. Perhaps some applications of serious statistics like Prentiss has applied, and greater use of the "continuous" data that I generated and that Carr and Bradbury also do (this volume), would be of benefit.

That "multiple lines of evidence" (Bradbury 1998; Carr and Bradbury, this volume) can be more accurate indicators of reduction realities than any single line of evidence is encouraging, since redundant measures, to a reasonable amount, can serve as internal checks to reliability (Prentiss, this volume). So clearly do the Carr and Bradbury and Prentiss papers demonstrate that combined "individual flake analysis" and "mass analysis" can explain reliably great amounts of debitage variability in predictable, stage-oriented interpretations, that at this point in time any large debitage set should include these two basic methods as an inclusive analytical tool. However, arguments can be made for these techniques and others depending upon the kind of information desired. For instance, my platform/no platform/scar count methodology has its limitations (Magne 1985), but it is also sensitive to certain kinds of production behavior information. This may be an appropriate place to clarify some questions about that method. I have been asked, or reviewers have questioned, why I chose platform scar counts as a means of classifying flakes with platforms (PRBs), when the platform scars are difficult to recognize, particularly with low experience levels; or why I developed the particular method I did; or why I did not use weight or size measures. As I explained then, I only counted platform scars on platforms with depths or widths greater than 2 mm unless the scarring was still discrete and clear on smaller ones. The reason I chose that variable was the same reason why I chose dorsal scar counts for shatter and not weight or length or any other variable—because the multivariate analyses revealed that those variables were the best predictors of reduction stages in my experiments. This result has been supported, especially the dorsal scar counts, by several other experimenters (see Amick and Mauldin 1989; Shott 1994). Carr and Bradbury here replicate my results of the numbers of flakes per event patterns by core/tool reduction techniques. Secondly, I did not employ multiple lines of evidence other than raw material type frequencies, simply because of the mass of lithic material I wished to examine—38 assemblages across four regions of interior British Columbia, including a total of 14,541 pieces of debitage, 861 tools, and 164 cores. This was done in a time when all my experimental data and archaeological data were initially collected on 50 case by 80 column recording sheets, transferred to IBM 80 column punch cards, read into a mainframe and then analyzed using custom FORTRAN algorithms or mainframe available statistical packages, again using punch card instruction sets, waiting often overnight for output, typing results with electric or manual typewriters, drawing graphs by hand and physically cutting and pasting text and tables and illustrations together. In the latter stages of my analyses, on-line editing of data and set up of analyses became possible, but even then in multiple-user computing rooms. So I dearly wanted to minimize analytical time (excuses, excuses).

Today, apart from the time necessary to acquire the data from the debitage itself, analyses are blindingly fast, so much more can be done. For instance, here Carr and Bradbury use a population of 80 simulated assemblages. In hindsight, the addition of weight or size classes to my basic classification certainly would have contributed positively to my interpretations of variability among Plateau housepit village, cache, processing, and plain old lithic scatter sites, but I'm not so sure still that the extra effort involved in doing so would have greatly increased the reliability or the significance of the patterning revealed. Being able to compare such a wide range of site types and assemblages meant that I had nearly the entire range of possibilities covered. This is a scaling issue. When large data sets allow confidence that the full scale is present, conclusions can in turn be made with high confidence. As Carr and Bradbury and others point out, no one individual attribute can accurately predict reduction stages, but some are more accurate than others. The comparative method, as basic a scientific tool as you can get, is greatly underrated in lithic analysis, but the single site/single knapper/single tool type approaches are by far more common.

An important point raised by Prentiss is the effect of "flake size goal," particularly in core reduction. This is obviously related to raw material characteristics such as the size of nodules or inherent fracture planes that might limit the size of blanks that can be removed (as shown in one of the best papers ever related to this limiting factor, by Wenzel and Shelley, this volume). Nonetheless, different knappers will desire different sized blanks for different intended products and to a certain extent their individual skill levels will influence their success in producing their intent. Intent of manufacture is an understatedly misunderstood source of variability. For the most part I contend that the intent of modern flintknappers is to conduct flintknapping experiments. Our intent is not to make tools to stay alive. To the extent that we can very precisely replicate nearly any tool type, any technique of manufacture (although there are some we haven't discovered and others we've surely invented), the intent of aboriginal knappers is still difficult to recreate. Perhaps that is the underlying reason for Sullivan's (this volume, Sullivan and Rozen 1985) strongly held view of a need for value-free classificatory methods. But my contention also includes recognition of the fact that there are only so many ways to break rocks and therefore we surely are able to identify the essential, technical manufacturing intentions all the way through the selection, reduction, use, and discard process.

The better we can measure those processes, the better we will be able to integrate lithic technological operations and rules into social transactions and patterns. Lithic experimenters have realized for some time that employing multiple knappers is a logical way to account for group variability (Magne 1985; multiple papers in Amick and Mauldin 1989; Ahler 1989b), yet we don't know clearly how the individual knappers might skew the group results. Nonetheless, the point that individuals do exhibit markedly different debitage results is worth repeating if only to expand the sample size of such experiments. With replicable methods and measures, a considerable database could conceivably be built of individual knapping events. But let's look beyond bifaces and let's look at other sources of variation as well, such as different stone characteristics, as discussed by Wenzel and Shelley (this volume).

As Carr and Bradbury and Prentiss here demonstrate, experimentation is continuing to increase its relevance to real archaeological issues. Although the days of looking for soft-hammer percussion flakes or pressure flakes are still with us even though we're not sure why knowing that would be meaningful, we are more and more often seeing confident applications of experimental knowledge to multiple assemblages. What I mean is that the percussor-type question is always posed as being self-evidently important, but it seems like a backwards approach. If we demonstrate that 80 percent of an assemblage was produced by soft-hammer flaking, then what? Have we not then just shown what type of tool was used to produce most of the assemblage? What is the relevance of that tool to the rest of the system? We need to make the link, if there is one, between the percussor tool type and higher order analytical and interpretive units. In our zealousness to reconstruct whatever we can, we do not always step back and ask if the result will be of any use. The even greater need is to link archaeological systematics with lithic technological ones, as Carr and Bradbury have done with their organization approach, here focusing on "level of production," which I see as a construct applicable to both highly localized or broadly regional settlement systems. By building on previous, replicable experiments, researchers are now approaching such problems as estimating the numbers of tools and cores produced in past events, recognizing biases such as over-representation of early stage reduction, and overcoming ambiguous areas of classification and interpretation. The degree of statistical methodological sophistication shown is remarkable and necessary.

In his contribution to this volume, Pecora modifies the Collins (1975) model with the concept of manufacturing/transport junctures, or pauses in the reduction process. An important point raised is that different kinds of junctures might have their own effects on mobility, depending on the junctures decided upon by the prehistoric populations at various points in their settlement system. These could be conditioned by such things as distance to raw material and immediate logistical considerations, although there are here and in other papers some problems with terminology. For example, what is a "non-formed tool artifact;" what kinds of artifacts are there that do not exhibit "technological characteristics;" and how can "flakes detached from bifaces" be identified when "flakes detached from the edges of bifaces" are another distinct category? This kind of landscapewide approach is what we need to continue to develop for large-scale results that will lead to cultural evolutionary knowledge.

Even if experimentation leads to objective classificatory or measurement methods, all lithic analyses benefit greatly from a firm personal grounding in making stone tools. Perhaps more than in any other paper, what we see in Whittaker and Kaldahl's paper is the advantage of tremendous first-hand experience in flintknapping, in having personal confidence in interpreting debitage morphology and artifact fracture patterning. In another instance of "multiple lines of evidence," the analysts apply size grading and debitage typology, as well as comparative analysis, to show that the debitage indicates strong biface derivation, and to conclude that most, if not all, bifaces indicated by the debitage were deposited there and not removed. Undoubtedly greater control over the effects of individual knapper behavior would be of use to the Grasshopper Pueblo instance, but this is a remarkable study that interconnects individual patterning and standardized debitage typology and size grading techniques with broader anthropological understanding.

Broader comprehension, and at large scale, is the goal of three important papers here. Rasic and Andrefsky describe an experimental application to understanding differences between two technological approaches, possibly linked to differing mobility strategies, but also allowing for the possibility that bifaces and microblade cores could be part of one settlement system, only used to solve different problems. Although the experimental sample set is small (one biface, one blade core), very interesting results on raw material efficiency, production rate, and size and shape consistencies are achieved. Obviously, severe environments pose restrictions on what people could do and when, and efficiency is a constant requirement. The Rasic and Andrefsky paper is a good contribution towards understanding what happened technologically in the early Holocene of the Pacific Northwest. One area to continue work along these lines is with other core types. Why focus on the possibility that bifaces are parent cores when we have many other amorphous, single- or multiple-platform cores in our assemblages, including those of the American Paleo-Arctic? Coincidentally, research I have been undertaking with Daryl Fedje at the high-resolution site of Richardson Island in Gwaii Haanas National Park Reserve and Haida Heritage Site, British Columbia, indicates that microblade technology may arise simply as a result of raw material stress. At Richardson Island, as sea levels rose, biface technology slowly declined, then microblade technology slowly increased in 17 levels over 900 years (Magne 2000).

Complementing that study, Wenzel and Shelley show that environmental conditions, including qualities of lithic sources, can greatly influence an entire technological tradition. This may be theoretically obvious, but empirical demonstrations are few. Again, here we see a combination of a classificatory approach with a size-grade approach, along with consideration of raw material quality. In this severe environmental situation, we see that the smaller debitage is of the highest quality; the reason is that it was used more completely. Looking at debitage in this way produces the excellent suggestion that experimentation should examine the products and by-products of experienced knappers using low-quality stone. Now that's something we have not done much of, although I might mention that I did include low-grade basalt and chert in my experimental design for application to Interior British Columbia Plateau assemblages (Magne 1985). In my view, the two blade technology papers should have a strong influence on North American blade technology studies, which suffer still from an overemphasis on culture-historical framework approaches.

I wonder, though, in seeking correspondences between lithics and settlement-subsistence-mobility patterns, if we are speaking the same language in various parts of North America. For example, Sievert and Wise suggest that the Kilometer 4 site resulted from a "specialized" economy, yet the Archaic period of the area included seasonal uses of coastal and inland areas and exploitation of a wide variety of fish, shellfish, birds, and sea mammals. Granted, the economy became increasingly specialized through time, but still the range of resources exploited is not so narrow in coastal environments and I think we need to better describe subsistence diversity. Nonetheless the patterns demonstrated at Kilometer 4 are remarkably similar to what we see in many instances on the northern northwest coast of North America—low mobility systems with rather simple stone tool kits. What is missing from consideration is the character of other parts of the overall technology, namely bone and wood tools. For it is there, on the Pacific Northwest coast, that assemblages become highly diverse, likely at the expense of the stone technology.

Methodologically, the approach to correlating lithic complexity with subsistence specialization uses many of the lessons learned in recent lithic studies. The overall sizes and mass of the tool and debitage assemblages, the preference for certain raw materials, and formal debitage and tool characteristics all provide intertwined clues as to settlement activities, duration of occupations, relative intensities of stone tool production, and actual stone tool uses. In short, the Sievert and Wise paper is an excellent example of an applied study where the researchers make use of what we do know about lithic variability rather than arbitrary analytical tools.

Tomka's paper puts a new spin on arguments relating effects of mobility on assemblage composition by considering the lithic technological effects of processing large amounts of food resources. This is a logical argument, and again in this volume, it is an excellent illustration of where thinking about mobility, logistics, and organization have brought us. While clearly this paper is not a discussion of debitage per se, it expands on the kinds of techno-economic models that debitage analyses need to relate to in a direct manner. Stone tools are not an end in themselves. I have small quibbles with Tomka's methodology. For example, what is an expedient tool versus a formal tool? Is a simple utilized flake really that much more expedient than a uniface or simple biface in the context of tool making generally? All three are really pretty easy to make. Maybe there should be a higher "cut-off" point so that only markedly difficult tools are defined as formal. Tool control effort and hafting benefits to processing tasks is something we certainly do not understand well, despite some initial promising studies by Stanford (1979) among others on elephant butchering with torque instruments attached to the stone tools. But here we may need to factor the relative strengths of prehistoric populations—Eugene Gryba's (Gryba 1988) method of hand-held channel flaking comes to mind—and I think we should sometimes try to provide for broader, not narrower control factors. Perhaps something more on the order of big versus small tools, with hafting/no hafting as the cross dimension, would be a better efficiency measure? One of Tomka's contributions here, to rephrase it, is that mobility in the general sense, and resource processing, should be seen as overlapping dimensions, each with their own extremes and effects. There were many ways to hunt and process bison, some involving solitary animal hunts, others mass kills. Winter or summer hunts could occur using jumps, pounds, canyon traps, bogging, and snow. Each would involve very different processing strategies and would have different lithic organizational requirements. His argument is essentially that processing considerations do not replace those of mobility, but that they are taken into account together.

I have the benefit of being a commentator in a strong volume, so my concluding remarks will address the strongest challenge, that posed by Sullivan's paper. In the face of these strong developments in positivist approaches to debitage analysis, where through greater understanding of the minute have we learned much about the whole, I take great issue with the notion that more should be learned by using arbitrary units of measure. On the contrary, I would point out that the trend is clearly for increasing integration of meaningful units of measure. The successful interests we see in this volume alone of applying technologically indicative debitage measures with controlled settlement and environmental indicators should lead to solid lithic-faunal-environmental data integration advances on very wide, if not global scales. On the whole I admit that Sullivan's paper and argument is confusing to me philosophically and historically. Now how could we not say that there has been clear and strong development of inferential and deductive methodology, given the set of papers presented here? Rather, despite Sullivan's insistence that "conventional" debitage analysis has restricted "ampliative inferences," all indications are that "conventional" approaches are working pretty well and are not stagnant, and that constant evaluation and improvement of methods are good things. Despite Sullivan's view, Shott has produced an excellent examination of the "history, theory, and method of debitage analysis" that can be used by students or anyone interested in knowing how we got where we are. Finally, I sense a fatal flaw in logic. First, nobody but nobody, including Holmes, has implied that debitage was deliberately produced with meaning. (Only modern flintknappers do that.) Secondly, while some may only presume that debitage has meaning, it has been firmly demonstrated that in fact it does; and finally, "interpretive content" (which is what we are looking for) is much different from interpretive "purpose." Much as with Dunnell's (1971) methods of systematic classification, which have been interpretively sterile when applied to lithic assemblages (see Whitlam 1980; Magne 1983), the most ambiguous results are obtained using value-free units that somehow magically acquire interpretive purpose.

Sullivan has serious problems with methods of confirmation, which is indeed a serious scientific concern, because he observes that confirmation methods are not perfect. No doubt elimination or nullification strategies are lacking in many archaeological analyses, but what we are doing here and what experimentation aims for, is correction of that problem. To counter Sullivan's argument as stated, I need to say that most lithic technologists seek to know why things are the way they are and to do so we had better have a firm understanding of the most basic principles. To do that requires confirmation through science. To me there is nothing "confirming" reduction stage measures with specific debitage attributes, in the sense of confirming preconceived notions (which Sullivan implies), if experiments conclude that objective measures do indeed relate strongly to objectively defined reduction stages. If they conclude no relationship exists, *then* we might try arbitrary ones to see if we could get lucky. Even if measures like early reduction stage percentages are not completely accurate, we're getting better. Plus, multiple assemblage comparisons across a spectrum of site "functions" allow for scaling of the results. We are starting to understand general assemblage characteristics, proportionate amounts are meaningful, and we may never get certainty in 100 percent of the debitage we are studying. As Shott (1994) and Teltser (1991) have said, most of this kind of work is probabilistic. Most science is. I miss the point of the whole argument, when in summary Sullivan tells us that interpretation-neutral units will tell us how mixed up assemblages are, while meaning-laden units will not. This is obviously not the case at Grasshopper Pueblo (Whittaker and Kaldahl, this volume). I could continue to point out inconsistencies but I think the point is made. The SRT appears to be a method that broadly works in some situations. But it's almost an accident. The experiments that support, enhance, and question its validity have been after the fact. That said, Sullivan's views might very well represent those of a significant number of practicing archaeologists. So be it—open discussion is healthy. Even if the SRT has only encouraged far more use of debitage as a source of information in the 15 years it has received widespread attention, it has been successful.

If we look at the history of North American debitage analysis, trends in scientific advancement are evident (Johnson 1978; Shott 1994). The 1990s were remarkable for debitage analyses in their experimental evaluations of the SRT, mass, and other classificatory methods, and the extent to which archaeological applications of debitage generally became more sophisticated. In large measure, digital technological advances have contributed to this phase of debitage research, in allowing cross application of methods and their refinement, using multiple knapping events, and using well-defined statistical methods. These papers I think represent where the bulk of lithic debitage studies are at in North America. They only begin to address larger issues such as technology as social agency or hunter-gatherer world views as reflected in technology, but they are necessary groundwork towards approaching those broader, anthropologically relevant interests in ways that are reliable and meaningful.

In beginning discussion of this volume, I asked myself whether the papers would be representative of the current status of North American debitage studies, and whether they would be a significant advancement from where we were 10 years ago when the Amick and Mauldin volume was produced, and I must conclude that they do. Here are some observations at the analytical level: consistent and unambiguous terminology is still an issue; replicability of measures, attributes, and experiments is much advanced over where it was 10 years ago; individual knapper variation is an avenue to pursue in far more depth; and combining size grade and typological approaches is very promising. At the middle-range level, methods are emerging that appear worthwhile, such as the juncture and processing approaches discussed here, and the potential is high to gain significant insight by relating lithic debitage to subsistence strategies. We have yet some naivety, some theoretical disagreement, some methodological advancement, some methodological confirmation, some local insight, and some regional and historical trends. I think that in the next 10 years we will see substantial developments along the lines of what has been going on in French Paleolithic studies with respect to *chaine operatoire* and agency studies, as outlined by Dobres and Hoffman (1999) and others. I believe we will have better understanding of the effects of social change and dynamics and environmental change on lithic technological systems and the roles of general technological systems (not just stone tool ones) in social systems. Improved debitage analytical methods and continuing establishment of clear relationships between tool and debitage remains and human behavior will play highly significant roles in these developments.

II

EXPLORING DEBITAGE AND ARCHAEOLOGICAL CONTEXTS

4

Where the Waste Went:
A Knappers' Dump at Grasshopper Pueblo

JOHN C. WHITTAKER AND ERIC J. KALDAHL

Room 246 at Grasshopper Pueblo, a fourteenth-century community in central Arizona, contained a dump of lithic tools and debitage amounting to over 41 kg of material. The full range of common lithic tools was represented, plus unusual evidence of the manufacture of large bifaces. The presence of many tools broken in manufacture, as well as their debitage, allows us to examine production sequences, estimate failure and production rates, and consider the differences in archaeological interpretation that might result from relying exclusively on either the debitage or the tools. In the wider Southwestern context, the Room 246 deposit is unusual both in its richness and in the presence of the biface material. The lithic artifacts, with contextual and other evidence, lead us to interpret the deposit as the result of a number of men knapping in a room dedicated to communal activities, with at least one knapper making unusual bifaces, perhaps for ritual use.

In the dark bottom floor of a two-story room in the center of a large pueblo, a pile of waste from stone tool making grew while the room above echoed to the sharp crack of breaking stone and the voices of knappers. Mixed with moldering bones and other refuse, it was eventually covered by the collapse of floors and walls. To the archaeologists 600 years later, this pile of discards is exceptional. Not only is it an unusually large concentration of interesting debitage, but it also contains examples of most of the normal stone tools made and used in the pueblo, plus an assemblage of typical small projectile points, and a very unusual group of large bifaces at all stages of manufacture.

The debitage produced in making stone tools is perhaps the world's first hazardous waste. Knapping produces copious debris in the form of large angular chunks, small sharp flakes, nasty little slivers, and lung-punishing dust. While prehistoric knappers were probably not alerted to the hazards of airborne particulates, people who go barefoot or in sandals are likely to be sharply aware of inconveniently distributed debitage. Some groups made efforts to remove it from habitation areas, or confine it to pits, dumps, and peripheral areas, although the surface of archaeological sites often shows that this was not a high priority.

Debitage can be a nuisance, but it is also a useful resource. People living in a stone-age site would have seen previously discarded flakes as convenient sharp edges, "expedient tools" to use the current jargon, and as blanks for making other tools. Debitage is of course also useful to us modern archaeologists: ubiquitous, imperishable, and uniquely informative about some human activities. However, debitage does not always yield its information readily. It is often found as scattered waste, built up over a long time, separated from the finished tools, and reflecting many events, people, and diverse activities. The rare situations where we have large deposits of debitage representing limited time spans and including at least some of the knapping equipment and the finished or broken tools the knapper was trying to make have been unusually informative.

ARCHAEOLOGICAL CONTEXT

The debitage "midden" from Room 246 at the prehistoric pueblo of Grasshopper is such a deposit. Grasshopper, in east-central Arizona, is a large pueblo in the late Mogollon or Western Pueblo tradition. Current interpretations (Graves et al. 1982; Reid 1989; Reid and Whittlesey 1997) suggest an initial occupation by a small population shortly before A.D. 1300. Regional patterns of aggregation resulted in rapid growth between 1300 and 1330, resulting in three main roomblocks and a number of outliers (Figure 4.1). There are more than 500 ground floor rooms, a great kiva, and enclosed plazas. After 1330 there is only limited evidence of construction, and Reid believes the community dispersed into the outlier rooms and satellite settlements, until the site was abandoned by 1400. In 30 years of summer field schools, the University of Arizona excavated about a fifth of the 500 or so rooms (Longacre et al. 1982; Longacre and Reid 1974).

Room 246 was a very complex room, excavated during the 1974 and 1975 field seasons under the supervision of Richard Ciolek-Torrello. Most of the contextual information used here is from our interpretations of the field notes and summary reports of the two sets of excavators (Adams et al. 1974; Deutchman et al. 1975).

Room 246 encloses the largest area of any room on the site except the great kiva. It was approximately 7 m long by 5 m wide, and two stories tall at abandonment. It was built as one of a group of "core" rooms that later grew to be Roomblock 3, but there are surfaces under the room that show use of the site before Room 246 was built. Room 246 was built early in the history of Grasshopper and continued in importance for a long time, with several episodes of remodeling and possible changes in function. See Whittaker (1984) for details of the stratigraphic sequence.

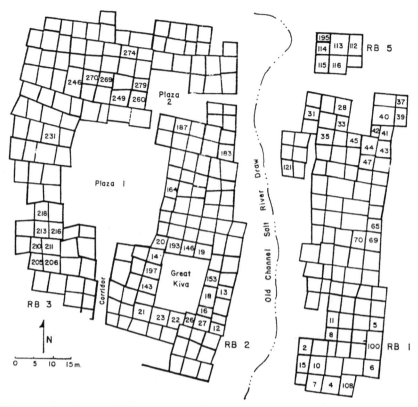

Figure 4.1. Grasshopper Pueblo, AZ P:14:1. Plan of the three main roomblocks with significant excavated rooms labeled. Room 246 is at the upper left in Roomblock 3.

When Room 246 was abandoned, it contained a complementary group of features that indicate what Ciolek-Torrello (1978) considered the suite of facilities necessary for a household. On the roof were mealing bins and associated equipment, with a slab-lined hearth in the center. The second-story floor also had a slab-lined central hearth, a mealing bin near the southwest corner, and clusters of pots in the eastern part of the northwest quadrant and near the east wall in the southeast quadrant. The ground floor had at least a partial prepared clay surface, but no fire features, and was apparently being used for refuse and storage. There was a group of pots in the northwest corner, and another pot cluster with manos and metates against the south wall. The ceramic and ground stone assemblages from Room 246 have not been analyzed. There were numerous other artifacts and waste scattered over this floor, but most of the lithic items were associated with the dominant feature, a pile of debris that occupied all of the northeast quarter of the room.

This "midden," designated Feature 5, is the source of the vast majority of the lithic artifacts from the room. As excavated, it was encountered at the level of the collapsed second-story floor, below which it apparently filled the entire northeast quadrant of the room. Its actual boundaries are not clear and artifacts were not always recorded as coming from the midden, even when they came from the northeast quadrant in relevant levels. Accordingly, some effort is necessary in tracing the midden material. Fragments of bifaces found in the room were usually recorded more precisely than other artifacts, and are all available for analysis. A detailed examination of their proveniences and of conjoinable pieces produced several clear patterns.

Most of the bifaces in all levels are from the northeast quadrant (55 out of 72 pieces). There are a few pieces from other quadrants at all levels, but specific coordinates for individually plotted artifacts show that most of these biface fragments were found near the northeast quadrant. The conjoinable pieces of bifaces and other items show that Feature 5 is a single homogeneous deposit at all levels. Pieces that fit together and were not modified after breakage are sometimes recorded as separated by one or even two stratigraphic levels. This is because these levels in the midden are arbitrary divisions formed by projecting a natural stratigraphic level (such as the collapsed second story floor) in one part of the room across a feature where that level did not exist. Vertical coordinates show up to 134 cm of vertical distance between conjoining fragments, although most are much closer to each other.

From the distribution of the bifaces and other evidence the midden can be assessed. From the field measurements and drawings the midden appears to be a half-conical pile in the northeast corner of the room, with its highest point against the east wall. The maximum height of the pile as excavated was about 1 m. The bottom rested on the last ground floor (Floor 1/Level 7). There are conjoinable biface fragments both above and below the apparent limits of the midden, but these are probably best explained as the result of disturbance—by rodents, features in the floor, and rain and muddy conditions during excavation. The excavators suggested that the midden materials were dumped through a hatch onto the second-story floor, but there is no evidence of a hatch, the pile is not centered in the room, and it does not appear to overlie the remnants of the second floor. More likely, the midden was on the ground floor and protruded through the rubble of the second-story floor when the floor and roof collapsed.

It is still not clear where the actual knapping was done. The dark ground floor without hearth, doors, or windows where the waste piled up is not likely to have been the work area. The second-story floor or roof is more likely. All the other lithic tools as well as the bifaces are concentrated in the northeast quadrant midden, and very rare on occupation surfaces elsewhere. If the roof or second-story floor were used as knapping areas, they appear to have been swept clean, at least of large pieces. As will be shown, most of the bifaces and points in the room were broken in manufacture, and much of the waste results from the production of these and other tools. Included with the large flakes and other material are hundreds of tiny flakes and minute debris, as well as a number of tools in apparently complete and usable condition. The small debitage suggests either that flaking was done on the spot, or that waste was carefully collected and swept up if the waste was moved. Most likely, it was not moved far. The whole items suggest that artifacts were stored here, or were lost at the site of use or manufacture, perhaps by being dropped among refuse.

There were pots on the ground floor around the midden area, apparently whole, so this room probably had a continuing storage function. It could not have been a very pleasant store room, as the midden contained large quantities of faunal remains, potsherds, ground stone, and other artifacts, suggesting that it was the final resting place of much general household refuse as well as lithic debris and related items. Almost as many mouse bones (130 MNI) were recovered here as in all the rest of the rooms together (Holbrook 1982). It was evidently an attractive habitat for vermin, either while edible refuse was being dumped into it, or after abandonment. The nonlithic artifacts from Room 246 have not yet been analyzed, and it will probably not be possible to resolve completely the questions of the relationship of the midden to its possible sources. It is probable that such debris was not moved far, and that a dark room with a smelly trash pile was not used as a work area. The best hypothesis seems to be that the upper habitation floor or the roof was the site of manufacture, and the waste was swept or dumped into the semi-abandoned room beneath, which served as a convenient household dump and perhaps as storage space for less valuable items, if the vessels there are actually complete.

THE LITHIC ASSEMBLAGE

Before discussing the lithic assemblage, a few contextual issues affecting the analysis should be mentioned. Following standard procedure at Grasshopper, the room was excavated in four quadrants with a cross-shaped balk separating them. The 1974 team excavated most of the room down to the ground floor (Level 7) except in balks and the northeast quadrant which contained the midden (Feature 5), and the 1975 team carried on from there. Some inconsistencies in recording and level designations resulted.

In 1974 fill around some features and most of the material from Feature 5 was screened through ¼-inch mesh, with every tenth shovelful from Feature 5 screened through ⅛-inch mesh. It is not clear from the records whether the rest of the room fill was screened. In 1975 all fill was apparently screened, and all of Feature 5, (Level 5 in balks and Level 6 in the entire northeast quadrant), was screened through ⅜-inch mesh. This differential screening may accentuate the concentration of lithic artifacts in the northeast quadrant. The distribution of large artifacts confirms the concentration, but it is now hard to estimate how much Feature 5 was spread over the rest of the room.

All of the recovered material was saved for analysis, including some 41 kg of lithic artifacts. However, the mass of material was not well sorted, and the field recording and later computer coding of some artifacts was inconsistent and often inaccurate, which means that provenience information on some pieces is not good. However, of 382 stone tools recorded by the excavators, only 29 were not located for analysis. All the bifaces were found. Where artifact counts differ from those given previously (Whittaker 1984), it is usually because in the course of the debitage analysis reported here, previously unrecognized retouched specimens were found.

Most debitage analyses aim to understand what kinds of tools were being made and used, even in the absence of those tools. The deposit in Room 246 has both debitage and tools, although we expect that at least some of the tools have been removed. We will discuss the tools first, then the debitage. A wide range of tools is represented, including most of the forms found at Grasshopper. More detailed information on the projectile points (Whittaker 1987a, 1987b) and the other tool types (Whittaker 1984) have been published elsewhere. Here we will make some general comments on the assemblage and briefly describe the unusual bifaces.

The lithic assemblage from Room 246, and from the rest of Grasshopper Pueblo, is outstanding for its diversity, quality, and quantity in comparison to most Southwestern sites. Grasshopper is only 4 to 30 km from a series of good chert exposures, which was probably exploited by all the sites in the region. The chert, derived from the Mississippian Redwall limestones (Finnell 1966), is exposed on the surface and in arroyos (Whittaker 1984). It occurs in nodules 10 cm to more than 30 cm in diameter, but large nodules are rare and usually flawed. They sometimes split into flat plates, which were used as blanks for some of the bifaces from Room 246. The chert is usually gray, but with much variation in color, banding, and the presence of fossils. The knapping quality varies from rather coarse with a sugary graininess to good with a smooth fracture surface, with a few pieces of outstandingly superior material. The bulk of the chert is of good quality, suitable for both bifacial reduction and pressure work.

As Table 4.1 shows, a wide variety of tools were made in Room 246. Some of the flake tools are very carefully finished; others are quite casual. Most were made on simple hard-hammer percussion flakes with large bulbs of percussion and well-defined points of impact on unprepared platforms. We suspect that many of the tools were used in craftwork in the room, but no use-wear analysis has been done. There are many cores (n=43), mostly with many flakes removed. About half (n=22) appear to be exhausted. Most cores were flaked expediently from a

Table 4.1.
Major Lithic and Related Tool Types in Room 246

Types	Number	Percent of Assemblage
Manufacturing Tools		
Antler flaking tools	26	
Shaft straighteners	14	
Hammerstones	76	
Flaked Stone		
Cores	43	12.5
Choppers	11	3.2
Flake knives	21	6.1
Scrapers	25	7.3
Miscellaneous flake tools	3	0.9
Drills	17	4.9
Large points	11	3.2
Small triangular arrowpoints	132	38.4
Small bifacial knives	4	1.2
Large bifaces	77	22.4
Total Flaked Stone	344	100.0

number of different platforms, and none show evidence of an effort to produce consistent series of regular flakes. Hard-hammer percussion was the major, if not the only technique used, and there was little or no platform preparation. As will appear later, this conforms to the evidence of the debitage. About a quarter (n=12) of the cores show signs of tool use: battering or microflaking of edges or steep retouch to make a scraper.

Knapping tools were common in Room 246. Seventy-six hammerstones were recorded, of which 45 were probably knapping hammers, although they were doubtless used for other things as well. They are mostly cobbles of quartzite or other tough material, with wear confined to ends or edges. The wear is mostly battering and crushing. It often forms facets, sometimes with striations at the edges from scraping the edge of the core during the follow-through of a blow. Some of the hammers have polish where the thumb and forefinger would have gripped them. All these wear patterns can be readily duplicated in experimental knapping. The rest of the hammerstones can mostly be called "pecking hammers." They are usually of cryptocrystalline material, often an exhausted core, with battering all over to the point that some are almost spherical. The cryptocrystalline materials of pecking hammers develop a rough surface from incipient fracture cones, which makes them unsuitable for knapping but effective in reducing a softer stone by pecking. They are common all over the site as are the manos and metates they would have been used to make.

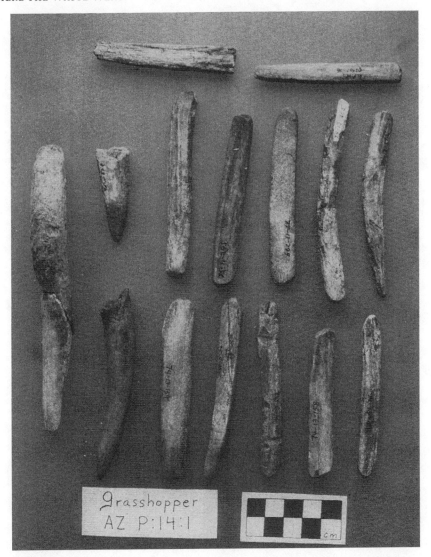

Figure 4.2. Antler pressure-flaking tools from Room 246. Both tine and cut antler flakers are represented.

There were also 26 antler knapping tools. Antler hammers or billets are not uncommon at Grasshopper; S. L. Olsen (1979) reports 43. These are short basal sections of antlers with wear facets, nicks, and scratches on the base resulting from knapping. There are three from Room 246. Pressure flakers are present in two forms, both identifiable by beveling wear and scratches on the tips (Figure 4.2). Flakers made from more or less unmodified tines are found at sites throughout America. Three were identified in Room 246. Cut antler flakers are less commonly

AZ P:14:1
Room 246   cm

Figure 4.3. Typical small arrow points from Room 246 show a diversity of form. The point second from left on the bottom is made of obsidian. The others are all local chert.

reported but are known elsewhere (Kidder 1932; Olsen 1980). These are small flat strips cut from the beam of an antler, with flaking wear on one or both ends. At Grasshopper they outnumber tine flakers 149 to 58 (Olsen 1979); there are 18 from Room 246. They require much more work than tine flakers, and have no obvious advantage, unless they were attached to a wooden handle to make a longer tool with a better grip and more leverage. Such compound pressure flakers are

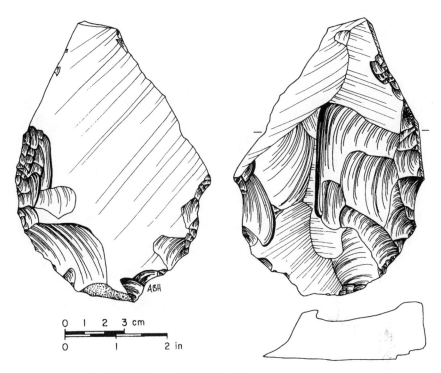

Figure 4.4. An edged blank (Stage 1 biface) from Room 246.

documented in historic California (Goddard 1904; Pope 1974; Schumacher 1951) and the prehistoric Southwest (Guernsey and Kidder 1921). Three other pieces of antler from Room 246 were cut or grooved and identified as blanks for flaking tools; there was other worked and unworked antler in the room as well.

The outstanding feature of the lithic assemblage in Room 246 is the large number of bifaces and points that seem to have been the focus of knapping effort. Small triangular arrow points make up about 38 percent of the flaked stone tools. The 41 finished points represent a wide variety of notched and un-notched forms typical of those found throughout the site (Figure 4.3). The points are made by pressure flaking and all stages of manufacture are represented. Ninety-one pieces appear to be unfinished points, usually discarded after breaks typical of knapping errors rather than impact damage (Whittaker 1987b).

Almost a quarter of the flaked stone tools in Room 246 are large bifaces or pieces thereof. As used here, the term "large biface" signifies a flat bifacial tool larger than 10 cm in length. There are 77 major pieces, of which 10 are unbroken bifaces. Many of the fragments conjoin, so the 77 pieces represent 60 individual bifaces. This is far more large bifaces than come from the rest of the site, or from any other Southwestern prehistoric pueblo of which we are aware.

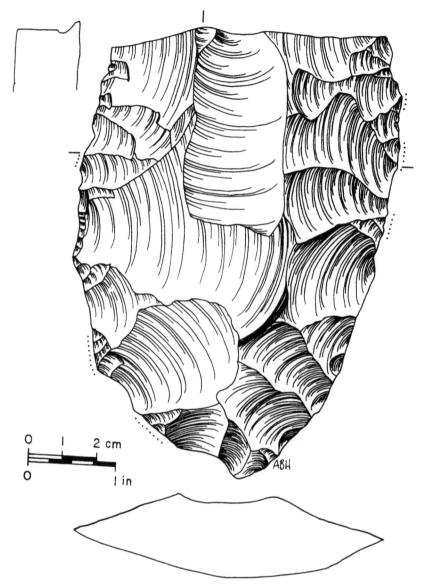

Figure 4.5. An early preform (Stage 2 biface) from Room 246. The large lengthwise flake is the only sign of further work after the piece snapped.

It will be convenient to describe the bifaces in terms of stages of manufacture (cf. Callahan 1979; Collins 1975; Patterson 1977; Whittaker 1994). Some (e.g., Callahan 1979) consider the unretouched blank as the first stage in biface production. This may be how a knapper sees it, but the archaeologist would be unwise to try to predict what a prehistoric knapper had in mind for an unflaked

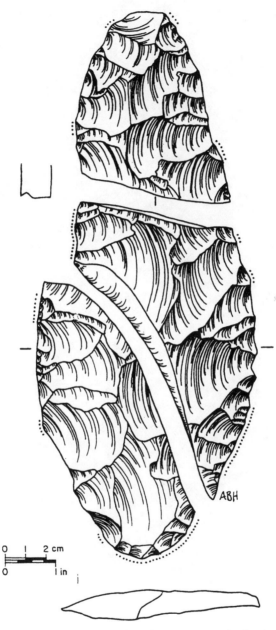

Figure 4.6. A thinned preform (Stage 3 biface) from Room 246, broken into three pieces by bending and perverse fractures. Dots indicate platform grinding on the edges.

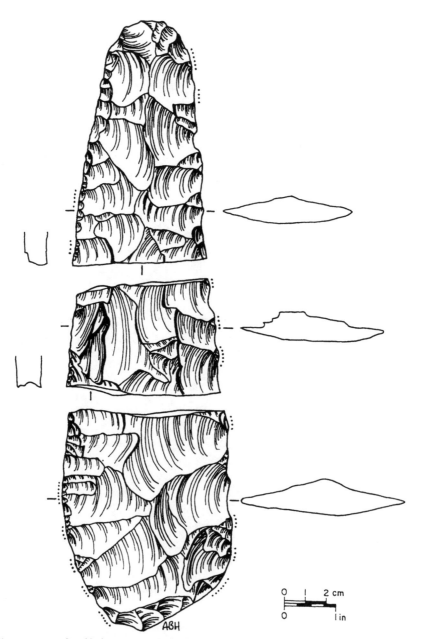

Figure 4.7. A refined biface (Stage 4 biface) from Room 246, broken by bending fractures while the knapper was trying to remove the large step plateau in the center. Dots indicate platform grinding on the edges.

Figure 4.8. Finished or nearly finished bifaces from Room 246. The two pieces in the lower left and the one on the lower far right are apparently finished and notched for hafting. The specimen in the upper right is unfinished but shows unusual pressure flaking.

nodule or an unretouched flake. In Room 246 there were a number of large flakes and pieces of nodules that could have been raw material for bifaces. Many other things could have been done with them, and they are not enumerated here.

In Room 246 there were four pieces we classify as Stage 1, or "edged blank" (Figure 4.4). At this stage, the knapper has begun to produce a bifacial edge on a suitable piece of material (one such piece weighed 880 g). A middle stage in biface manufacture is often called the "preform." For this analysis it is useful to subdivide preforms into two stages: Stage 2 "early preforms" (Figure 4.5) have completely bifaced edges but are irregular and essentially unthinned; at this point thinning is the main goal of the knapper. There are nine examples. One typical specimen weighed 325 g. Another 19 bifaces can be called Stage 3, "thinned preforms" (Figure 4.6). They are still not regular, but major thinning is in progress (two such pieces each weighed 200 g). Stage 4, "refined biface" is represented by 25 bifaces (Figure 4.7). These are fairly thin and flat, with a symmetrical form but with jagged untrimmed edges and large areas of ground platform remaining along edges. A weight range was observed in finished forms from 90 to 270 g. The average weight on seven complete specimens was 160 g.

Only three bifaces appear to be finished, having a symmetrical form, and edges shaped and regularized, with jagged platform remnants trimmed off. They also have narrowed bases with shallow notches, presumably for hafting (Figure 4.8). As most of the bifaces are unfinished, the desired final form is uncertain. The three apparently finished specimens are of middle size for the assemblage, and thicker and more lenticular in cross section than some unfinished examples. Two are tapered lanceolates, bipointed, with maximum width close to one end. The third finished biface is shorter and broader, with a rounded tip and distinct stem. Several of the unfinished bifaces (Figure 4.9) suggest that another form was attempted: a long, thin, flat biface with one edge straight and the other slightly convex. These tend to be over 150 mm long, 50 mm wide, and 10–15 mm thick, slightly longer and thinner than the two finished lanceolates. However, the longest biface was 302 mm long before it broke into three pieces as it neared completion.

The bifaces were worked by percussion with antler hammers or soft hammerstones, producing large, flat, expanding flake scars. The platform remnants on bifaces and flakes are often extensively ground, especially in the later stages when more care was necessary. There was a tendency to overdo the grinding on thin edges, and a number of bifaces had crescentic bites removed from the edges when excessively strong platforms were struck. Pressure-flaked tools are very common at Grasshopper, and sometimes show great skill, but there is almost no pressure work on the bifaces. One extremely narrow biface has part of one edge finished with large but narrow and regular scars that would be difficult to produce except by pressure flaking. The other pieces, including the finished bifaces, seem to have been worked by percussion alone.

AZ P:14:1
Room 246   cm

Figure 4.9. Large bifaces from Room 246 at Stages 3 and 4, broken by bending or perverse fractures typical of errors in percussion manufacture. The three lower specimens suggest that a long narrow form was the goal.

Only six bifaces show visible signs of use. One finished biface (74-13-11) has polish along edges that are microflaked and dulled. Two other pieces have battering and dulling along an edge. One of these is a finished biface (74-13-125); the other is a thinned preform. Three pieces have microflaking along steep angled breaks, apparently from being used to scrape wood or other hard material after the biface broke. Of these, one each is at Stage 1, 2, or 3, and the latter has also had steep scraper retouch added along one edge.

The patterns of breakage and discard are consistent with the manufacturing context. The more a biface was worked, the more likely it was to be broken as it became thinner and more fragile. Most of the bifaces were broken by bending or perverse fractures (Cotterell and Kamminga 1979; Crabtree 1972; Tsirk 1979). Perverse and bending fractures in particular are often caused by striking a platform that is too strong or too high above the center plane of a biface, or by striking too far in from the platform. Eleven bifaces were discarded unbroken, but five of these had other problems that would have made them difficult to finish. Only the three finished bifaces, two refined bifaces, and one thinned preform show no obvious reason for discard.

Good pieces of material were selected to make bifaces and only three were discarded because of poor material or breakage due to flaws. In the case of the pieces broken by flexing and by perverse fractures of undetermined origin, the knapper probably struck an inaccurate blow or failed to support the biface as he struck it. In several cases, striking too strong a platform flexed the biface, and in one example, the biface broke as the knapper repeatedly tried to remove a step fracture (see Figure 4.7). One unbroken Stage 4 piece was apparently discarded because the knapper failed to remove a step, leaving an ugly thick spot and a notched edge. Three pieces in the first three stages were abandoned when the knapper could not thin them satisfactorily.

Similar patterns can be seen by looking at problems that did not cause the discard of bifaces. Material flaws and excessive thickness were problems that were usually overcome or resulted in early discard. As the bifaces became thinner, there were more likely to be problems related to platform preparation on the edges. A higher percent (40 percent) of almost finished bifaces were simply broken, reflecting their fragility and the fact that to get that far, most other problems had to have been overcome.

The bifaces are probably the work of a limited number of knappers, perhaps only one or two. The projectile points from Room 246 were a diverse group, and because there were other limited contexts with sets of points, notably burials, it was possible to compare groups of points in terms of variations in form and in the patterning of flake scars produced by knappers' habits of holding and working points. This analysis suggested that while many of the sets from burials and elsewhere were the work of individual knappers, the diverse points from Room

246 were probably produced by many knappers (Whittaker 1984, 1987a). Although attributes of form and flake scar patterning distinguish individual knappers of bifaces (Gunn 1975, 1977), it was not possible to perform a similar analysis on the bifaces. There are no other assemblages in the pueblo to compare to these, only isolated pieces, and most of the bifaces were discarded unfinished.

Nevertheless, the material and treatment of the bifaces is quite uniform, enough so to suggest one or a few individuals with a consistent knapping strategy (cf. Young and Bonnichsen 1984). The flaking and platform preparation is consistent, especially in emphasizing strongly ground platforms. Although the flake scars are not uniform or patterned, control of thinning and terminations is fairly good, despite the biased view presented by discarded failures. The large, thin pieces demonstrate considerable skill, although some have avoidable mistakes, such as excessively strengthened platforms leading to damaged edges or bending fractures, and repeated step terminations that left unremovable thick spots. On the other hand, the forms are not very consistent, nor is the progression of pieces through different stages of manufacture. One could suggest that, as with the points, there were multiple knappers whose technology and approaches were similar, but whose products varied. However, while points are ubiquitous throughout the pueblo, it is worth emphasizing again that the bifaces are unique. If multiple knappers were indeed involved in production, an explanation that accounts for the spatial restrictiveness in this tool form's production, storage, and discard must be offered. This is a subject to which we will return in our interpretations.

The treatment of some of the discards is also odd. It is not surprising that some were used as tools, just as were many other pieces of material from the pile of waste. However, several pieces that were too narrow or too flawed to be made into either the lanceolate or the crescentic finished forms show biface work after one would expect them to have been abandoned. Other large fragments that could have been reworked into successful bifaces were discarded. The lack of pressure flaking is also not typical of the other flint work at Grasshopper and in Room 246. One admittedly speculative explanation of these facts is that the bifaces in Room 246 may be the work of a knapper (or knappers) who was fairly skillful and adept at the techniques of soft-hammer flaking, but who was perhaps experimenting with an unusual large form rather than turning out an accustomed product.

DEBITAGE

With so many tools to work from, can the debitage tell us anything more? We attempt to examine several questions by integrating debitage data with information provided by the tools in Room 246:

(1) The tools from Room 246, especially the bifaces, form an unusual assemblage, not just for the site, but also for the Southwest as a whole. How does the debitage assemblage compare to other Grasshopper assemblages and other Southwestern material?

(2) Would the debitage by itself suggest the same kinds of activities and products as the tools?

(3) What can we infer from the debitage about the scale of production, especially of the unusual bifaces?

As noted earlier, the 41 kg of lithic artifacts were collected under slightly different excavation protocols, over two seasons of excavation. There was no obvious way of taking a statistically random sample of the debitage lots (about 85 bags of varying sizes). Accordingly, 12 numbered bags were selected for analysis. They comprise most of the material labeled as coming from Geological Level 6 (secondary refuse between second story floor and ground floor) in the northeast quadrant of the room, which was entirely midden material, plus about a third of the material from Geological Level 5 (labeled "second-story floor fall" but actually midden material in the northeast quadrant). These lots were all from work in 1975, and thus are most of the material from a limited vertical and horizontal provenience, excavated in a limited time by the same team. It should be a reasonably representative chunk of the reasonably homogeneous midden, and for analytical purposes, we will have to treat it as such, with some reservations. There are, for instance, some differences in bag contents, some having more large flakes, others more smaller flakes, which we think represent different episodes of screening and sorting during excavation and initial analysis. The field school washed and sorted all artifacts and entered them into a crude computerized catalog system, but the records are poor and the sorting of bulk artifacts erratic. However, the sample analyzed includes large numbers of small flakes, suggesting that the collection was fairly complete.

The analyzed sample weighs 6,297 g, and includes some 4,147 pieces of debitage. The sample was 17 percent of the total weight of debitage from Room 246 (36.694 kg). This material was analyzed in several different ways at different times by the two authors. Our different approaches are both current among lithic analysts, and arrived at similar conclusions, supporting each other but relying on differing comparisons. Whittaker sorted the debitage into standard technological categories: shatter (angular fragments without flake traits); normal flakes (flat platforms, point initiations, large bulbs, relatively thick); biface thinning flakes (edge platforms, diffuse bulbs, thin and expanding, multiple flat dorsal scars); and indeterminate flakes (mostly lacking platforms). Within these categories, the pieces were size-graded by fitting on a grid into five size grades (<1 cm, 1–2 cm, 2–4 cm, 4–6 cm, and >6 cm), and also sorted by presence/absence of cortex and presence/absence of platform. Kaldahl categorized debitage as shatter, complete

TABLE 4.2.
Major Assemblage Categories as Percentages of Assemblage Weight and Count
(Whittaker Data)

Category	Percent of Assemblage Weight	Percent of Assemblage Count	Count	Percent with Category Cortex
Material with cortex	NA	8.6	357	NA
Flakes with cortex	NA	8.0	313	NA
Shatter	12.9	5.7	240	18.0
Normal flakes	44.1	12.8	530	21.9
Biface thinning flakes	21.6	47.4	1966	5.1
Indeterminate flakes	21.3	34.5	1431	6.8
Total Flakes	87.1	94.2	3907	8.0
Total Assemblage	100.0	100.0	4147	8.6

flake, broken flake, or flake fragment (after Sullivan and Rozen 1985), and recorded individual weight, length, width, thickness, and some platform attributes. As the two analyses were compatible but somewhat different, we specify which analysis produced the following information.

Tables 4.2 and 4.3 characterize the debitage assemblage, and a number of important trends can be readily seen. Both by weight and by count the assemblage includes a high proportion of biface debitage. Many of the biface thinning flakes are small, so they are 47 percent of the assemblage count but only 22 percent of the weight. The numerous biface thinning flakes are also rarely cortical, while the generally larger normal flakes are more likely to have been removed from near the surface of the core. Shatter is relatively rare because of the high quality of the chert; large angular pieces are sometimes produced in initial work with a nodule, but are often solid enough to be used for further reduction.

These trends are echoed in Kaldahl's analysis. In his dissertation, Kaldahl (2000) analyzed lithic debris from four contexts at Grasshopper, two earlier sites nearby, and seven other sites in the Silver Creek and Hay Hollow Valley areas, a total of 68 assemblages from 10 different pueblos. Kaldahl's analyses provide some of the basis for our statements about the unique nature of the Room 246 assemblage, but for the purposes of this paper, we will confine our comparisons of Room 246 to a single similar context: Room 269. Because the assemblage from Room 269 is in the same site, spatially and chronologically close, based on the same raw materials, and deposited under similar conditions, it is the assemblage most comparable to that in Room 246, which makes the differences even more striking.

Room 269 was "two doors down" (see Figure 4.1) from Room 246, and was

TABLE 4.3.
Debitage by Size Categories (Whittaker Data)

Debitage	<1 cm	Percent	1–2 cm	Percent	2–4 cm	Percent	4–6 cm	Percent	>6 cm	Percent
Shatter	0	0.0	182	75.8	47	19.6	6	2.5	5	2.1
Normal flakes	24	4.5	164	30.9	253	47.7	79	14.9	10	1.9
Biface thinning flakes	955	49.1	613	31.5	335	17.2	41	2.1	2	0.1
Indeterminate flakes	555	38.8	609	42.6	253	17.7	13	0.9	1	0.0

TABLE 4.4.
Basic Technological Types, Percentages in Rooms 246 and 269 (Kaldahl Data)

Technological Type	Room 246	Room 269
Shatter	13.4	20.8
Core	0.4	5.9
Flake	82.7	70.3
Notched flake	0.1	
Retouched: unidirectional	1.1	0.5
Uniface	1.1	0.5
Retouched: bidirectional	0.8	2.0
Biface	0.3	
Total	100.0	100.0

built as part of the same construction event. Also a two-story structure, Room 269 had few features on the first-story floor. On the second-story floor, a hearth and a cluster of pots were recovered (Ciolek-Torrello 1978). Chipped stone debitage from the dark understory was analyzed in order to contrast the two assemblages. In Table 4.4 the basic technological types used in Kaldahl's analysis underscore Whittaker's observations regarding the paucity of shatter relative to flakes. More flakes were apparent in the Room 246 assemblage, driving down the relative percentages of shatter. The retouched and facially thinned pieces recorded above encompass those pieces, often unfinished blanks or tools that were broken in the production process, which were encountered amidst the general debitage. These do not include the formal tools such as the large bifaces or the projectile points.

While analysis using the debitage categories of Sullivan and Rozen (1985) can incite great passion among debitage analysts, Kaldahl finds it a useful comparative tool. In Table 4.5, the debitage category percentages illustrate some distinctions in the flintknapping activities that generated the deposits in Rooms 246 and 269. While complete flake frequencies between the two rooms were similar, the broken flakes and flake fragments in Room 246 constituted 40 percent of the assemblage, in contrast to 30 percent of the assemblage in Room 269. Higher proportions of broken flakes and flake fragments would suggest an assemblage with more thinned pieces, which were more susceptible to breakage. This is completely consistent with the biface production activities implied by the formal tool assemblage. The lower frequencies of shatter in the Room 246 assemblage are quite apparent in this contrast. The lower proportions of shatter suggests that the knapping activities which created the Room 246 trash deposit derived from less heavy percussion activities from the early stages of cobble and core reduction. The patterns in the Table 4.5 debitage data can be interpreted to reflect the important

TABLE 4.5.
Debitage Category Percentages in Room 246 and 269 (Kaldahl Data)

Debitage Category	Room 246	Room 269
Complete flake	46.5	48.7
Broken flake	3.5	10.6
Flake fragment	36.5	19.0
Shatter	13.5	21.7
Total	100.0	100.0

TABLE 4.6.
Platform Type Percentages in Room 246 and 269 (Kaldahl Data)

Platform Type	Room 246	Room 269
Cortical platform	2.8	3.6
Single noncortical platform	50.7	67.6
Dihedral platform	8.2	7.2
Faceted platform	10.7	1.8
Crushed/Unidentifiable platform	27.6	19.8
Total	100.0	100.0

trends, but Whittaker would like to point out that the uninformative debitage categories defined by Sullivan and Rosen fail to clearly convey the distinctive nature of the Room 246 assemblage which is evident at a glance to any flintknapper.

We conclude then with two sets of evidence that support the above two inferences. Our first inference is that much of the refuse deposited in Room 246 derived from biface production debris, primarily the large bifacial tools. Perhaps the most telling and clear argument for this can be observed in the platform types recovered (Table 4.6).

Having analyzed tens of thousands of debitage pieces from other Puebloan sites, we can say with some confidence that flake platforms are overwhelmingly cortical or simple single-facet noncortical platforms. For example, at the Pueblo IV site of Bailey Ruin, just to the north of Grasshopper Pueblo on the Mogollon Rim, 2,300 chert pieces with platforms were analyzed (Kaldahl 2000). Of those, only 2.1 percent had dihedral or faceted platforms. In contrast nearly 19 percent of the Room 246 assemblage had faceted or dihedral platforms. The neighboring Room 269 had 9 percent of those platform types. Flakes with heavily prepared dihedral and faceted platforms are most often produced during biface manufacture. Biface knapping also generates many flakes with crushed platforms.

Our other inference is that the flintknapping activities that generated the trash in Room 246, beyond biface production, involved the production of flake

TABLE 4.7.
Cortical Coverage Category Percentages in Room 246 and 269 (Kaldahl Data)

Cortical Coverage	Room 246	Room 269
0%	93.0	85.6
1–10%	3.9	10.4
10–50%	2.8	4.0
50–90%	0.1	
90–100%	0.1	
Total	100.0	100.0

blanks, with less evidence for the earliest reduction stages and heavy hard-hammer percussion. This is further supported in an assessment of cortical coverage on artifacts (Table 4.7).

In Room 246, about 7 percent of all pieces had some cortical coverage, versus the 14.4 percent of artifacts recovered in Room 269. The debris in Room 269 had more shatter and greater amounts of cortical coverage indicative of an assemblage with more early stage reduction debris. The Room 246 assemblage, in contrast, with less cortical coverage and less shatter, had debris from somewhat later steps in the reduction process. Moreover, the higher proportions of faceted platforms, broken flakes, and flake fragments underscore our interpretation that the Room 246 assemblage derived from more biface tool and retouched tool production.

Within the context of Grasshopper Pueblo, we can consider what the debitage shows about lithic manufacture. Table 4.1 showed the distribution of major tool types within Room 246. Most come from the midden deposit. The tool assemblage shows that production within Room 246 focused on two main types of artifact, the large bifaces described earlier, and the small triangular arrow points typical of Grasshopper. Both are found at all stages of manufacture, and most pieces show the kind of breaks typical of manufacture errors. The debitage assemblage conforms to these patterns, with high percentages of readily recognizable biface thinning flakes, and high rates of flake fracture, platform preparation, and platform damage. Half of the biface thinning flakes are less than 1 cm in maximum dimension, and some of these small flakes are probably pressure flakes from point manufacture, although we can expect that the bulk of the pressure debitage from the points, being very small, would not have been recovered.

Small triangular projectile points like those from Room 246 are ubiquitous throughout the site, but large bifaces are very rare. There are only a handful of pieces that may be related to the bifaces from Room 246. One is a wide flat ovate biface from Room 269. It is similar in workmanship to those in Room 246, but better. It is heavily patinated on one surface and lightly patinated on the other, thus probably older than the unpatinated bifaces in Room 246. Since the two rooms are part of the same construction and habitation unit, it is tempting to speculate that this biface was the model for the assemblage in Room 246, but of course this is untestable. There are also three fragments of middle stage bifaces. One is from Room 270, which is next door to Room 246, and may derive from the debris in Room 246. The others are from fill in the Great Kiva and cannot be confidently connected to Room 246. Other pieces that could be related to Room 246 are a stemmed ovate from Room 70 that resembles the one described above, and a stemmed crescentic form from Room 41, which is of different chert and finished by pressure flaking. Bifaces like those from Room 246 were not found in the more than 600 burials excavated at Grasshopper, nor are they normal finds at other sites in the region. Perhaps very few actually left the room.

The bifaces in Room 246 did not leave any characteristic discard that allows an easy estimate of missing finished pieces in the manner in which tranchet sharpening flakes have been used to estimate adze production at Colha (Hester et al. 1983). We can however examine some parameters through the mass of debitage. Finished bifaces from Room 246 weigh between 100 and 200 g. Pieces of chert suitable for making them would weigh between 500 and 1,000 g. Accordingly, we might expect that the 60 bifaces recovered in the room should have produced between 18 and 54 kg of debitage. By weight, about 22 percent of our debitage sample is biface debitage (Table 4.2). This is a minimum, since many of the indeterminate flakes are probably broken biface thinning flakes; the early stages of biface manufacture with hammerstones would have produced many flakes we would put in our "normal flake" category, and waste flakes of all sorts were consumed to make the points and other tools in Room 246. If our sample is reasonably representative, a half to a quarter of the 41 kg of debitage in Room 246 derives from biface manufacture, say 9 to 19 kg. It seems that the debitage in the room probably came from not many more bifaces than are present. There is at least no reason to assume that any large number were finished and removed.

INTERPRETATIONS

Room 246 contains the largest single deposit of lithic waste at Grasshopper. Such deposits often suggest specialized craft workshops, but there are a number of arguments against such an interpretation in Room 246. Although the lithic material was the most notable aspect of the deposits in Room 246, and the only part that has been analyzed, the midden actually contained much more. The ground floor of Room 246 was used for storing and discarding all sorts of things—whole or partial pots, bone tools and waste from their manufacture, manos and metates as well as hammerstones probably used to work them, sherds, food remains, and other household debris, and waste and tools from lithic crafts and related activities. The lithic debris itself includes most of the diverse flaked stone tool types found at Grasshopper. Whittaker has shown elsewhere (1984, 1987a) that the numerous projectile points are diverse in forms and flaking patterns and represent the work of a number of knappers. Because there is little to compare them to, it is difficult to analyze the bifaces with the same techniques that showed the diversity of the points. Our impression, as discussed earlier, is that they are perhaps the work of a single knapper or a few knappers working in close association with each other, pursuing the production of similar forms. This is suggested by the unique nature of the bifaces, as well as consistency of technique, particularly the use of heavily ground and isolated platforms and a tendency to damage bifaces by endshock and excessively lipped thinning flakes. The traits of the bifaces, and the probability that few were completed and removed, suggest a competent knapper who was working on an unusual kind of artifact. The bifaces suggest an experimental industry; eccentric rather than specialized.

Ciolek-Torrello (1978, 1985) examined the distribution of artifacts and features in rooms across the site to produce a functional classification of rooms. Many households apparently occupied suites of two to three rooms or floors with complementary features that indicate storage, habitation, and manufacturing activities. Room 246 can be interpreted as the space of a single family or similar social unit, occupying a vertical suite of complementary floors. Some arrangement of horizontal suites with floors in surrounding rooms that are not all excavated cannot be ruled out, but at abandonment at least, the ground floor no longer opened into its neighbors. Such suites can be described as "multiple room households," which at Grasshopper typically include a specialized habitation room plus one or two rooms for storage and manufacture (Reid 1989:85; Reid and Whittlesey 1982). Such rooms as 246, with long occupations spans and a high incidence of manufacturing evidence, are often in what Ciolek-Torrello (1978) calls "central zones." These are areas of the pueblo centrally located around architectural features of special social significance such as plazas and the Great Kiva.

Room 246 also shows some unusual features suggesting communal uses. It is enormous, and when built, enclosed a pair of ovens. There were niches in the north wall, and human, macaw, and hawk burials under the floors. The midden material also reflects common use of the room. The projectile points represent the work of a number of knappers, distinguished by form and by flake scar patterns (Whittaker 1984, 1987a, 1987b). There are also a number of diverse shaft straighteners, which also suggest multiple craftsmen. The midden contained an unusual number of bird bones, including parts of two macaws, turkey, quail, pigeon, owls, jay, and raven (Olsen 1980). These could have provided feathers for ceremonial use or for arrow fletching. The midden, and the room as a whole, also had unusual numbers of exotic materials and ornamental items, including worked shell, turquoise, steatite, bone, and quartz crystals. All of these are frequently found in burials and other ceremonial contexts, and like the stone tools, may represent male craft activities.

The clan or moiety house in modern pueblos (Dozier 1965; Eggan 1950; Hawley 1950; Hill 1970) is probably the best analog to Room 246. Among modern pueblos these are rooms that may have no architectural distinctions and are sometimes occupied by the head family of a clan or sodality. Ceremonial paraphernalia is often kept here, and such rooms may be used for meetings and some ritual. Kivas and clan houses may also serve as gathering places for men of the clan or ceremonial society, and both secular and religious craft activities may take place there.

In recent times knives and chipped stone tools have been used ceremonially by Puebloan people. Cushing in 1879 documented a ceremonial dance at Zuni where participants carried "huge, leaf-shaped, bloodstained knives of stone . . ." (Cushing 1970:47). Later, Stevenson (1904:41) and Bunzel (1932a:528) both discussed the Zuni Stone Knife Society, whose principal deity is a figure with wings like knives. A parallel figure at Acoma is Flint Bird who wears a coat of stone knives (White 1932:172). Bunzel (1932b:873) noted in her study of Zuni katsinas, that some katsina accouterments included hafted stone knives. Stevenson (1904: 173–174) described a ceremonial bundle that contained two obsidian knives, one of which was 10 cm in length. Stone knives are reported to be part of anti-witchcraft ceremonials (Darling 1998). Large stone knives were probably not produced by Puebloan people during the last 150 years. But stone tools, whether heirloomed or scavenged, continue to play an important part in ceremonial life. The large knives of Grasshopper Pueblo, by virtue of their size and lack of evident use, could well have been one part of a ceremonial society's ritual paraphernalia.

Ritual paraphernalia production and maintenance by ceremonial societies historically occurs in highly restricted loci, usually within the integrative structure that houses that ceremonial society (e.g., Lange 1968:291; Parsons 1925a:55–58, 1925b:112; Stephen 1936:101–112; White 1932:71, 82, 130–131). In cases where production activities are not carried out in a ceremonial room, they may be carried out in the household of a society's leader (Lange 1968:311). Perhaps the best account of ritual paraphernalia production, maintenance, and storage in the ethnographic literature is Bunzel's discussion of katsina mask production at Zuni (Bunzel 1932b:848–856). The masks of individuals are produced by the ceremonial society leaders and artisans in kivas. Production takes several days and involves numerous rituals. A mask is subsequently stored in the home of its owner. Prior to a dance, the kiva chief will collect the members' masks and take them to his home, where assistants to the chief remove all previous paint, feathers, and other decorations and then refurbish them (Bunzel 1932b:892–893).

Upon the death of a mask's owner, the mask is undecorated over the course of several days and buried (Bunzel 1932b:856).

Clearly ritual paraphernalia production, maintenance, and discard are spatially restricted. There is every likelihood, then, that a prehistoric ritual society would have similar spatial restrictions on their production and use behaviors. Given recent ethnoarchaeological studies of the disposal of ceremonial items (Walker 1995), there is also every reason to expect that the discard of ceremonial items, once their use-lives are complete, would have occurred in spatially segregated contexts. These ethnographic examples lend themselves well to explaining the unusual production of large bifaces in Room 246. As a potential meeting space for a ceremonial society, the areas in and around Room 246 may have been a "clubhouse" for people belonging to the same ritual organization. While passing the time in each other's company, the production of projectile points by assembled flintknappers is a likely occupation. Others have made similar arguments about projectile point production in Pueblo ceremonial rooms (Hill 1970; Martin et al. 1967). This interpretation conforms well to Whittaker's (1984, 1987a) study that documented manufacturing diversity in the projectile points of Room 246. Beyond producing projectile points, one society member or several produced ritual paraphernalia, which probably included large bifacial knives for display in ritual performances. These ceremonial items would be expected to have spatially restricted production and discard contexts, as was observed for the large bifaces of Grasshopper Pueblo. The relationship between prehistoric Western Pueblo societies and historically documented ritual societies, such as the Zuni Stone Knife Society, is an intriguing relationship to consider.

CONCLUSION

The broad agreements between information from tools and debitage is encouraging for those trying to interpret debitage alone, although had the knappers in Room 246 concentrated on small projectile points instead of bifaces, the normal recovery techniques used in this excavation would surely have retrieved much less debitage evidence. Had the bifaces been removed from the room, we would have known little about their form, because they are an unexpected and rare artifact. However, the debitage alone would have provided a powerful set of clues in the forms and sizes of flakes, the distribution of cortex, and the attributes of platforms, all reflecting the production of large bifaces.

The debitage and tools dumped in a dark storage space at the bottom of Room 246 reflect important activities in the prehistoric pueblo and even the more general social milieu. Some waste was disposed of safely and conveniently under the rooms where it was made. Convenience rather than care is probably the important principle here; the deposit appears dominated by sharp stone debris, but was actually much more diverse. In the case of the bifaces, there may have been restrictions on the disposal of ritually sensitive craft products and their waste. The large quantities of waste, much of it still usable, and the careless loss of many finished tools, suggest that raw material and knapping labor were relatively cheap. The knappers at Grasshopper had easy access to plentiful high-quality chert. The midden is fairly homogeneous, and probably indicates only a short period of activity. Personal knapping experience shows that vast quantities of debitage can be produced in a short time, from relatively few pieces of stone, especially with several knappers at work. The large bifaces would have taken an hour or two to make (Whittaker 1994; Whittaker and Stafford 1999). If one knapper made most of the 60 bifaces, we are not talking about one event, but the span represented is more likely to be days than years. Several knappers probably worked in some sort of convivial setting, consistent with ethnographic male-oriented activities in clan houses and other communal structures. They turned out typical tools for their time and culture, but with a degree of variability that shows individualism, and even eccentricity was not suppressed.

5

Alaskan Blade Cores as Specialized Components of Mobile Toolkits: Assessing Design Parameters and Toolkit Organization through Debitage Analysis

JEFFREY RASIC AND WILLIAM ANDREFSKY JR.

Bifaces, used as specialized tools and as cores, were a primary component of the mobile toolkits employed by prehistoric hunter-gatherer groups in North America. In some toolkits, however, particularly those in the American Arctic, prepared blade cores were also common. The use of blade core technologies has generally been explained in cultural historical terms (e.g., Paleoindian versus Paleo-Arctic) or in terms of a simple functional argument—blade cores offer a more efficient means of utilizing lithic raw materials. Through analysis of debitage assemblages produced from bifacial and prepared blade core reduction experiments, we show that blade cores and bifacial cores are both efficient means of utilizing lithic raw materials, yet they differ in a variety of other ways. These differences are discussed in terms of the costs and benefits presented to prehistoric toolmakers and users. Given this set of costs and benefits, the technological choices favored by prehistoric people may shed light on the situational and organizational contexts in which these technologies were used.

Lithic analysts typically measure a variety of flake attributes and assemblage characteristics in an attempt to understand prehistoric technological behavior. Many of these studies seek to identify processes that prehistoric individuals may have been aware of but to which they gave little attention. For example, our interest in discovering stages of reduction, types of percussors, or reduction strategies would probably have been quite amusing to a prehistoric knapper.

Other parameters, however, that we archaeologists explore would have been very relevant to that individual. The size and shape of detached pieces and the amounts of usable material produced relative to waste were probably major concerns to prehistoric tool users. It is from this perspective that we examine characteristics of experimental debitage assemblages produced from two comparable core strategies: bifacial cores and blade cores.

While the role of bifaces, as cores as well as specialized tools, in the technologies of mobile hunter-gatherers has been widely discussed (Andrefsky 1991; Boldurian 1991; Goodyear 1979; Hofman 1992; Kelly and Todd 1988; Kelly 1988; MacDonald 1968:65–66; Parry and Kelly 1987), blade cores were also important components of some mobile toolkits. Blade cores are commonly found in Alaskan archaeological assemblages ascribed to mobile hunting and gathering groups, and it is clear that blades were used in some cases by Clovis people—the archetype of highly mobile hunter-gatherers (Collins 1999; Green 1963). The role of blade cores within the technological repertoires of these groups, however, has not received much attention and hence it is not well understood. Though research on core and blade technology abounds, it has largely focused on reconstructing production techniques (e.g., Crabtree 1968; Del Bene 1992; Flenniken 1987a; Kobayashi 1970; Sheets and Muto 1972; Sollberger and Patterson 1976) or on the use of core morphology or production techniques as culture historical markers (e.g., Anderson 1970; Andrefsky 1987; Hayashi 1968; Magne 1996; Mobley 1991; Morlan 1970; Wyatt 1970). Several studies have addressed functional or organizational aspects of blade technologies, but these have generally concentrated on agriculturalists or groups with low residential mobility (e.g., Arnold 1987; Clark 1987; Odell 1994b; Parry 1994; though see Bamforth and Bleed 1997; Bleed 1996; Eerkens 1998; Wenzel and Shelley, this volume).

An interesting issue, then, is how blade core reduction strategies are incorporated into the technologies of mobile foragers, or in other words, why are core and blade strategies sometimes used in place of or in addition to more common bifacial core strategies? We acknowledge that historical factors play a role in determining which technologies are known to a group of people. However, in this case we suggest of greater importance in explaining technological variability in the archaeological record is the fact that blade and bifacial reduction strategies offer different sets of costs and benefits that would have been advantageous in different situational contexts. Prehistoric tool users, therefore, would have selected among these available technologies based on such considerations as immediate and expected task requirements, and the availability and characteristics of lithic raw materials, and within the context of constraints imposed by mobility organization and the structure of subsistence resources. Our goals in this essay are to highlight the unique features of each reduction strategy and then to suggest contexts in which these attributes may have been advantageous to prehistoric tool users.

HIGH-LATITUDE FORAGERS AND CORE DESIGN

One region in North America in which blade cores are especially common among mobile hunter-gatherer groups is Alaska. The use of bifacial technologies is also widespread in the region and we use archaeological assemblages from this area, specifically northwestern Alaska, as a model for our reduction experiments and to provide a starting point for discussion of core design. We emphasize, however, that our goal is not to replicate any specific reduction technology, but rather to explore the economics of core strategies in general. We acknowledge that there are many specific blade production techniques even within this region (Anderson 1970; Andrefsky 1987; Owen 1988), as there are a variety of bifacial reduction techniques, yet we are concerned with general characteristics that are more or less common to all techniques within these categories. In comparing the costs and benefits among core strategies at this general level we simply hope to generate some testable predictions for the situational and organizational constraints that influence the selection of reduction strategies.

Blade technology is defined here as a lithic production strategy in which a stone nucleus is shaped, often in a highly patterned manner, to facilitate the purposeful and repeated detachment of blades: long, narrow detached pieces with parallel lateral edges. Many techniques, including pressure, indirect percussion, and direct percussion, have been used in the North American Arctic to produce blades (Owen 1988). Blades come in a variety of sizes and in this region the smallest—usually based on an arbitrary size cutoff—are referred to as microblades. In this paper we are concerned only with these small blades or microblades since larger blades were probably used in different ways.

A biface is defined as a tool that has two surfaces (faces) that meet to form a single edge that circumscribes the object (Andrefsky 1998:76). Both faces contain some flake scars that travel at least halfway across the face. Bifacial cores are considered to be bifaces that functioned, at least occasionally, as a source of usable flake tools or flake blanks targeted for further modification.

MOBILE TOOLKITS

We chose to examine and contrast blade and bifacial cores because these are the two most common core strategies employed in the transported, personal toolkits of mobile foragers. Such mobile toolkits, according to Kuhn (1994:427), are those items that are continuously carried by individuals, as opposed to gear that is made expediently, or tools that may be transported but are cached at fixed locations. Such implements are equivalent to what Binford (1979:262–263) labeled personal gear, and which he characterized as being (1) carried in anticipation of future use rather than made in response to tool needs, (2) heavily curated (i.e., manifesting high levels of care in maintenance, recycling, and reuse), and (3) produced through a process of staged manufacture, the stages of which often occur in different places and at different times (Binford 1979). Alaskan blade cores, as well as bifacial cores, should be considered as components of mobile toolkits. They were carefully made, often of the highest quality raw materials (Anderson 1970), and are known to have been transported great distances from the geologic source of the raw material (Malyk-Salivinova 1998). Also, their reduction was often staged, with successive episodes of production, use, and maintenance being performed at different locations.

Because mobile toolkits are transported, their design is constrained to a large degree by considerations of portability relative to potential utility. This concern with portability is critical since, in addition to tools, people must also carry other essentials such as food and shelter. Thus, greater weight transported in the form of tools translates into less weight carried in other necessities. This is an especially relevant concern to logistically organized collectors (Binford 1980), as prehistoric Alaskans most likely were, since food and materials would have been regularly moved to residential camps, rather than moving camps near resource locations.

Portability can be attained in several ways, but all seek to maximize the utility derived from a toolkit in relation to its size and weight. One way to achieve this is to design a single implement for multiple functions. Aspects of this design consideration, in reference to functioning tools rather than cores, have been labeled by Shott (1986) as versatility and flexibility. Versatility refers to the number of functions a tool is designed for and flexibility refers to the ability of a tool to be modified for tasks other than that for which it was designed. Both strategies increase the number of options available to tool users from a given implement and hence can serve to increase utility. We use the term *versatility* in this paper to refer to the number of different types (sizes and shapes) of blanks a core can produce. A versatile core, for example, can produce blanks that range from large to small, thick to thin, and curved to flat. Following Shott's (1986) terminology, a flexible core would be one that could be recycled into a tool which functions other than as a core.

Another way to maximize utility derived from tools or cores is through efficient use of lithic materials, which may reduce tool-stone requirements and allow for reduction in the size and weight of toolkits, or prolong periods between quarry visits. We suggest that this latter concern, the frequency of retooling, was probably a consideration regardless of how "embedded" resupply trips were, since this task nevertheless entailed some energy and opportunity costs.

While being mindful to considerations of portability, prehistoric people also

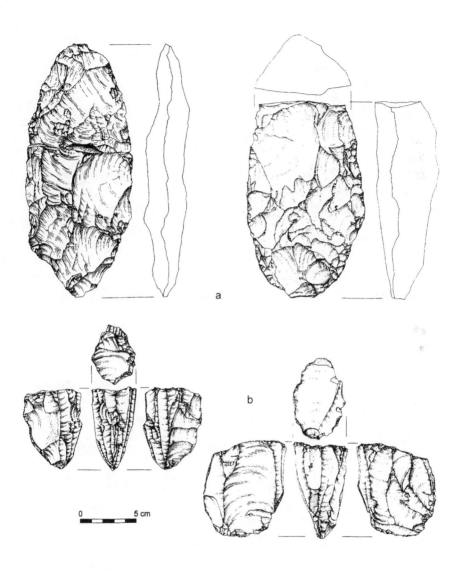

Figure 5.1. Archaeological specimens from northwestern Alaska that were replicated in this study: (a) bifacial core, (b) blade core.

needed to design toolkits to meet specific functional needs. The most basic function of chipped stone cores is to provide cutting edge in the form of flake tools or tool blanks. Whether an implement acts as a knife, a projectile, scraper, chopper, or drill, the essential function is cutting. Thus, maximizing the amount of cutting edge produced from a given mass of core material should have been an important design goal for mobile toolkits. As already mentioned though, there are a variety of cutting tasks, and for each there is an optimum type of cutting edge. A good scraping edge, for example, is morphologically different from an edge well suited to slicing. In some situations a variety of edge types may be desired in a toolkit, and thus flexibility in terms of the types of blanks one can produce from a core may also have been an important design goal. In other situations, consistent production of a specific type of cutting edge may have been ideal (see Tomka, this volume).

In sum, transported cores are expected to entail characteristics that allow them to produce the maximum amount of appropriate cutting edge relative to transport costs. With these design considerations in mind we now discuss the characteristics of detached pieces produced from blade core and biface reduction strategies.

CORE REDUCTION EXPERIMENTS

We replicated a blade core and a bifacial core modeled after artifact types recovered from archaeological sites along the Wrench Creek drainage in the western Brooks Range, Alaska (see Figure 5.1). Several large bifaces, interpreted to have served as cores, were recovered from the Tuluaq site, which is dated to at least 10,000 B.P. In Alaska the use of bifaces as cores, however, occurs until quite recent times. Binford (1979:262) describes their use among the ethnohistoric Nunamiut:

> Informants always spoke of carrying "cores" into the field; as they put it, you carry a piece that has been worked enough so that all the waste is removed, but that has not been worked enough so that you cannot do different things with it. . . . That the items being described by the informants were cores, was made clear by many references to the removal of flakes radially around the disc for use in butchering animals, the manufacture of scrapers from flakes struck from the "long side" of the oval, and the fact that once you had reduced the core down to a very small size you had a "round scraper."

Several sites in the Wrench Creek drainage have also yielded blade cores. Some of these specimens are small, pressure-flaked, wedge-shaped microcores typical of the American Paleo-Arctic Tradition that is thought to date from 8,000 to 10,000 years ago (Anderson 1984). Other blade cores are larger, oval-platformed specimens, which were probably reduced with a percussion technique. Cores of this type are found throughout the Brooks Range (Hall 1975:67; Solecki 1950:67, 1996) though none are from dated contexts. Technologically similar cores elsewhere in Alaska, such as those from the Ugashik Narrows phase on the Alaskan

Peninsula, date between 9,000 and 7,500 B.P. (Henn 1978). It is these percussion-flaked, oval-platformed cores that our experiments most closely replicate.

Archaeological specimens from Wrench Creek, both bifacial and blade cores, appear to have been produced with a percussion technique. The archaeological specimens are all made from chert, though of different types. Blade cores are exclusively made with high-quality, fine-grained, glassy cherts. Bifaces, in comparison, are often made with tougher and coarser-grained cherts, though some are also of the fine-grained variety.

The replicated bifacial core was produced from an obsidian cobble with a direct free-hand percussion technique (Crabtree 1972) using either a quartzite hammerstone or a moose antler billet. The replicated blade core was produced from an obsidian flake blank with direct free-hand percussion using a siltstone hammer. In both experiments, the goal was to produce as many usable flakes as possible. Reduction ceased when the knapper could no longer produce usable flakes without a change in reduction strategy, for example using bipolar reduction.

During the experiments, debitage was collected after each blow to the core and was labeled with a corresponding sequence number. The blade core replication was divided into six stages; each consisting of twelve hammer blows, and the bifacial replication was divided into seven stages of ten strikes. This collection technique enabled each piece of debitage to be assigned a specific sequence number or a range of sequence numbers from which it was produced and it allowed us to monitor changes in the character of detached pieces through the reduction sequence.

We divided the debitage set into two major categories. Flakes were defined as detached pieces with a single identifiable dorsal surface and a single identifiable ventral surface. All other specimens were classified as angular shatter. For all specimens large enough to be caught within a ¼-inch hardware mesh, we used a sliding caliper and recorded three simple size attributes to the nearest millimeter: maximum linear dimension, maximum width (the greatest dimension perpendicular to the maximum linear dimension), and maximum thickness. Additionally, we measured weight to the nearest 0.1 g on an electronic balance.

We acknowledge that obsidian fractures differently than does chert and that our experiments most likely did not exactly replicate the variation in debitage produced by the prehistoric knappers who worked the Wrench Creek bifaces and cores. We do not see this as a major obstacle, however, since the purpose of the experiments was not to duplicate the archaeological materials, but rather to compare general characteristics of bifacial and blade core reduction strategies. Additionally, it should also be noted that, when available, obsidian was used prehistorically in Alaska for both bifacial and blade core technologies (see, for example, Clark and Clark 1993).

TABLE 5.1.

Stage Data from Biface and Blade Core Reduction Experiments

	Bifacial Core	Blade Core
Blank form	Cobble	Flake Blank
Blank weight	2057.9 g	270.0 g
Core Shaping Stages		
Stages Zero–Two (biface); Stages One–Two (blade core)		
Weight of usable flakes	1472.9	101.1
Weight of waste material	85.2	14.7
Number of usable flakes	66.0	26.0
End of stage core weight (formed core)	499.8	270.0
Core Reduction		
Stage Three		
Weight of usable flakes	127.4	61.7
Weight of waste material	29.9	4.6
Number of usable flakes	23.0	12.0
End of stage core weight	342.5	223.7
Stage Four		
Weight of usable flakes	79.8	65.6
Weight of waste material	26.0	4.1
Number of usable flakes	35.0	12.0
End of stage core weight	236.7	154.0
Stage Five		
Weight of usable flakes	59.7	31.5
Weight of waste material	25.1	4.7
Number of usable flakes	18.0	11.0
End of stage core weight	151.9	117.8
Stage Six		
Weight of usable flakes	44.5	32.5
Weight of waste material	13.6	4.2
Number of usable flakes	17.0	10.0
End of stage core weight (depleted core)	93.8	81.1
Totals (Stages Three–Six)		
Usable debitage weight	311.4	191.3
Waste debitage weight	94.6	17.6
Number of usable flakes	93.0	45.0
Number of blanks:formed core weight (blanks/g)	0.186	0.166
Usable debitage weight:total debitage weight	0.767	0.916

EXPERIMENTAL RESULTS

We quantified three aspects of lithic production for both bifacial cores and blade cores: production rate, raw material efficiency, and size and shape of detached pieces. Furthermore, changes in these parameters were monitored through the reduction continuum beginning with fully prepared but unworked cores and progressing to depleted cores from which no additional usable flakes or blades could be gained. The initial core-shaping stages were not included in the following calculations since our interest was in transported cores. We assume that, prehistorically, the initial core-shaping portion of the reduction continuum would be performed at or near the raw material source and only formed cores would be incorporated into the transported toolkit. Table 5.1 lists summary data from the experiments.

Raw Material Efficiency

We monitored the raw material efficiency of blade and bifacial core strategies three ways and found that both bifaces and blade cores are efficient producers of usable products. Since the sizes of original nodules and formed cores were variable—the blade core is only about half (54 percent) as massive as the bifacial core—we calculated measures of raw material efficiency relative to core mass. Usable items were arbitrarily defined as those flakes measuring at least 25 mm in maximum dimension. Items smaller than 25 mm in maximum dimension and all pieces of angular shatter were classified as waste.

One way to assess the efficiency of a core reduction is by calculating the number of usable items produced relative to the mass of the formed core. By this measure we found the bifacial reduction to be more efficient, producing 0.19 blanks/g compared to 0.16 blanks/g for the blade core. This apparently slight difference may be more meaningful if we consider a hypothetical toolkit made entirely of blade cores or bifaces with a total weight of 5 kg. In such a case, the blade cores would produce 800 usable items compared to 950 usable items from an equal mass of bifaces. It is difficult to judge whether this degree of difference would have been recognized and valued by prehistoric tool users.

Other measures of raw material efficiency favor the blade core strategy. If raw material efficiency is measured by comparing the weight of usable flakes as a percentage of total debitage weight, we see that 90.7 percent of the blade core debitage is usable and only 76.7 percent of the bifacial core debitage is usable (see Table 5.1). Since this measure of efficiency considers only debitage, however, the weight of the exhausted core—which has also been transported—is not taken into account and therefore this may not be the most accurate assessment of core efficiency. A better measure of efficiency considers the weight of the exhausted

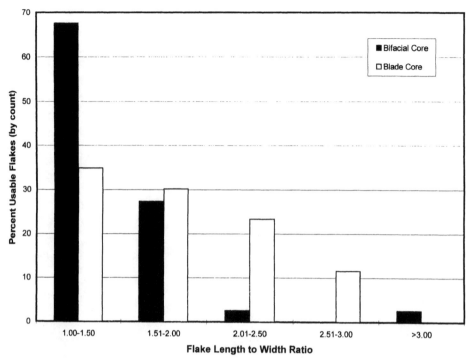

Figure 5.2. Shape categories of debitage produced from experimental blade and bifacial cores.

core. Since the utility of the exhausted blade core is rather limited and should be considered as waste, the "exhausted" bifacial core is now a thinned bifacial implement, and its mass may be considered useful. We considered the exhausted blade core as waste and the exhausted bifacial core as usable. Under these parameters the blade core efficiency is reduced to 70.9 percent compared to the bifacial core at 62.4 percent (see Table 5.1). The blade core is still more efficient though only marginally so. These findings are in accordance with similar studies that have found bifacial cores to be roughly as efficient as blade cores in terms of the useful products they supply (Flenniken 1987a; Morrow 1997).

SHAPE AND SIZE CHARACTERISTICS OF DETACHED PIECES

An obvious, and perhaps the essential difference between blade core products and those from bifacial cores is in the shape of detached pieces. We characterized flake shape by calculating length to width ratios for all usable flakes and found significant differences in the shapes of core products. Figure 5.2 shows that, as one might expect, the highest percentages of detached pieces from the blade core

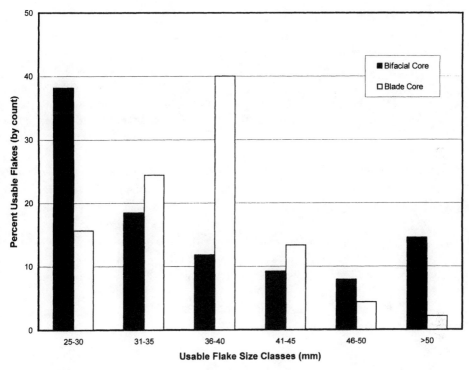

Figure 5.3. Flake size distribution of experimental blade and bifacial core products.

are long and narrow and thus have higher length to width ratios. Bifacial core products, in comparison, tend to be roughly equal in length and width. A chi-square test of the counts of usable flakes in each length to width class for both core types shows a significant pattern (X^2=27.52, df=4, p<0.001).

The maximum size of usable core products is of course limited by the dimensions of the core. Our experiments, however, suggest that a unique design feature of blade cores is their ability to maximize the size of blanks relative to core size. Consistently larger blanks can be produced from a blade core than from a comparably sized bifacial core. Figure 5.3 shows significant patterning (X^2=21.26, df=5, p<0.001) in the size distribution of usable flakes from the two core reduction experiments. Although the larger bifacial core did produce flakes larger than the largest flake from the blade core, these were few in number. The greatest proportion of usable blanks from the bifacial core is in the smallest size class, while the greatest proportion of usable flakes derived from the blade core is from a range two size classes larger. This is surprising since one would expect debitage size to be sensitive to core size (Tomka 1989), and therefore, given that the bifacial core in this experiment was nearly twice as large as the blade core, one would expect the larger core to produce greater numbers of larger flakes.

PRODUCTION RATE

Time was recorded at various stages throughout our reduction experiments and although great differences in production rates between core strategies were noted, the results are presented here with reservations. Production rate was measured as the number of usable flakes produced per minute of reduction time. In several blade core reductions performed for this study, production rates ranged from 7.2 to 10.7 blanks per minute. The single bifacial reduction for which we recorded time produced only 2.5 blanks per minute.

While it is tempting to conclude that blade core reduction is significantly more efficient than bifacial reduction by this measure, experimentally derived production rates should be viewed with caution since a host of factors such as raw material qualities, and the skill and experience of the knapper, particularly his or her familiarity with a given production mode, could drastically influence such estimates. Among prehistoric groups in which the production of chipped stone tools was a regular activity from a young age, the time spent producing blades or usable flakes was perhaps insignificant, especially in comparison to much more time consuming hafting tasks (Keeley 1982:800). Furthermore, staged reduction of toolkits would have allowed tool production to be scheduled so as not to conflict with subsistence or social activities (Binford 1979; Torrence 1983).

CHANGES IN CORE PRODUCTS THROUGH THE REDUCTION SEQUENCE

An important design consideration for a transported and curated item such as a core is how its performance will change through its use-life. We assessed this quality in terms of uniformity of detached pieces (the similarity in shapes and sizes of blanks produced during different portions of the reduction continuum) and consistency (changes in these proportions over the course of the full reduction continuum).

One simple way to evaluate the consistency of core products is to chart the total weight of usable blanks produced during each stage of the reduction process. Figure 5.4 shows a significant difference between the core types in this respect (X^2 =6.48, df=3, 0.1>p>0.05). The bifacial core shows a steady decrease in total weight of usable flakes produced during successive stages of the reduction process. In contrast, the blade core reduction, although it shows a drop in usable flakes between Stages four and five, exhibits less variability than the bifacial core.

The uniformity of core products among our experimental assemblages differs as well. Size variability among individual blanks is greater for bifacial products than it is for blade core products. Since the mean maximum dimension of flakes from each experiment is very similar, a direct comparison of the standard devia-

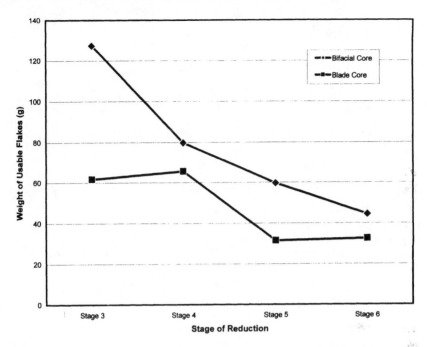

Figure 5.4. Total weight of usable blanks produced through blade and bifacial core reductions.

tion values for the mean maximum dimensions is reasonable. Table 5.2 lists the mean maximum dimensions and standard deviations of maximum flake dimensions for both core types and demonstrates that there is greater variability in flake size within the set of bifacial core products, with standard deviations ranging from 10.82 to 16.02 mm, than in the group of blade core products, in which standard deviations range between 4.87 and 5.43 mm.

DISCUSSION

As might have been predicted before this study was performed, the products of blade core reduction are distinctly different from those derived from bifacial reduction. We hope, however, that some of the specific ways in which they differ, the ways in which the products change through a reduction continuum, and how these differences would have been meaningful to prehistoric people have been elicited. A remaining challenge is to determine how the costs and benefits presented by biface and blade core technologies influenced the technological choices made by prehistoric tool users. These choices are thought to have been made in response to a variety of situational contingencies and organizational constraints faced by prehistoric people. An understanding of the limitations and benefits of

TABLE 5.2.

Size Variability of Usable Flakes from Blade and Bifacial Core Reductions

Stage of Reduction	Mean Maximum Dimension (mm)	Maximum Maximum Dimension (mm)	Minimum Maximum Dimension (mm)	Standard Deviation
Blade Core Reduction				
3	39.08	48	29	5.43
4	37.16	51	27	6.42
5	35.00	44	25	4.97
6	33.80	41	25	4.87
3–6	36.26	51	25	5.68
Bifacial Core Reduction				
3	39.78	86	25	16.02
4	28.82	104	25	12.06
5	35.33	68	25	11.14
6	34.53	60	25	10.82
3–6	34.62	104	25	12.83

different technologies sheds light on the problems prehistoric people were attempting to solve and in turn provides a more detailed picture of prehistoric life. We first summarize the characteristics of these core strategies and then discuss two sets of factors that may have been important in selecting from among them: lithic raw material constraints and considerations related to tool function and maintenance.

SUMMARY OF BLADE CORE AND BIFACIAL REDUCTION CHARACTERISTICS

The blade core reduction in this experiment was found to be an efficient use of raw materials as measured by the number of usable items produced from a given core mass, and as measured by the proportion of usable debitage relative to waste products. It was also found to consistently produce a high proportion of long and narrow detached pieces that were relatively uniform in both size and shape. Furthermore, these characteristics were found to hold true through the entire reduction continuum; the size and shape of the first blades removed were similar to that of blades produced at the end of the reduction sequence. A unique feature of blade cores seems to be the ability to maximize the size of detached pieces relative to the size of the core.

Our bifacial reduction experiment shows that a bifacial core strategy can also be judged an efficient use of raw material as measured by the number of usable flakes relative to core mass. In regard to the shape and size of usable detached pieces, those produced from the entire bifacial reduction sequence were found to be more variable than those obtained from blade core reduction experiment. As well, the size and shape of usable flakes from the bifacial core were more variable during each portion of the reduction continuum when compared to equivalent portions of the blade core sequence.

RAW MATERIAL ECONOMY

Our experiments support previous findings (e.g., Flenniken 1987a; Morrow 1997) that demonstrate bifacial and blade core reduction to be a similarly efficient means of utilizing lithic raw materials. This refutes a commonly accepted notion that blade cores are superior to all other reduction strategies in terms of raw material economy (see Bar-Yosef and Kuhn 1999). The use of blade core technology, therefore, cannot be explained simply as a choice in favor of a more efficient technology. We do believe, however, that the size of available lithic raw material packages may be relevant. Since blade cores maximize the size of detached pieces relative to core size they can produce more large blanks than a similarly sized bifacial core. For example, a hypothetical blade core with a height of 4 cm can supply numerous blades that are nearly 4 cm long, while a 4-cm-long biface—the size of a typical dartpoint—would hardly be considered a core since few flakes of usable size, and probably none approaching 4 cm, could be obtained from it. As such, the blade core strategy is one option for supplying cutting edge in situations where suitable lithic raw materials occur only in small nodules. Even in cases where large nodules are available it would seem that smaller pieces of stone are almost always more abundant and more easily procured, thus reducing procurement costs for blade core materials.

SPECIAL PURPOSE AND GENERALIZED CORE TECHNOLOGIES

An overall picture that emerges when looking at the characteristics of blade and bifacial core reduction strategies is one of a specialized technology compared to a generalized and versatile technology. Small blade and microblade cores are specialized implements. They served one function—a source of usable detached pieces—and these pieces came in a narrow range of shapes and sizes that were useful for a relatively narrow range of functions. The range of uses for which blades can be used or modified for is largely dependent on their size, with larger blades offering more options. With small blades, as used in this study, and more so with even smaller pressure-flaked microblades, the delicate, acute edges would be useful only for light-duty cutting and graving tasks (Hutchings 1996). While microblades in Alaska are occasionally found to have been retouched into tools (Owen 1988), these items are relatively uncommon, and it is thought that small blades and microblades were typically used without modification (other than sectioning to obtain straight segments) as insets in slotted bone or antler projectile points (Ackerman 1996a, 1996b; Larsen 1968). They may also have been used in hafted cutting implements analogous to the crooked knives used by Alaskan Eskimos into the historic period (Murdoch 1892:160; Nelson 1899:94). Due to their small size and acute edges, however, chopping, scraping, sawing, or heavy graving functions are not efficiently undertaken regardless of the haft design.

In contrast to the narrow role of blade cores, bifaces themselves could serve as cores or tools, and the flakes detached from them could be used in a variety of ways as well. As cores, bifaces provided flakes of various shapes that could be used for diverse tasks. Unlike small blades, these flake blanks could also be further modified into a variety of more specialized tools such as cutting, scraping, boring, and piercing implements (Andrefsky 1998; Frison and Bradley 1980; Kelly 1988; Morrow 1996; Stanford and Broilo 1981; Wilke et al. 1991). Additionally, the bifacial core itself was useful as a relatively massive, durable-edged tool that could be extensively resharpened (Jones 1980; Kelly 1988; Ohel 1987). When the bifacial core has been reduced in size so that it can no longer provide useful blanks, it could be cycled into a formed tool such as a projectile point or hafted knife (Frison and Bradley 1980; Hofman 1992; Wilke et al. 1991).

One aspect of core design raised in this study, and one that illustrates how blade and bifacial cores differ in terms of their specialization, is the way core products change through a reduction trajectory. Numerous studies show that flake size generally decreases through a biface reduction continuum (e.g., Bradbury and Carr 1999; Ingbar et al. 1989; Magne and Pokotylo 1981; Stahle and Dunn 1982). This is the very nature of a reductive technology, and for this reason the ability of a bifacial core to produce flakes large enough to be useful will decrease through its use-life. Thus a biface can only serve the dual purposes of tool and core for a limited portion of its reduction trajectory. Furthermore, compromises must be made in terms of flake removals that produce usable flakes and those that maintain the effectiveness of a bifacial tool. For instance, the removal of a large flake blank may affect the symmetry and edge angle of a biface and hence degrade its suitability for specific tasks. Although its usefulness as a core will diminish over time, the fact that a bifacial core can be laterally cycled into a specialized bifacial implement such as a projectile point or knife, provides the user of that tool with additional options.

In comparison, a blade core has one purpose—the production of useful detached pieces. No compromise in design is required since the core serves a single function. Consequently, the configuration of the core (i.e., the platform shape, overall core morphology, platform to face angles, etc.), once established, can then be maintained with relatively little variation (relative to other reduction strategies) throughout the entire reduction sequence. This allows consistent production of detached pieces, which vary little in size and shape.

General aspects of the context in which cores were used, and which may have affected the types of core strategies chosen prehistorically are (1) the ability to predict specific kinds of tool-using activities, and (2) the types of tasks to be performed. The greater flexibility of the biface strategy would seem to be of value when the exact nature of tasks to be performed is not known. The ability to make blanks of various shapes and sizes from a biface would allow one to cope with a wide variety of tasks. However, the costs of this flexibility may include greater time requirements for production of these items, some cost in terms of portability, and in some situations increased procurement costs of suitable lithic raw materials. These costs would be warranted in situations where people were faced with scarce or unknown lithic resources or when the types of tasks likely to be required were not easily predicted, for example, when people are entering new and unfamiliar territories, when rapid environmental changes are occurring, or when the structure of the resource base is characterized by unpredictable fluctuations in resource availability (Hiscock 1994; Kelly and Todd 1988).

More routinely, the need for a flexible and generalized core strategy, such as the bifacial core strategy, may be dictated by the range of expected tasks during a particular excursion. For logistically organized hunter-gatherers the range of potential tasks that one must be prepared to perform is expected to increase with increases in the duration/distance of a given foray (Binford 1977). A schematic of this relationship is shown in Figure 5.5. On longer or more distant forays, the range of expected activities is wider and specific activities that may be performed are more difficult to predict, hence a more flexible, generalized toolkit, which may have included bifacial cores, would have been useful.

The use of blade cores, on the other hand, because of their specialized nature, would be dictated more by the types of tasks that were expected. The combination of standardized products, production efficiency, and limited function seen with blade technology, would be well suited to activities in which specific activities are reliably predicted, and where processing volumes or time stress place a premium on efficient tool use and tool maintenance (Tomka, this volume). Time constraints on production and tool maintenance are typically of concern when the scheduling of resources is unpredictable and thus opportunities to utilize down time in order to "gear up" are not available (Bleed 1986; Torrence 1983). In such situations, blade cores would allow quick production of standardized replacement parts that would facilitate tool maintenance. Under other conditions—for

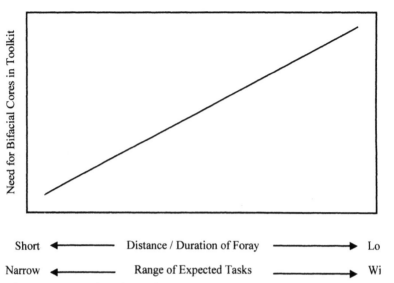

Figure 5.5. Expected conditions for the inclusion of bifacial cores in transported toolkits.

example, when potential tool uses (and thus required blank forms) varied widely, were unpredictable, or required blank forms not obtainable from blade cores—blade core technology alone would be insufficient.

As can be seen, blade core and bifacial core strategies offer different costs and benefits to tool users, however we see no reason why both strategies would not have been incorporated into a single toolkit. In fact, given the limited range of products derived from blade cores, other types of tools or cores were almost certainly required in all but the most specialized activities. We suggest that the relative proportion of these items may have differed according to a variety of situational and organizational constraints. In the Arctic, where marked seasonal fluctuations in resource availability is the norm, one might expect toolkits to vary according to seasonally specific activities and subsistence strategies. One might envision, for example, one toolkit for mid-summer encounter hunting and another for fall intercept hunting. One implication of this contention is that some of the variability seen in archaeological assemblages—even seemingly fundamental technological variation—may be due to such situational and organizational constraints. Thus, the presence or absence of evidence for basic technologies, such as blade core reduction, in an assemblage is not necessarily a good trait for use as a chronological or cultural marker. Blade cores may be more accurately viewed as specialized components of a toolkit that was possibly used only in very specific situations. It is hoped that additional work along these lines will better isolate just what these situations were.

ACKNOWLEDGMENTS

An earlier version of this paper was originally presented at the 1999 annual meeting of the Society for American Archaeology. We thank Marty Magne for his insightful comments on that earlier manuscript. Some of the ideas presented in this paper were developed during discussions with Bob Gal, Jeff Flenniken, and Bill Parry. Their ideas are gratefully acknowledged. Fieldwork on Wrench Creek was conducted by National Park Service archaeologists from the Western Arctic National Parklands. A grant from the National Park Service's Shared Beringian Heritage Program contributed to the project's success.

6

A Generalized Technology for a Specialized Economy: Archaic Period Chipped Stone at Kilometer 4, Peru

APRIL K. SIEVERT AND KAREN WISE

Until recently, chipped stone artifacts from the south-central Andean coast have not been studied systematically, partly because lithic density is low and the artifacts are largely informal. In this paper, we examine the lithic assemblage from Kilometer 4, an Archaic period site occupied from approximately 8,000 to 3,000 B.P., and characterized by increasing sedentism and specialization on marine resources. We analyze the lithic assemblage from Kilometer 4 to assess how manufacture and form may be influenced by raw material availability, mobility, and projected functional needs. Differences in the technology for three excavated areas at Kilometer 4 suggest that a combination of factors work together to influence the overall organization of Kilometer 4 lithic technology, with functional requirements being crucial. We find that the assemblages represent generalized and informal industries manufactured using locally available raw materials and expedient reduction techniques. The generalized and informal nature of the lithic assemblage is in marked contrast to what is usually portrayed as a highly specialized overall technology in the region. Thus it appears that generalized, informal lithic technology can be an important component of a specialized overall technology.

Archaeologists usually make extensive use of the chipped lithic materials found at prehistoric hunter-gatherer sites in their attempts to identify chronological markers, reconstruct subsistence, assess patterns of mobility, and understand the overall organization of technology. The focus is often on formal tools, which tend to be functionally specific and stylistically interesting (see, for example, Knecht 1997). Chipped stone debitage, which is nonformal, irregular,

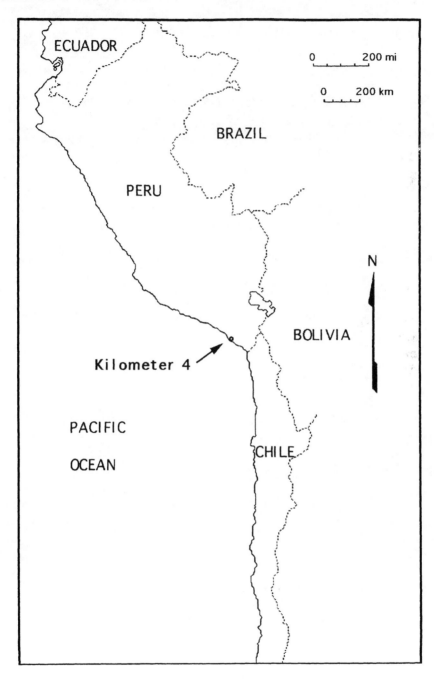

Figure 6.1. Andean coast showing location of Kilometer 4.

and not always pretty, nevertheless makes up the bulk of lithic assemblages. Debitage, generated through lithic reduction is often viewed as a by-product in the manufacture of other more formal tools. However, in cases where the overall organization of lithic technology is geared toward informal artifacts, the production of flakes and fragments may be an important end in itself.

Research at Archaic period (roughly 10,000–3,000 B.P.) hunter-gatherer-fisher sites on the south-central Andean coast (Figure 6.1) has produced relatively few formal lithic tools, in spite of what is generally argued to be a specialized technology focused on the exploitation of marine resources (Llagostera 1979b, 1989). In an attempt to understand the role that lithics play in the overall organization of technology for early people in the region, we analyze the lithic assemblage from Kilometer 4, a Middle to Late Archaic period site near Ilo, Peru.

The south-central Andean coast in northern Chile and southern Peru presents one of the driest deserts in the world, juxtaposed to one of the earth's richest coastal marine fisheries. The waters of the south-central Andean coast teem with marine and coastal life, creating easily exploitable intertidal and subtidal zones, and vast fishing grounds off-shore. The terrestrial environment consists of tracts of barren coastal desert, dissected by narrow river valleys and small springs. In addition, inland oases of seasonal fog-fed vegetation, *lomas*, provide rich patches of plant and animal resources during the winter months (Rundel et al. 1991).

Human occupation of this environment began during the Paleoindian period (Nuñez 1983, 1989b; Nuñez et al. 1983), and by the Early Archaic period, around 10,000 years ago, numerous sites had been established along the coast (Keefer et al. 1998; Lavallée et al. 1999; Llagostera 1979a; Sandweiss et al. 1989, 1998). Throughout the Early and Middle Archaic periods, coastal sites consisted of small, apparently seasonally occupied camps with small groups of circular structures, midden areas, and informal cemeteries. Fishing, shellfishing, hunting or trapping birds, and hunting marine and terrestrial mammals provided the faunal resources used by Early to Middle Archaic people (Keefer et al. 1998; Llagostera 1989; Nuñez 1983; Rasmussen 1998; Sandweiss et al. 1989, 1998; Schiappacasse and Niemeyer 1984). By around 5,000 to 4,000 B.P., coastal settlements began to be permanently occupied by groups focusing their energies on fishing (Llagostera 1979b, 1989; Wise 1990, 1997).

Archaeologists working on the Archaic period outline some general trends in Archaic period prehistory (e.g., Aldenderfer 1989; Llagostera 1989; Nuñez 1983, 1989a, 1989b). These include (1) relatively early separation of the cultural tradition and seasonal rounds of the coast from that of the nearby highlands; (2) Early to Middle Archaic (10,000 to 5,000 B.P.) settlement patterns characterized by seasonal and repeated use of sites located near the ocean, at river mouths and springs, with seasonal use of inland areas including river valleys and lomas; (3) sedentary coastal fishing villages appearing by the Late Archaic period, after around 5,000 B.P.; and (4) subsistence focused largely on the marine environment, especially on fishing, but including shellfishing, the exploitation of birds, and possibly hunting of sea mammals.

There have been few comprehensive analyses of technology for the coast, but Llagostera (1979b, 1989) argues that highly specialized coastal technology in the south-central Andes facilitated maritime specialization and fishing in particular. Several studies have included lists of types of tools present at different time periods (see Muñoz 1982; Nuñez 1983). Research on lithic assemblages from specific sites has generally been limited to descriptive presentations that include illustrations of a few formal tools, including projectile points and other bifaces (see, for example, Bird 1943; Muñoz et al. 1993; Sandweiss et al. 1989; Schiappacasse and Niemeyer 1984). A projectile point typology developed at highland sites excavated over 30 years ago (Ravines 1972) remains the main reference on Archaic period lithic technology in the region, while Bird's (1943) work is the most detailed study of formal tools from the coast. No in-depth analyses that include debitage have been published to date.

The analysis presented here is intended to form a baseline for other lithic studies in the region and demonstrate that a fundamental level of debitage analysis can provide needed information regarding site differences and the overall organization of technology at hunter-gatherer-fisher sites. Furthermore, we need to understand something of the character of debitage at the coastal habitation sites before we can even begin to understand its potential relationship to both maritime technology, and to the projectile point-bearing sites that pepper the lomas inland from the coast. We chose the Kilometer 4 site because it is a large, well-studied site with excavated strata that include both Middle and Late Archaic period contexts. The site offers the prospects of tracking change in lithic technology in a situation of increasing specialization on marine resources, as well as increasing sedentism.

It is not our intention to try and interpret the mobility and seasonality patterns at Kilometer 4 by looking at the lithic artifacts. Instead, we have interpreted changes in mobility and resource focus using other criteria, such as living floor preparation, intensity of occupation, and faunal data. We then evaluate the effects these characteristics may have on raw material selection, artifact form, and artifact function.

KILOMETER 4

Kilometer 4 is located northwest of the town of Ilo, Peru (Figure 6.1). The site covers an area of roughly 10 ha and is located approximately 50 m from the present-day beach (Figure 6.2). It extends across a relatively flat area adjacent to the beach, well up into the hills that begin several hundred meters inland. At the

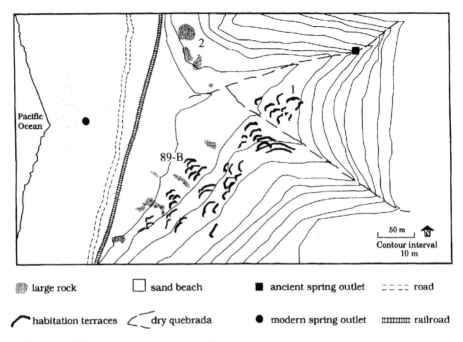

Figure 6.2. Kilometer 4 site map showing locations of excavated zones.

northeastern edge of the site are the remains of a small ancient spring. The site contains the remains of at least 50 domestic terraces, varying in size from 4 to 10 m across. The location of Kilometer 4, directly on the beach, with its own source of potable water, is virtually ideal for a fishing village. The sandy and rocky beaches directly in front of the site are today popular spots for both fishing and shellfishing, attracting both land-based line fishermen and boats using nets near the shore. The seasonal vegetation, lomas, lie several kilometers inland in the coastal cordillera.

Excavations were conducted at Kilometer 4 in 1989 (Wise et al. 1994), 1992, 1993, 1994, and 1996 and have revealed the presence of a vast midden area, the stratified remains of houses built on domestic terraces, and three separate cemetery areas. The site appears to span the Middle and Late Archaic periods, with the Late Archaic period occupation being intensive and long. All areas of the site that have been excavated to sterile soil contained between approximately 1.0 m and 2.5 m of cultural deposits. While across most of the site these deposits appear to have accumulated between approximately 5,000 and 3,500 B.P., one area has been dated to between roughly 8,000 and 6,000 B.P.

The earliest, or Middle Archaic, area that we examine here is designated as

Zone 2 (Figure 6.2). This area had been disturbed by heavy machinery during and after the construction of a road and a railroad, but excavations and cleaning of over 60 sq m conducted in 1993 and 1994 revealed the presence of a cemetery area underlain by a series of occupation surfaces and features, some of them undisturbed. A charcoal sample taken from one of the lowest strata was dated at 8,030 ± 100 B.P. (Beta 77947, uncalibrated), while another wood charcoal sample from one of the higher strata dates to 6,220 ± 70 B.P. (Beta 77951, uncalibrated). Zone 2 is characterized by light midden and by domestic features consisting of ephemeral surfaces with some postholes, small pit features, and possibly the remains of a circular shelter floor. This set of occupation layers is interpreted as a seasonal and nonintensive occupation. Chipped lithic artifacts are present in Zone 2, but are dispersed and sparse.

The Late Archaic period deposits at Kilometer 4 contain dense concentrations of cultural debris compared to those found in Zone 2. Late Archaic domestic features at Kilometer 4 consist of small circular houses placed on purposefully constructed domestic terraces. Several terraces have been tested, and excavations in the area known as Zone 1 revealed details of the construction and use of residential areas during the Late Archaic period. In Zone 1 (Figure 6.2), over 60 sq m were excavated, including a full house floor, which represents one of at least seven layers of houses built sequentially on the same terrace. Each terrace surface was built using fill consisting of redeposited shell midden. Uncalibrated radiocarbon dates for the upper levels of Zone 1 range between 3,970 ± 80 B.P. (Beta-77948) and 3,240 ± 60 B.P. (Beta-77943). Lithic artifacts are extensively distributed throughout these levels and include a range of debitage and formal tool types.

Approximately 50 sq m of a second Late Archaic period area (Zone 89-B) were also tested. Uncalibrated radiocarbon dates of 3,750 ± 60 (Beta 52796) and 3,760 ± 70 B.P. (Beta 52797), seem to indicate this area was occupied at a time when the population appears to have been sedentary and focused on fishing. Zone 89-B also included a single isolated burial containing the skeletal remains of a 45- to 50-year-old male interred with bone, stone, shell, hide, and textile artifacts (Wise et al. 1994). This area also produced a concentration of lithic materials, interpreted in the field as an activity area for lithic manufacture, the only such area found on the site.

These three excavated areas, Zones 1, 2, and 89-B, all contain evidence of domestic activity and therefore offer an opportunity to examine variation in site structure and use as it affects lithic technology. Furthermore, they provide the opportunity to study the character of lithic debitage in situations of increasing sedentism, and increasing focus on specific subsistence resources. These three excavation areas also offer the opportunity to examine how lithic debitage in each area relates to the formal tools recovered.

VARIATION IN LITHIC ASSEMBLAGES

Analysts have worked to identify and understand the factors that account for variation among lithic assemblages and have focused on three factors in particular—raw material availability, mobility, and stone tool function. The following section briefly reviews some of the recent thinking about how these factors may affect the overall appearance or organization of lithic assemblages.

RAW MATERIAL AVAILABILITY

The first requisite of any lithic technology is stone. The quality and quantity of available stone for chipping affects the choices made regarding material selection and conservation (Andrefsky 1994a; Roth and Dibble 1998). Materials can be acquired by several means, including planned collection trips to quarries, opportunistic collecting, or trade. Raw material collection strategies will condition the reduction strategies used to produce finished tools. For example, raw materials collected during trips to quarries or other collection locales may be partially reduced first, to lessen the overall mass toted. In such cases, evidence of initial reduction may reside primarily at the quarry or collection site, while at the habitation sites there could be relatively less debitage compared to artifacts classified as tools. Materials collected via trade may be acquired as finished or partially finished tools and, again, debitage levels might be relatively low. Debitage may be more plentiful in locations where habitation occurs at sites near lithic resources, reflecting the greater amount of debitage produced in manufacturing blanks or cores, which may then be taken or traded away. What to expect in situations where there is an adequate supply of lithic raw material suitable for chipping nearby, but it is neither of superb quality nor highly abundant is less clear, but researchers have tried to formulate general patterns. Andrefsky (1994a) summarizes some possible relationships between raw material availability and tool formality as follows: (1) high quality and low abundance correlates to high tool formality (high tool to debitage ratio), (2) high quality and high abundance leads to a range from high to low formality (variable tool to debitage ratio), and (3) low quality leads to low formality (low tool to debitage ratio) regardless of whether the material is plentiful or scarce. While this may indeed be true in some cases, other factors must also come into play.

Raw material quality and quantity act as limiting factors in determining strategies for reduction. For example, material having small nodule size is often processed using bipolar techniques when small size limits reduction using hand-held hammers (Andrefsky 1994b; Goodyear 1993; LeBlanc 1992; Shott 1989). Bipolar reduction may be visible archaeologically when bipolar flakes, large amounts of angular debris, and bipolar cores are identified (Jeske and Lurie 1993).

Also, in areas where lithic material is rare or difficult to obtain, conservation of materials as indicated by resharpening, recycling, and retooling can be expected (Bamforth 1986; Jeske 1989, 1992; Nassaney 1996; Thacker 1996; Torrence 1983). In sum, raw material availability will affect reduction strategies and logistics, as well as conservation and reuse of lithic tools, and these effects can be visible archaeologically.

MOBILITY

Settlement patterns provide the infrastructure for raw material acquisition and subsequent artifact manufacture because site location and seasonality will determine when and where people encounter raw materials, and what those materials may be needed for. Mobile versus sedentary groups face different decisions regarding scheduling activity to either collect materials or manufacture lithic tools. Over the last 15 years, analysts have shown that in some cases, highly mobile hunter-gatherers tend toward higher degrees of formality and curation, while sedentary populations use an overall lithic technology marked by expediently produced and casually maintained lithic tools (Kuhn 1994; Nelson 1991; Odell 1994b, 1996; Parry and Kelley 1987). Often the reason hails back to questions of availability. Sedentism allows the opportunity to stockpile, thereby increasing the abundance of raw materials available on site (Johnson 1996; Odell 1996).

If this general model holds, for highly mobile groups we would expect more formal tools as well as more signs of maintaining these tools, including bifacial flakes, resharpening flakes, and recycled tool types.

FUNCTIONAL EXPECTATIONS

The way tools look, the raw material selections made, and discard behaviors all depend on how and where tools will be used. During the 1980s interest in functional analysis of stone implements was boosted by technical developments in use-wear analysis (for reviews see Grace 1996; Shea 1992; Yerkes and Kardulias 1993). More recently, lithic analysts, especially in the New World, have focused more on issues of mobility and planning than function. Tomka (this volume) challenges the assumption that mobility determines formality, reiterating that formality is more likely to be related to the functional needs of the tool. Torrence (1994) reminds us that functional needs should be addressed to a greater degree.

While subsistence may dictate the overall functional requirements for any chipped stone industry, other activities also employ lithic tools. Lithic tools are

TABLE 6.1.

Chipped Lithic Assemblage from Kilometer 4

Area	Count	Column Total	Weight (g)	Column Total	Average Piece Weight (g)
			Debitage		
Zone 2	261	6.7%	776.8	10.4%	2.98
Zone 1	2607	67.3%	4545.2	61.0%	1.74
Zone 89-B	1005	25.9%	2130.3	28.6%	2.12
Subtotal	3873	100.0%	7452.3	100.0%	1.92
			Tools		
Zone 2	32	14.0%	3376.2	31.6%	105.51
Zone 1	110	48.2%	6270.6	58.6%	57.01
Zone 89-B	86	37.7%	1047.3	9.8%	12.18
Subtotal	228	100.0%	10694.1	100.0%	46.90
Total	4101		18146.4		48.82

often needed to make other implements or objects of fiber, bone, shell, wood, and stone. Other uses may be more difficult to assess, especially if they involve ceremonial functions such as display, use in performing specific rituals, or mortuary activities (Sievert 1992). When looking at function, a range of potential uses must be considered.

Function may also contribute to whether or not overall technologies appear generalized or specialized. "Generalized" technology would be adapted to multiple functions, while "specialized" technology is conceived as technology having specific or exclusive functions. As subsistence strategies shift toward situations of higher specialization, this may be reflected in the overall organization of lithic technology. Torrence (1983) posits that if people use a large range of resources, tool diversity will be low, to allow maximum flexibility and versatility. As people focus on a narrower range of resources, we might expect the innovation of new tool types that perform exclusive functions. Potential characteristics of specialized lithic technologies might include high intensity of use, limited kinds of materials processed using stone tools, and functionally limiting characteristics of the tools. More generalized technology would be versatile and exhibit greater variety in materials processed, few limiting characteristics, but can include either formal or nonformal tool types.

For an Archaic period coastal site such as Kilometer 4, we identify changes in lithic use over time. This variability most likely stems from a combination of factors governing raw material availability, mobility, and subsistence resource focus, rather than any one factor in particular. We expect that the later occupation at Kilometer 4, believed to be more sedentary and highly specialized on marine resources, will offer higher tool diversity, and at least some tools that point directly toward utilization of marine resources.

CHIPPED STONE AT KILOMETER 4

Our goals in the analysis of chipped stone at Kilometer 4 were to determine the kinds of lithic implements used by Archaic period inhabitants, the strategies they used for manufacture, and the choices they made in using lithic artifacts. We separated the assemblage into *debitage* (unmodified lithic waste) and *tools* (retouched pieces, specially prepared unmodified flakes, and pieces with significant edge damage). Characteristics recorded for this assemblage include raw material, artifact size, amount of cortex, morphology, and formality (measured by ratios of formal to nonformal artifact categories).

The chipped lithic assemblage from the three excavated zones at Kilometer 4 comprises 4,101 artifacts, with 3,873 pieces of debitage, and 228 tools (Table 6.1). All were collected during excavation using quarter-inch screens. As lithic assemblages go, that from Kilometer 4 is small. Total weight of chipped stone for over 150 sq m of excavation to an average depth of over 1.0 m is only 18.1 kg.

The amount of debitage is small in all three zones; however, the density of lithic materials in Middle Archaic Zone 2 is especially low. Even though Zone 2 simply has a lower density of stone tools, the weight per debitage artifact is the highest at nearly 3 g. It also has the largest tools, weighing an average of over 105 g per tool.

Zone 1, the largest excavated area, yielded the greatest amount of material. The assemblage from Zone 1 came from several levels of domestic terrace occupation and midden spanning 5,000–3,000 B.P. The fill for restructuring domestic terraces in Zone 1 comes from adjacent Late Archaic shell midden. Contexts here are likely to be mixed, without discrete activity areas. We expect to find a representative range of lithic artifact forms. Zone 1 accounts for over 67 percent of the debitage (by count). However, less than half the tools recovered from all three areas came from Zone 1. By weight, the amounts of debitage and tools from Zone 1 appear nearly equal with 61 percent of the debitage and nearly 59 percent of the tools. Zone 1 artifacts weigh, on average, one-half as much as artifacts from earlier Zone 2 at 57 g/tool.

Zone 89-B also sampled Late Archaic domestic occupations and contains an identifiable concentration of lithic materials. The area yielded just over one-quarter of the debitage, and over 37 percent of the tools from the three areas combined. By weight, this zone has nearly 29 percent of the debitage, but only

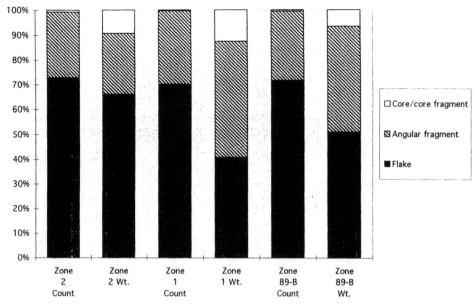

Figure 6.3. Counts and weights of three debitage form types at Kilometer 4.

10 percent of the total tools. Tools from Zone 89-B are on average smaller than those from the other two zones as indicated by the very low average tool weight at 12.18 g.

To summarize, the Middle Archaic Zone 2 produced a very small amount of rather large debitage and tools. The Late Archaic period Zone 1 yielded comparable percentages of debitage and tools by both count and weight. This might be expected of a long term and intensive occupation in which lithic manufacture and use continue on a small scale throughout a great span of time. In the other Late Archaic zone, 89-B, debitage counts and weights are comparable; however, tool weights are unusually low.

DEBITAGE FORM

Several aspects of the debitage, including form, size, and amount of cortex, may shed light on the overall lithic technology at Kilometer 4. Morphology of debitage can be used to interpret several factors, including reduction sequence, chipping technique, or desired product. Debitage types found at Kilometer 4 include flakes, angular fragments, and cores and are distributed as shown in Figure 6.3. Flakes are defined here as relatively thin pieces exhibiting striking platforms, bulbs of percussion, or compression rings. Angular fragments are thick pieces without clearly defined striking platforms or bulbs of percussion. Pieces having

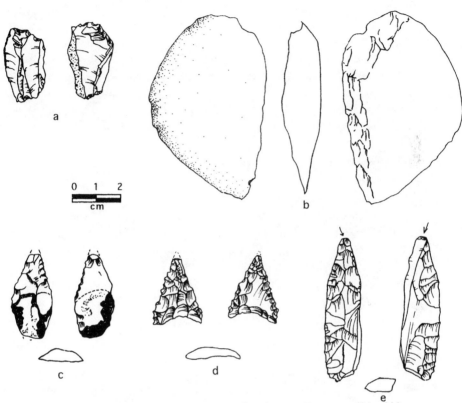

Figure 6.4. Lithic artifacts from Kilometer 4: (a) bipolar core, K4-256.01, (b) cobble cortex tool, K4-9844.03, (c) unifacial projectile point with hafting mastic, K4-4417, (d) projectile point with concave base, K4-2335, (e) burinated projectile point, K4-2950.

multiple platforms and/or significant platform preparation were classified as cores. We do not have information regarding flake breakage so we interpreted the overall proportion of flakes on the basis of weight as well as count. As shown by the columns in Figure 6.3, when the three zones are compared on the basis of artifact count, they appear similar. Debitage in the three zones clearly differ by weight, with Middle Archaic Zone 2 having the highest proportion of flakes. Zone 2 may be weighted toward larger flakes. For the Late Archaic zones, flakes account for less than 50 percent of the assemblage by weight. Angular fragments tend to be more massive than flakes, and especially large angular fragments, along with somewhat smaller flakes, could easily account for the lower flake weights recorded for Zone 1.

The use of bipolar technique should be considered for Kilometer 4, partially because it is known that at least some of the chalcedony found at the site occurs in small nodules. Jeske and Lurie (1993:138, 153) found experimentally that bipolar reduction results in a lower percentage of flakes among the debitage than does hard-hammer reduction, as well as a higher incidence of damage and crushing on multiple edges. Jeske and Lurie (1993:153) produced 49.8 percent flakes using bipolar reduction, compared to 82.3 percent flakes using a hard hammer. Flakes in the three zones at Kilometer 4 account for 70.1 percent to 72.8 percent of the total debitage count. These percentages of flakes, although lower than that produced experimentally using a hard hammer, are much higher than for materials produced experimentally by bipolar reduction by Jeske and Lurie. Although few individual flakes (n=3) could be unambiguously attributed to bipolar reduction, Zone 89-B yielded at least one artifact that appears to be a bipolar core (Figure 6.4a). Therefore, although some evidence for bipolar reduction is present, it does not appear to be the primary reduction technique used.

We have data on the presence of bifacial thinning flakes, probable platform rejuvenation flakes, and bipolar flakes for a subset of the debitage assemblage primarily from Zones 1 and 89 (n=900). Bifacial thinning flakes have characteristic faceted and narrow platforms coupled with intersecting flake scars on the dorsal face from prior flake removal. Platform rejuvenation flakes are defined as pieces produced in the process of reworking the striking platform on a core and were identified by the presence of dorsal crests consisting of scars with overlapping stepped or hinged terminations, suggesting why the platform needed trimming in the first place.

The assumption usually made is that debitage morphology suggests the desired outcome of knapping. For example, the presence of bifacial thinning flakes is testimony to the production of bifaces and retouched tools even if those tools are not found. Very few bifacial thinning flakes were identified among the subset of 900 flakes (n=17). Zone 1 has 2.8 percent bifacial thinning flakes, compared to 0.8 percent for Zone 89. There are also two retouched bifacial thinning flakes recorded among tools and if these are included, then bifacial thinning flakes account for 1.3 percent of the total from Zone 89. None was noted for Zone 2.

A very small number of platform rejuvenation flakes (n=23) testifies to some core reduction having occurred at Kilometer 4. In the subset for which we have the data, 2.4 percent of the flake assemblage for Zone 1, and 2.8 percent for Zone 89-B consist of platform rejuvenation flakes, indicating consistency between these two zones. No apparent platform rejuvenation flakes were recorded for the earlier Zone 2.

Core fragments (n=17) are equally divided between both Late Archaic areas. Only two core fragments are recorded from Zone 2. Because the Zone 2 excavations were relatively large, overall low flake weights and lack of platform or thinning flakes suggest that relatively little lithic tool manufacture occurred in the Middle Archaic Zone 2.

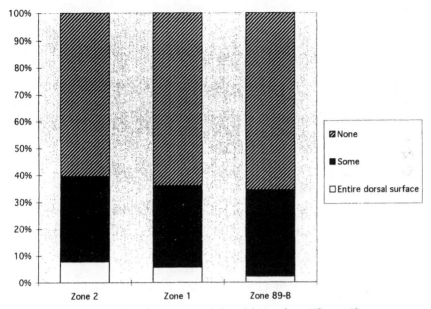

Figure 6.5. Incidence of dorsal cortex recorded on debitage from Kilometer 4.

Cortex. The amount of cortex present on flakes is an attribute that can provide a rough guide to the degree of reduction that has occurred (Andrefsky 1998:102). Since flintknapping is a subtractive process, more cortex can be expected to characterize products of the first steps in knapping a core, with an understanding that the presence or lack of cortex does not correlate directly with any specific point in the reduction of individual artifacts (Shott 1996a; Tomka 1989). For example, cortex often remains on bifacially worked artifacts such as projectile points. Furthermore, cortex need not be present, even on the first pieces removed from a nodule, because raw material may simply not have much cortex. At Kilometer 4, we are not interested in looking at the absolute amount of cortex on the lithic debitage, but rather, at variation among cortical incidence for the three excavated zones.

Kilometer 4 flakes, for which information on cortex was available, were divided into three very broad categories based on the amount of dorsal cortex present. They either had no cortex, some cortex, or cortex covering nearly the entire dorsal face (Figure 6.5). These categories coincide roughly with some versions of the so-called triple cortex typology that makes use of tertiary, secondary, or primary flake categories (see Shott 1996a and Sullivan and Rozen 1985 for discussion of consistency in using this terminology). Across the site, there are varying proportions of flakes having 100 percent dorsal cortex. Zone 2 has the highest at

7.3 percent, while Zone 89-B has only 2.2 percent, and Zone 1 falls between at 5.7 percent. For pieces with some dorsal cortex, the percentages for the three zones appear similar with 31.7 percent of the assemblage for Zone 2, to 30.2 percent of the assemblage for Zone 1, and a high of 32 percent of the assemblage for Zone 89-B. Pieces with no cortex are naturally the most common. Middle Archaic Zone 2 yielded 60.5 percent with no cortex, while the Late Archaic Zones 1 and 89-B have 64.1 percent and 65.7 percent, respectively. Although amounts of cortex are fairly similar overall, the earliest context, Zone 2, has the highest proportion of flakes with 100 percent dorsal cortex, and the lowest percentage with no cortex. The lowest percentage of cortical flakes was recorded for Zone 89-B, which also had the highest proportion of flakes having no cortex.

Two factors may account for the variation in the presence of cortical flakes between the three zones. First, Zone 89-B has relatively high percentages of debitage from igneous materials, which tend toward tabular fracture patterns, and can be collected as slabs without any cortex. Second, we believe that there is simply less lithic reduction occurring during the habitation recorded in Zone 2, and little bifacial reduction. Again, because lithic reduction is subtractive, less overall reduction would yield a smaller proportion having no cortex, compared to the zones where bifacial reduction appears to occur.

Size. Artifact size can also be used to help interpret reduction (see Andrefsky 1998:99–100). Shott (1994:90) writes that while ". . . it is trivial to observe that flakes tend to become smaller but more numerous as reduction proceeds . . . debris size distributions . . . still vary in form and in slope, the rate at which frequency and size interact." This variation can easily relate to the type of reduction occurring, and therefore give size some potential for reconstructing behavior. For example, Patterson (1990, 1997) has proposed a log-linear model indicating that, for bifacial reduction, flake percentage (using a logarithmic scale) plotted against size (using a linear scale) yields a straight line graph. This seems useful in cases where discrete knapping episodes are indicated. We suspect that such a model is unlikely to work well in situations where alternative knapping strategies are used together within the overall lithic technology, and where the evidence of these strategies is mixed. Nevertheless, it will be interesting to see how the three areas sampled differ in respect to artifact size.

We used five size classes based on maximum dimension and these are graphed in Figure 6.6. For all zones, most artifacts fall between 1 and 2 cm in maximum dimension. Zone 1 has slightly more artifacts in this category at 64.3 percent, compared to 54.8 percent for Zone 2, and 50.9 percent for the 1989 excavation. What stands out is the almost total lack of artifacts less than 1 cm in maximum dimension for Middle Archaic Zone 2. The line graphs for Zones 2 and 89-B are nearly identical in shape, with the exception that Zone 2 has virtually no small

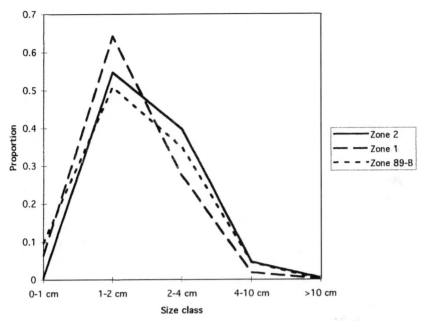

Figure 6.6. Comparison of size classes for debitage from Kilometer 4.

flakes (less than 1 cm in maximum dimension). Zone 1 stands out in that there are relatively more flakes in the two smaller size classes.

Larger artifacts between 4 and 10 cm in length are present in equal proportion in Zones 2 and 89-B. The greater proportion of somewhat larger artifacts recovered from the 1989 excavation compared to the other Late Archaic area, Zone 1, is therefore consistent with interpreting it as containing more discrete debris from lithic production. Although the debitage is essentially larger from this zone, there is very little cortex. Raw material may have been partially reduced elsewhere, or it had little cortex to begin with. Again, Zone 89-B may contain evidence of lithic manufacture, but the overall amounts of debris present are still far below what one would expect for a long-term flintknapping activity area. This suggests that the lithic concentration represents a short-term lithic processing event (for a discussion of this topic, see Pecora, this volume).

In sum, the following characteristics of the debitage can be outlined. First, lithic density is low across the site, but extremely low during the Middle Archaic period. Second, several types of reduction strategy appear to be occurring, with little to no bifacial reduction in Middle Archaic zone 2. Most of the reduction across the site appears to be geared to the manufacture of flakes and fragments, some of which may be turned into a variety of rather informal tools, unifaces, and later in the sequence, bifaces. Third, there is slight evidence for bipolar reduction, but it is not prevalent. Therefore, the lithic technology appears to

TABLE 6.2.
Tool Forms at Kilometer 4

Tool Type	Zone 2		Zone 1		Zone 89-B		Total		Potential Uses
	Count	Column Total (%)	Count	Column Total (%)	Count	Column Total (%)	Count	Column Total (%)	
Cobble cortex tool	14	45.2	22	20.6	12	14.0	48	21.4	Scrape, cut, butcher, dig
Retouched, damaged piece	6	19.4	34	31.8	41	47.7	81	36.2	Cut, butcher, scrape, pry, engrave
Uniface	8	25.8	13	12.1	15	17.4	36	16.1	Scrape hide, wood, bone
Biface	2	6.5	10	9.3	8	9.3	20	8.9	Knife, preform
Projectile point	1	3.2	24	22.4	6	7.0	31	13.8	Shoot, harpoon, knife
Other	0	0.0	4	3.7	4	4.7	8	3.6	Engrave, pry
Total	31	100.0	107	100.0	86	100.0	224	100.0	

Note: excludes four cobble cortex cores.

involve a mixed set of reduction techniques. It is apparent that the three areas sampled do differ in terms of reduction strategies used. Perhaps the reasons for this can be clarified by examining the modified tools that were found.

TOOL FORM

Artifacts classified as *tools* include the following types, listed in increasing level of formality: flakes or fragments with edge damage or retouch, cobble cortex tools, irregular unifacial tools or scrapers, symmetrical unifacial tools, bifaces, and projectile points (Table 6.2). These tool types present a range of forms and potential uses.

Retouched flakes and fragments account for over 36 percent of the total tools for the site. There are differences, however, in the relative contribution of these common tools between the Middle Archaic and the Late Archaic periods. In Zone 2, only 19.4 percent of the tools are retouched flakes or fragments. This number jumps to 31.8 percent for Late Archaic Zone 1, and even higher, to 47.7 percent for Late Archaic Zone 89-B.

Other than retouched flakes and fragments, the most prevalent tool type at Kilometer 4 is the cobble cortex tool (Figure 6.4b). A total of 48 were recovered (Table 6.2). For the Middle Archaic zone, these tools account for over 45 percent of the tool total. In the Late Archaic zones, the proportion of these tools drops to 20.6 percent for Zone 1, and 14 percent for Zone 89-B. This artifact type is consistently made from unmodified or retouched cortical flakes from igneous or quartzite cobbles. Water-rounded dorsal surfaces suggest that the cobbles came from the beach, and because there are so few cores (n=4) on site, the flakes were probably removed at the beach as well. Cobble cortex tools at Kilometer 4 range in size from 26.3 mm to 196.0 mm in length. The production of these flake tools was the object of a flintknapping strategy designed specifically to utilize coarse-grained materials. It was clearly the major component of the lithic manufacturing strategy during the Middle Archaic period, and, while still important during the Late Archaic, was supplemented to a greater degree by other strategies, including bifacial reduction.

Unifacial tools consist primarily of a range of steeply retouched tools in a range of forms. There are tools that resemble end scrapers, while others appear shovel-shaped, semicircular, or very small and thin. Nearly 26 percent (n=36) of the tools from Zone 2 fit into the uniface category 2. This incidence drops to nearly 12.1 percent for Zone 1, and rises to 17.4 percent for Zone 89-B. Many of these tools would have been suitable for hafting.

The most highly formalized tools are projectile points. Fragments of 31 projectile points are present, 1 from Zone 2, 24 from Zone 1, and 6 from Zone 89-B. Even so, these are not always finely bifacially worked. There are points with unifacial

Table 6.3.
Tool Formality

	Debitage	Tools	Tool/Debitage Ratio	Formal Tools	Percent Formal
Zone 2	261	32	0.123	11	34.4
Zone 1	2607	110	0.042	47	42.7
Zone 89-B	1005	86	0.086	29	33.7
Total	3873	228	0.059	87	38.2

and minimal bifacial retouch (Figure 6.4c–d). In fact, 29 percent of the projectile points recovered from the three zones are either unifacially worked, or unifacial with shallow retouch on the opposite face. Other bifaces appear to be preforms and this also suggests that some bifacial reduction was practiced at Kilometer 4. There is little evidence for recycling of broken projectile points. One exception is a point that suffered an impact-derived burination that effectively split the tool. The burin scar was then used as a scraping edge (Figure 6.4e).

Overall, we see a decided increase in the number of projectile points in the Late Archaic compared to the Middle Archaic occupation. This represents an increase in tool formality and overall diversity, and may signify a fundamental change in tool use or maintenance. The change from Middle Archaic to Late Archaic also corresponds to a reduction in the dependence on cobble cortex tools, and on unifacial or scraping types of tools in general.

Formality

Tool formality can be gauged by looking at the ratio of designated tools to debitage, and by looking at the relative proportion of the most highly formal tools among designated tools. For our purposes, formality refers to the regularization of lithic tool types. Several factors contribute to formality, including tool symmetry, standardization, and the degree of modification. Formal tools are defined to include only projectile points, bifaces, and fairly symmetrical unifacially worked pieces. Cobble cortex tools and retouched or edge-damaged flakes or fragments qualify as informal tools for this study.

Table 6.3 shows the ratio of tools to total debitage for each of the three zones as well as the proportion of "formal" tools to total tools. Overall, at Kilometer 4, the tool-to-debitage ratio is 0.059 while the formal tool percentage averages 38.2.

Middle Archaic Zone 2 has the highest tool-to-debitage ratio at 0.12. Zone 2 is thought to represent a generalized economic system involving a greater degree of mobility and seasonal use of the site. Finding a higher proportion of "tools" in respect to debitage may suggest a somewhat higher degree of curation and would

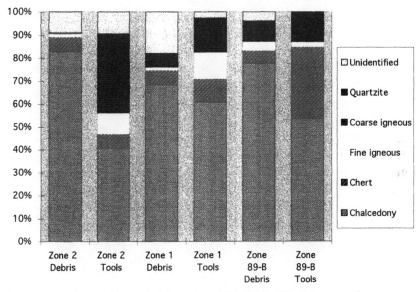

Figure 6.7. Raw materials recorded for tools and debitage at Kilometer 4.

fit with a model in which systems of higher mobility engender the use of formally modified but versatile tools. Approximately one-third of the tools for Zone 2 fit into the formal tool category, while 40 percent are cobble cortex tools classified as informal.

The Late Archaic components present a different picture. Zone 1 has by far the lowest ratio of tools to debitage, but it also has the highest percentage of formal to total tools at nearly 43 percent. This can be accounted for by the higher percentage of projectile points, the most formal of tool types. Tool-to-debitage ratios for Zone 89-B falls between Zones 1 and 2, at 0.086. Zone 89-B has 34 percent formal tools, more in keeping with Middle Archaic Zone 2 than with the other Late Archaic area.

Therefore, while the formal tools for Zone 2 are weighted toward unifaces, the tools of Zone 1 are weighted toward projectile points. The Late Archaic therefore presents an increase in formal tools within the suite of tool types used.

RAW MATERIAL

There are several types of material available locally as shown in Figure 6.7. The most prevalent is a grayish white to light brown chalcedony that can be found at several outcroppings along washes or *quebradas* near Kilometer 4. Chert is also present at the site and was distinguished from the chalcedony on the basis of translucent quality and luster. The chalcedony/chert cluster is overall of good quality with few inclusions and internal fracture planes, and an even cryptocrystalline grain. Igneous material such as basalt is available in outcroppings along the Ilo coast. A fine-grained red andesite occurs in the Moquegua highlands (about 2,500 m elevation) upriver from Ilo. Nodules of these highland materials, as well as moderately fine-grained quartzite can be found in the quebradas and among the cobbles that line the beaches. Therefore, the presence of highland materials need not signify cultural contact with highland populations, or long distances traveled. Coarse-grained igneous material such as granite is also available among beach cobbles. Other materials are found in extremely small quantities and these include quartz, jasper, and obsidian. With the exception of the obsidian, all of these are occasionally found as nodules in quebradas or along beaches.

Across the site, chalcedony made up 71 percent of all raw materials. Chert comprised 6 percent, coarse igneous material 5 percent, fine igneous 2 percent, quartzite 1 percent, and the remainder, other or unidentified. There was relatively little variation in this overall pattern in the different excavated areas of the site, although the percentages of each raw material type used to make tools did vary.

In Middle Archaic Zone 2, 82 percent of the debitage is chalcedony (the highest among the three zones), but only 41 percent of the 32 tools are made from this material. Coarse-grained igneous material and quartzite make up another 34.4 percent of the tool assemblage, mostly in the form of cobble cortex flake tools. Among the three zones, Zone 2 has the highest proportion of igneous debitage. Chert accounts for approximately 6 percent of both the debitage and tool categories. Fine-grained igneous material comprises over 9 percent of the tools. This contrasts with the complete lack of coarse igneous debitage, only one quartzite flake, and four pieces of fine igneous debitage.

Chalcedony is also the most common material from Zone 1, accounting for nearly 68 percent of the debitage, and 61 percent of the tools. Coarse materials including both igneous rock and quartzite are recorded for 6 percent of the debitage and 14.5 percent of the tools. Chert debitage amounts to 6.4 percent, while tools of chert make up 10 percent (n=11). Fine igneous material makes up only 1.4 percent of the debitage, but nearly 12 percent of the tools. In Zone 1, the raw material composition of the debitage closely reflects the composition of the tool assemblage.

In Zone 89-B there is a much higher percentage of chert tools than would be expected given the debitage composition. Chalcedony is still the most common, comprising almost 78 percent of the debitage, but was found in only 53.5 percent of the tools. Chert makes up only 5.5 percent of the debitage, but was used for over 31 percent of the tools. Coarse materials make up 8.7 percent of the debitage assemblage and nearly 13 percent of the tools. If the lithic concentration in Zone 89-B can be attributed to discrete lithic reduction episodes, then even a short interval of flintknapping with igneous rock could produce a concentration. In Zone 89-B, there is at least one case in which two flakes refit, again supporting the possibility of a discrete lithic activity area.

In sum, the materials used at Kilometer 4 are all locally available. Usage of these local raw materials remains relatively constant over time if we look only at the debitage. However, between the Middle and Late Archaic periods, there is an increase in the use of chert for making tools, although this is not reflected by the relatively constant incidence of chert debris. It appears as though chert tools may be entering the site in finished form later in the occupation. Coarse materials are used almost exclusively for making a particular artifact type, the cobble cortex tool, the manufacture of which leaves little debitage. Differences in raw material use for Middle Archaic Zone 2 as opposed to the Late Archaic areas are probably attributable to changes in seasonal site usage. However, the differences in raw material usage between Late Archaic Zones 1 and 89-B may depend more on variation in activities or tasks conducted in the two separate areas. Zone 89-B, also a domestic area, probably represents a more discrete set of activities. Zone 1, sampling a set of sequential floors and mixed fill, probably gives us a representative sample of materials used at Kilometer 4 throughout the Late Archaic period. All materials remain locally available throughout the term of occupation. Therefore, the changes in raw material use between the Middle and Late Archaic may depend on functional requirements of the lithic industries.

FUNCTION

In looking at the functional correlates to the debitage assemblages from Kilometer 4, the first question becomes—what is it these people need to be doing with stone tools? During the Middle and early Late Archaic, the people at Kilometer 4 appear to collect and use a wide variety of terrestrial as well as marine resources. Data indicate an increasing focus on small schooling fish (anchovy and herring) by the Late Archaic period. Bone artifacts include awls, net or fishing line weights, bird bone tubes, some of which are decorated with etched lines, small bird bone flutes, and bone beads. There are a few wooden artifacts, and several cactus spine fishhooks. Elsewhere along the Andean coast, bone and shell fishhooks have been recovered. There is some evidence for the use of bird skins and hide at Kilometer 4 as well. Textile technology is fairly well developed as indicated by cordage and netting. In addition, shelters were made and relatively flat habitation terraces were created. Ultimately, people died and were buried.

Given this range of potential activities, we outline several tasks and activities that seem necessary in order to accomplish them. We can then assess how well the tool types present at Kilometer 4 are able to meet these needs. Essential tasks include cutting or sawing, and scraping activities. Cutting will be required during butchery, hideworking, and plant processing. Sawing should accompany wood-working and boneworking. Scraping tools will be expected for softening hide, and shaping wood or bone artifacts. Furthermore, food collection, shelter construction, terrace maintenance, and burial may all require digging.

Potential uses for the stone tool types recovered at Kilometer 4 are shown in Table 6.2. There are clearly tools that can serve to perform all of the activities suggested above. However, other materials might also be used. For example, expedient cutting or scraping tools can be made from shell, which is ubiquitous on the site. Digging can be accomplished with sticks, but it could also employ some of the larger cobble cortex tools.

The most obvious activity requiring projectile points is shooting. Projectile points found at coastal sites are stylistically similar to points collected from scattered sites in the inland lomas areas that supported terrestrial mammals. Therefore, projectile point loss or discard would be expected on the lomas to a greater extent than on the coast. However, since lomas sites have not been systematically tested, we know very little about the debitage there, and whether or not it presents evidence for bifacial reduction, resharpening, or recycling. As fishing technology expanded on the coast, more projectile points might be adapted to harpooning for fish and sea mammals.

The precise role that the cobble cortex tool industry plays remains uncertain. Some appear to be used in a scraping activity as indicated by worn and abraded edges, striations perpendicular or oblique to the edges, and edge damage. Others with thin fine edges and striations parallel to the edge may have served cutting and sawing functions. The great size range of these artifacts makes it likely that they were used in more than one type of activity. Donnan and Moseley (1968) suggest that these served in processing and perhaps scaling fish, and Sandweiss (1992) reports finding a scale adhering to one of these tools. As yet, no experimentation has been done to reproduce the wear patterns from processing fish on such flakes. Cobble cortex tools appear to represent a generalized tool type, one with high versatility and durability, along with low cost because the materials can be found along the beach. They appear to be useful for a wide variety of tasks including cutting, scraping, and even digging. Exhibiting no hafting traces or elements, they were probably handheld. They are clearly the most important tool type in the Middle Archaic, but are used less throughout the Late Archaic in favor of a wider variety of unifacial and bifacial artifacts.

SUMMARY

We have presented a preliminary analysis of lithic materials from Kilometer 4. The amount of chipped lithic materials recovered is relatively small, especially when compared to the larger amounts of chipped lithic debitage recovered from

Early to Middle Archaic period highland sites in the Osmore River system, such as Asana (Aldenderfer 1998). Again, in interpreting the relative lack of chipped stone tools for Archaic period contexts at Kilometer 4, we return to the effects of raw material availability, mobility, and function.

RAW MATERIAL AVAILABILITY

The people of Kilometer 4 have adequate local raw material for chipping, but as populations grew, access to specific quarries or resources may have changed. Although amounts of debitage from different materials remain relatively constant through time, there are two major changes seen in the selection of raw materials between Middle Archaic and Late Archaic occupations. First, in Late Archaic occupations, chert tools become more common. However, since there is no increase in the proportion of chert debitage, these chert tools may not actually be made at the site. Second, the use of coarse materials for tools declines. This is related to the lower percentages of cobble cortex tools recovered from the Late Archaic occupations.

Indeed, the overall low density of lithic artifacts could be explained in part by the presence of alternative choices of raw material such as shell. While the presence of alternate material choices may keep the incidence of lithic totals consistently lower, it cannot explain the changes observed in the lithic assemblages at Kilometer 4 between Middle Archaic and Late Archaic contexts. For these changes, structural differences in the types of activities occurring and in the types of occupation may be more important.

MOBILITY

Middle Archaic settlement at Kilometer 4 is thought to be seasonal. Few remains from terrestrial mammals are present, and the lack of technology used in hunting terrestrial mammals is not surprising. There is virtually no evidence for projectile point production or discard for the Middle Archaic at Kilometer 4. If terrestrial resources were important to the more mobile Middle Archaic inhabitants, they needed to go elsewhere, probably to inland lomas, to acquire them.

During the Late Archaic period, occupation appears to become more sedentary as the inhabitants focus more heavily on marine resources year round. Two effects on the lithic industry are possible. First, longer periods of occupation might encourage tool users to bring what hunting or harpooning tools there were into the site for retooling or maintenance. This would involve repair or replacement of both hafts and points, and provides one explanation for the greater proportion of projectile points deriving from Late Archaic contexts, especially Zone 1. A second effect would involve the addition of tools and equipment for year-round, rather than seasonal activities. For the Middle Archaic occupation we probably sampled only a piece of the total settlement system. For the Late Archaic, we have probably sampled a larger portion of annual domestic activities. Therefore, an increase in tool diversity would not be surprising. Increase in tool diversity in the Late Archaic period also supports Torrence's (1983) argument for greater diversity of tool types in economies focused more on specific resources. Of course, an increase in tool diversity will depend on tool function.

FUNCTION

There are clear changes in the function of tools over time. Low incidence of retouched flakes and high incidence of primarily unifacial artifacts in the Middle Archaic give way to retouched flakes and projectile points later on. Middle Archaic tools appear geared to a variety of scraping and cutting tasks. In fact, the toolkit for the Middle Archaic contains scraping or generalized scraping and cutting tools, and very little else. From this concentration, it may appear that tool use during the Middle Archaic was more highly specialized, if by specialized we mean focused on a narrower range of activities (i.e., scraping). Again this makes sense if the site was only seasonally used for the exploitation or processing of specific marine or coastal resources. The question becomes, what are they processing? Possibilities include fish, hides, and/or wood. It may be that the functional requirements simply do not necessitate highly formalized, specialized tools, and for these reasons the lithic technology for Middle Archaic Zone 2 appears minimal and expedient, leaving little debitage.

In Late Archaic occupations, represented by Zones 1 and 89-B, the range of tool types increases to include more bifacially produced types, and small amounts of the production debris that go along with them (bifacial thinning flakes and preforms). A greater number of projectile points, especially those with barbs (Figure 6.4d), may indicate greater use of harpoons. On the other hand, the longer-term Late Archaic occupations, while also specializing on marine resources, may still retain the equipment needed for logistical seasonal hunting trips. The difference here is that these tools now find their way to the site as a result of its function as a more permanent home base.

CONCLUSION

Overall, the chipped lithic assemblage in itself does not appear to be overtly specialized for a maritime economy. There are few obviously specialized chipped lithic tools, with the exception of harpoon points (which could easily be geared toward hunting). Most of the tools and tool types are versatile cutting or scraping tools. While the chipped stone technology does not appear specialized, technology clearly designed for fishing is present. There are ground stone fishing weights or *pesos* that were produced by pecking and grinding basalt splinters into bi-pointed plummets. Other tools used specifically for the procurement of marine resources include fishhooks of cactus spine and composite hooks made from either bone or stone shafts to which barbs are attached.

It may be that a maritime economy, especially one focusing increasingly on schooling fish depends less on chipped stone tools than on other technology such as nets and cordage. This factor, as well as the availability of alternative raw materials could explain the generally low densities of chipped stone. As the inhabitants become more sedentary, a greater variety of lithic reduction strategies appear, including some bipolar reduction and bifacial thinning. For the Late Archaic, heavier focus on marine resources could account for the greater variety of tools used. Diversity might also follow from increased sedentism, which might allow more tool maintenance activities to occur at the site. During the Late Archaic period there is less use of the versatile cobble cortex tool type so common in the Middle Archaic, and later assemblages overall become more formal. These changes between Middle and Late Archaic contexts appear to be related to changes in the functional requirements of the assemblage, due in part to both increased sedentism and increased resource specialization. Even so, as the subsistence economy becomes specialized, the lithic assemblages remain multipurpose and flexible, in other words, generalized.

We have modeled the changes in lithic technology between the Middle Archaic and the Late Archaic contexts for the coastal site of Kilometer 4 in southern Peru. Although we find variation in the organization of lithic technology between three different areas of the site, we do not believe that any single factor of raw material availability, mobility, or function can explain the differences. It is more likely that changes in subsistence and mobility result in a complicated set of combined effects on the lithic technology.

7

What Put the Small in the Arctic Small Tool Tradition: Raw Material Constraints on Lithic Technology at the Mosquito Lake Site, Alaska

KRISTEN E. WENZEL AND PHILLIP H. SHELLEY

In most technologies, one of the most important elements of organization is the material available to utilize in production. Before the first flake could be removed to begin the manufacture process resulting in a finished tool, prehistoric flintworkers had to consider a number of factors related to the deposition, occurrence, and quality of lithic raw materials. Characteristics of lithic resources were fundamental components of the technological process. This research presents a simple and direct method of examining the relationship between lithic resources and the organization of stone tool technology. A comparison of cultural materials (debitage and artifacts) from the Mosquito Lake site in northern Alaska with the noncultural materials of a lithic quarry provides some interesting insights into the influence of raw material on the organization of technology within the Denbigh Flint Complex (4,300–3,500 B.P.). The results of this analysis indicate that the selective interplay of climatic variation, characteristics of lithic resources, and distribution of other resources influenced the selection of small tools that are a hallmark of the Denbigh Flint Complex and the broader Arctic Small Tool tradition (5,000–1,000 B.P.). More importantly, this research demonstrates that it is possible to isolate attributes sensitive to raw material variables in simple yet effective analysis.

Unfortunately, we understand very poorly the use of stone as a raw material.
(Jochim 1989:107)

It is surprising that this statement by Michael Jochim was made in a volume where the majority of papers conclude that the organization of lithic technology directly reflects specific aspects of human behavior (Torrence 1989a). If the basic component of lithic technology, namely the stone that comprises the tool, is not understood, any behavioral explanations derived from variability in flaked stone technology are suspect. Before the first flake could be struck on the trajectory towards a finished tool, prehistoric flintworkers had to consider a number of factors related to the deposition, availability, and quality of raw materials. In the 11 years since the publication of the *Time, Energy and Stone Tools* volume, lithic researchers have tackled the beast of human reason and intention with all the force of a Folsom hunter hurtling a spear at a bison. From experimental replication of tools and their use to ethnoarchaeological studies of modern hunter-gatherer groups to complex mechanics experiments, lithic researchers have expanded their investigative scope to incorporate many different theories and methods in the quest to comprehend the relationship between human behavior and the objects comprising the archaeological record.

In this new research climate, mobility continues to occupy center stage, often obscuring the larger picture of organizational behavior. The advances of the last 20 years in lithic research have contributed to deeper investigation of stone tool technology and the teasing out of variables influencing its organization in prehistoric cultures. However, the recognition of the complexity of technology has not led to a rapid movement forward to address other aspects of behavior. Progress in lithic research has been complicated by the lack of adequate theory to address a wider range of issues and the continued use of methods derived from settlement system studies (Jeske 1996).

The limitations imposed by the traditional mobility approach to studying technology have often relegated raw material to a cursory role. However, evidence from Andrefsky (1994a, 1994b) challenged the traditional association between tool types and settlement patterns. In an examination of sedentary and mobile groups in regions of different lithic resource availability, he found lithic material to be the primary constraint on organization. His study and the work of others (Hayden 1989; Ingbar 1994; Owen 1988) demonstrate the advantage to be gained in considering the role of raw materials in organizational studies.

This study uses a simple and direct approach to examine the problem of raw material constraints on technological organization via the examination of a debitage sample from a Denbigh Flint Complex site in Alaska. Due to the relative youth of Arctic archaeology, much time has been devoted to the construction of typologies and culture-histories using variability in stone tool morphology and style. However, as Bielwaski (1988) and Nagy (1994) have noted, the theoretical frameworks applied to develop these chronologies often do not adequately address the problem of variability in lithic technology.

The problem of interpretation in Arctic prehistory is best exemplified by the unique situation of the Arctic Small Tool tradition (ASTt) and the Denbigh Flint Complex. The discovery of tiny lithic implements representing a bifacial and blade technology confounded researchers upon their discovery (Giddings 1964). The appearance of this distinct industry across Alaska, Canada, and Greenland at approximately 5,000 years ago is followed by a period of relative continuity until its rather sudden disappearance at around 1,000 years ago (Dumond 1977; Giddings and Anderson 1986). The Denbigh Flint Complex represents the earliest manifestation of the ASTt, with coastal sites at Cape Denbigh in the northern Bering Sea to large habitation sites in the interior of Alaska at Onion Portage (Anderson 1984), Punyik Point (Irving 1964), and Kurupa Lake (Schoenberg 1985). The microlithic tools are assumed to be an adaptation of a mobile group following a seasonal cycle based on the primary subsistence resources of the region: caribou, anadromous fish, and sea mammals (Anderson 1984; Dumond 1977; Mason and Gerlach 1995).

The variability at the attribute and artifact level of Arctic Small Tool tradition assemblages has served as a foundation for constructing chronologies, as well as inferring subsistence and settlement patterns. However, these interpretations and classifications have often utilized ill-defined functional and stylistic attributes that are not clearly understood (Bielwaski 1988; Nagy 1994). In fact, variation within ASTt assemblages is often greater than that between assemblages (Anderson 1970; Giddings and Anderson 1986). It is important for researchers to sort out the variability to avoid weaker behavioral interpretations or faulty chronologies.

The abundance, quality, and accessibility of raw materials are important factors influencing the flaked stone strategies employed by prehistoric peoples. While this may seem a self-evident point, it often becomes lost in the analysis as researchers juggle many different variables in technological studies. Andrefsky (1994a) and Hayden (1989) have noted that while many lithic studies linking mobility patterns with technological organization have been useful, they often neglect the influence of raw material, particularly in linking the characteristics of local quarries and other lithic sources to the archaeological evidence available. In this study, debitage and artifacts from an archaeological site are examined along with local quarry data to identify attributes sensitive to the characteristics of a raw material source.

Materials from the Mosquito Lake archaeological site in northern Alaska (Figure 7.1) can provide insights into the influence of raw material on the organization of technology within the Denbigh Flint Complex. The site was excavated in the 1970s as part of the Alyeska Pipeline Project (Kunz 1977). Situated on a bedrock lobe in the Atigun River Valley, the site yielded over 30,000 lithic artifacts suggesting a large lithic workshop area, especially given the lack of features (some charcoal deposits and remnant hearth rings). Thirteen localities were assigned to the Denbigh Flint Complex on the basis of diagnostic artifacts and supporting radiocarbon dates spanning 3,500 B.P. to possibly as late as 2,135 B.P.

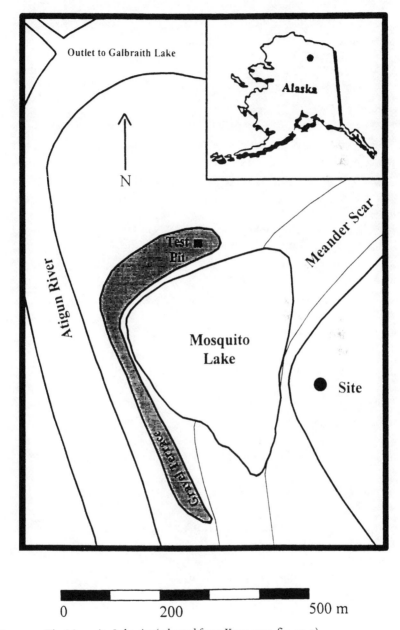

Figure 7.1. The Mosquito Lake site (adapted from Kunz 1977, fig. 49-3).

(Kunz 1977). This analysis focuses on the relationship of one factor, raw material, and investigates its effect on technological organization within the Denbigh Flint Complex localities at the site.

THE MODEL

Three objectives provide the framework for the model. First, manufacturing sequences at the Mosquito Lake site will be reconstructed to describe the stages and techniques of lithic manufacture present on site. It cannot be disputed that the organization of technology in any culture reflects situational adaptations that optimize human expenditure of time and energy (Torrence 1989b). Thus, the presence or absence of certain technologies reflects solutions to particular problems, such as the availability of lithic raw material. Second, the quarry materials will be described in relationship to the materials at the site. In order to evaluate the technological strategies present at the site, it is necessary to examine the characteristics of the lithic raw materials in the region. Finally, attributes sensitive to raw material constraints will be identified through simple statistical analysis.

In this model, it is necessary to operationalize a series of assumptions in order to focus the attribute analysis on raw material factors. The specification of these antecedent conditions provides for proper evaluation of the results and the implications of results.

The fundamental assumption of this study is that lithic technology is a reductive strategy that favors the selection of high-quality raw materials. The lithic production sequence begins with a piece of stone that is subsequently worked into a desired object through the removal of material. This places certain requirements on the raw materials utilized in order to minimize errors and energy expenditure, particularly in areas of limited lithic availability. To solve this problem, the inherent qualities that cannot be manipulated by the flintworker in production are instead controlled through the selection process. Experimental studies and ethnographic observation have allowed archaeologists to infer certain requirements for toolstone. High-quality raw materials must be of adequate size and shape, homogeneous, cryptocrystalline, vitreous, and isotropic (Crabtree 1972). While it may be possible to improve the isotropic qualities of toolstone through heat treatment, characteristics such as small or inappropriate nodule size require different strategies in technique and stone tool design.

It is assumed that the Denbigh Flint Complex materials are the remains of a mobile hunter-gatherer group following a seasonal cycle based on time-sensitive sources. Based on the archaeological and ethnographic data (Dumond 1977; Giddings 1964; Giddings and Anderson 1986), Denbigh Flint Complex peoples were a flexible group with a versatile economy that allowed them to utilize both interior and coastal resources. The strongest argument for this assumption is the simple fact that options are limited in the Arctic. The primary resources for the last 10,000 years have been caribou in the interior, sea mammals on the coast, and anadromous fish (salmon) along drainages. The lengthy ethnographic record indicates that most Iñupiat groups have followed a seasonal cycle based on sealing and/or whaling in the late spring/early summer with caribou hunting and/or salmon fishing taking place during the summer, fall, and winter (Anderson 1984; Dumond 1977, 1984). In addition, the settlement distribution and assemblage composition of Denbigh Flint Complex sites indicate a mobile group following a seasonal cycle with temporary settlements at the coast and along lakes, and semipermanent dwellings located along rivers of the interior (Dumond 1977; Giddings 1967).

It is this assumption of mobility that has been implicitly accepted as an explanation for the unique technology of the Denbigh Flint Complex and the Arctic Small Tool tradition. However, in this study the assumption serves as an antecedent condition, not an explanation. Assuming that seasonal variation impacted the economic strategies of the group allows assessment of the constraints imposed by the availability, abundance, and quality of raw materials in such a system.

Environmental evidence from the end of the Pleistocene to modern times suggests that the region has remained relatively uniform over the last 10,000 years. While environmental data suggest several short yet significant climatic shifts, the overall character of the landscape has not changed significantly (Mason and Gerlach 1995). However, while these climatic changes may not have radically changed the variety of flora and fauna present, they may have altered their distribution, which may have influenced cultural development in the region (Mason and Gerlach 1995).

The north slope of the central Brooks Range is an area of temperature extremes and intense wind and storm activity. This climate has hindered extensive human occupation of the area. Summers are short and cool, with freezing temperatures possible every month of the year. The winter freeze-up begins around mid-September with break-up ending sometime in late June, and a very brief thaw season between May and June (Mull and Adams 1985; Watson 1959).

The temperatures throughout winter and summer are generally low, as is the precipitation. Wind is a major factor throughout the year, with velocities reaching up to 48 kph, causing severe wind-chill temperatures and contributing to poor visibility in the winter (Wahrhaftig 1965). Precipitation in the area is variable and is increased at the boundary between the Brooks Range and Arctic foothills to the north.

As a result of the combination of glacial activity and cold temperatures, the ground is perennially frozen. In fact, it is possible for the region to be frozen for up to eight months a year (Table 7.1). Thus, despite the extensive chert-bearing

TABLE 7.1.

Summary of Annual Climatic Values from North-Central Alaska, 1975–1979

	Brooks Range	Arctic Foothills
Total Degree-Days (5-year)		
Thawing	453–1189	760–1125
Freezing	2173–3888	4225–5412
Thaw Season		
Length	87–131	104–139
Starting dates	May 3–June 10	May 18–June 27
Precipitation (mm)		
Frozen	57–181	87–110
Unfrozen	117–292	52–157
Total	295–450	140–267
Temperature (EC)		
Mean	−6.9 to −5.9	−11.1 to −6.2
Range (extremes)	−37.8 to +26.1	−53.3 to +30

Adapted from Mull and Adams 1985, table 1.

formations within the Brooks Range, these lithic sources may have been seasonally restricted due to the freezing temperatures in the fall and winter.

EXPECTATIONS

A total of eight expectations were defined for the attribute analysis of debitage and artifacts and complementary study of lithic raw material sources. The first set of expectations deals specifically with the effects of raw material on lithic technology. The second set of expectations addresses the strategies utilized by prehistoric toolmakers dealing with raw material constraints.

Despite the location of the Mosquito Lake site near a prehistoric quarry, it is expected that the predominance of poor-quality materials (inadequate size, irregularities, etc.) and limited seasonal availability of lithic materials constrained the organization of technology. The influence of these factors on the Mosquito Lake assemblage will be reflected in the following ways:

(1) Locally available raw materials will be primarily of poor or average quality and limited size dimensions. The results of a size and quality assessment survey of unmodified raw material at the quarry are expected to correlate with the debitage from the cultural site.

(2) The assemblage will contain a high frequency of lithic shatter and incom-

plete flakes due to the poor quality of material. The presence of a large amount of lithic shatter reflects the intensity of production, which may be related to quality (Shelley 1990). A high frequency of incomplete flakes, particularly the absence of platform remnants due to crushing, also suggests a high rate of failure in flake removal.

(3) High-quality lithic debitage will be dimensionally smaller in relationship to poor-quality debitage. In a size class distribution of complete flakes, high-quality materials will predominantly be smaller relative to poorer quality flakes.

(4) High-quality local materials will be reserved for formal tool production. Formal tools are defined as those artifacts requiring a significant time investment in manufacture (Andrefsky 1998; Tomka, this volume). It is expected that standardized tools, which require greater attention in manufacture, will be comprised of a combination of high-quality local and nonlocal materials.

Given these expectations regarding the quality and abundance of raw material, a secondary set of expectations can be derived. If raw materials are of poor quality and, additionally, limited in accessibility due to climatic factors such as frozen ground nine months of the year, then toolmakers can be expected to maximize raw materials. Maximization is a concept developed within optimization studies, which utilizes cost-benefit models (Torrence 1989b). However, in this study, maximization is used less formally and is simply defined as the efficient use of raw material. Maximizing strategies are expected to be reflected in the following ways:

(1) A high frequency of blades will be present in the assemblage. The adoption of a blade technology provides more cutting edge by increasing the number of uniformly shaped implements derived from a piece of lithic raw material (Rasic and Andrefsky, this volume; Sheets and Muto 1972). Additionally, the standardized form of blades allows them to be easily used in composite tools (Giddings 1964).

(2) Platform remnants will display a high frequency of abrasion and microflake removals. In order to minimize failure in flake removal, toolmakers can invest extra time in the preparation of core platforms. The presence of a high degree of remnant preparation indicates an emphasis on minimizing failure due to raw material influences, such as low availability and poor quality materials.

(3) Cortical flakes will occur in low frequency. Despite the location of the site near the quarry, it is expected that due to the poor quality of materials available, toolmakers were forced to conduct extensive testing at the quarry to find appropriate materials (Shelley 1993). Thus, the presence of a low amount of large cortical flakes and a high frequency of small interior flakes suggest a workshop focused on later stages of manufacture, with primary reduction taking place elsewhere.

(4) Nonlocal materials will be present as formal tools and as late stage reduction debitage. It is expected that nonlocal materials will be of a higher quality

and, therefore, the use-life extended via resharpening and repair. These tools include microblades, bifaces, endblades, sideblades, burins, and burin spalls. Any nonlocal debitage most likely represents later reduction stages, such as resharpening and maintenance debris.

METHODS

A raw material survey of the quarry was conducted following methods developed by Shelley (1993). Secondly, an attribute level analysis of debitage (n=2,204) and tools (n=393) was conducted on a sample of the Mosquito Lake lithic assemblage. The statistical analysis addressing the eight expectations comprised the final step.

Efforts to reconstruct the dynamics of past human behavior are complicated by the limited knowledge regarding the origin of lithic raw materials recovered archaeologically (Shelley 1993). In order to identify the effects of lithic raw material availability and quality on technological organization, it is necessary to identify and analyze the lithic sources within the immediate area of a site. Thus, a raw material survey was conducted in the vicinity of the site to locate primary and secondary lithic sources.

Previous archaeological and geological investigations had identified several isolated tectonic blocks of green-gray chert associated with the limestone member of the Triassic Age Otuk Formation within the Atigun Gorge (Kunz 1977; Mull and Harris 1985; Von Krogh 1977). These blocks had been exposed due to faulting and were eroding out from terraces in primary context. They were also present in secondary context within drainages around the source.

After identifying the presence of chert in the general survey, the next step was to conduct an analysis of the raw materials in the various contexts identified. Following the methods described by Shelley (1993), two separate survey areas were identified to adequately describe the available sources from different settings. First, a 20 by 20 m square was laid out on a terrace. All tool-quality stone greater than 5-cm maximum dimension was analyzed for size, shape, and quality. Second, a 100 m linear transect was surveyed along a drainage to describe the characteristics of materials in alluvial settings. All secondary deposits of appropriate size were analyzed for size, shape, and quality. A total of 110 pieces were analyzed.

The maximum dimension (length), maximum dimension perpendicular to length on the same plane (width), and dimension perpendicular to the plane of length and width (thickness) were recorded on all nodules. The qualitative data recorded included an estimate of roundness using an established template (Waters 1992) and quality. Quality assessments (high, medium, low) were based on the homogeneity and isotropic characteristics of a piece.

The high number of lithic artifacts from the Mosquito Lake site necessitated

TABLE 7.2.
Radiocarbon Dates from Mosquito Lake (Kunz 1970)

Locality	Sample No.	Date B.P.	MASCA Correction
2	GX-4075	2705 ± 160	910–930 ± 170 B.C.
3	GX-4080	2135 ± 160	330–370 B.C.
4	GX-4079	2425 ± 160	510–560 ± 170 B.C.
5	GX-4104	2665 ± 155	880–900 ± 165 B.C.
8	GX-4250	3515 ± 160	2040 ± 170 B.C.

the selection of a sample for analysis. From the 13 Denbigh localities described, 5 were selected for sampling. The term *locality* does not refer to an activity area, which may reflect different site functions and complicate analysis, but rather to discrete excavation units. These localities all had associated radiocarbon dates within the Denbigh Flint Complex period (Table 7.2).

Formal tools are defined as artifacts that require energy and skill to manufacture, such as endblades, sideblades, burins, microblades, and bifaces (Andrefsky 1994b, 1998). They are tools in standardized form, shaped for hafting, which require a preconception, or a "mental template" prior to manufacture. They are distinguished from "expedient" tools, such as flakeknives and retouched flakes, which can be manufactured spontaneously with minimal preparation. Because debitage was the primary focus of the study, the analysis of formal tools was very basic. The attributes recorded were raw material type (a visual identification and association with documented samples from formations), quality, condition (complete or incomplete), and length and width.

The analysis of debitage provides much more information on the process of manufacture, particularly in understanding raw material constraints. Debitage studies can identify techniques, technological traits, and manufacturing stages present at an archaeological site (Andrefsky, this volume; Carr and Bradbury, this volume; Crabtree 1972). The classifications utilized in this attribute-level analysis were constructed based on the research interest in variables related to raw material.

The metric attributes of length, width, thickness, and weight were recorded on each piece of debitage. Length was measured along the proximal-distal axis on the ventral face of the flake, width was measured along a line perpendicular to the length axis, and thickness measured at a line perpendicular to the width. When the proximal-distal axis could not be determined, length was measured on the longest axis. Weight was recorded to the nearest tenth of a gram, although the data were not used in analysis.

Raw material type classifications were based on visual similarity to samples derived from different lithic formations in the region. These samples are stored at

TABLE 7.3.
Summary of Eight Expectations and Results of Analysis

Expectation	Result	Comments
Raw Material		
Locally available raw materials will be primarily of poor quality and limited size dimensions	Negative	Material primarily of moderate to low quality and average size
High frequency of lithic shatter and incomplete flakes	Positive	Shatter comprises over 30 percent of debitage assemblage and incomplete flakes account for 70 percent of debitage; majority of terminations are hinge and step (70 percent)
Flake size and quality correlated	Positive	Two smallest size classes account for highest frequency of high-quality material
High-quality materials reserved for formal tool production	Positive	Majority of formal tools (80 percent) high quality
Maximization		
High frequency of blades	Positive	30 percent of artifact inventory comprised of microblades and retouched blades
High frequency of platform preparation	Negative	Majority of platforms prepared, but not correlated with raw-material quality
Cortical flakes in low frequency	Positive	Less than 5 percent of debitage sample
Nonlocal materials present as formal tools and late-stage reduction	Positive	98 percent of formal tools of nonlocal materials and 50 percent of late-stage debitage

the Eastern New Mexico University Lithic Laboratory. This system of typing materials to formations is considered preferable when feasible because it allows distinction of local and nonlocal materials. The lithic resources of the Brooks Range region are well documented and described, thanks to the extensive geological work of Mull and Adams (1985), Mull and Harris (1985), and the archaeological investigations of Shelley (1993) and Kunz (1977).

Raw material quality assessments were based on the homogeneous and isotropic characteristics of a piece. High-quality lithic materials were defined as being of adequate shape and size, cryptocrystalline, and free from inclusions,

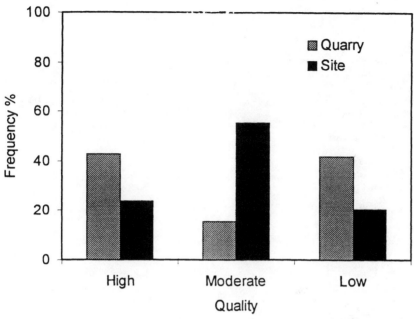

Figure 7.2. Raw material quality distribution from quarry (n = 110) and site (n = 2,138).

cleavage planes, and weathering damage. Obviously, in the debitage analysis, size and shape could not be addressed, but the other characteristics were used in classification. Moderate-quality materials are those pieces with minimal flaws that did not inhibit the isotropic properties of the stone. Debitage and quarry stone with minor inclusions and flaws were classified as moderate. Low-quality materials were those pieces with substantial flaws in the form of inclusions or cleavage planes and materials with substantial frost damage.

RESULTS OF ANALYSIS

The eight expectations defined prior to data collection and analysis are summarized in Table 7.3. Six expectations were supported by the data from the Mosquito Lake site. The most intriguing results are discussed in the following section.

Based on the quarry survey, the locally available cherts were of adequate size and shape, but variable quality. The predominant form types using Zingg's (1935) shape classification are disk and roller forms, with an average mean length of 11.9 cm, width of 7.5 cm, and thickness of 4.7 cm. The rocks examined at the quarry vary substantially in quality, with the majority primarily of moderate and low quality (Figure 7.2). In a Kolmogorov-Smirnov two-tailed test, there is a statistically significant difference between the quality frequencies of the quarry sample and the debitage sample. This suggests that prehistoric flintworkers may

TABLE 7.4.

Size Classes of Complete Flakes Sorted by Raw Material Quality

Quality	1–10 mm	11–20 mm	21–30 mm	31+ mm
High	82	39	10	1
Moderate	178	125	34	10
Low	44	60	24	24

$X^2 = 63.49, p < 0.001, df = 6$

TABLE 7.5.

Termination Type Frequency

Termination Type	N	Percent
Feather	178	29.6
Hinge	218	36.2
Step	206	34.2
Total	602	100.0

have been selecting higher quality pieces from the quarry and transporting them to the site for further reduction. Evidence of primary reduction in the form of nondiagnostic lithic scatters with large cortical and early-stage reduction flakes was recorded at the quarry, supporting this inference.

Size class of complete flakes provided some very intriguing results. Complete flakes from the site were sorted by raw materials quality into two size classes (Table 7.4). The distribution of moderate- and low-quality flakes across size classes is rather uniform, with the highest frequency of high-quality flakes in the smaller size class. A Kolmogorov-Smirnov two-tailed test yielded statistically significant difference between the cumulative proportions of the two flake size classes.

The Mosquito Lake assemblage also contained a high frequency of lithic shatter and flakes with hinge and step terminations. The presence of a large amount of limited attribute flake fragments (LAFFs) and limited information lithic fragments (LILFs) reflects a high intensity of production, which may be related to production (Shelley 1990). This shatter comprises over 30 percent of the entire assemblage sample. Poor-quality materials are more likely to shatter and/or result in unsuccessful flake removals during reduction due to flaws. Flake termination type also indicated the presence of poor-quality lithic material. Feather, hinge, step, indeterminate, and missing classifications were used in analysis. The high frequency of hinge and step terminations (Table 7.5) are certainly suspect, given the great skill represented in the finished artifacts of the Denbigh Flint Complex. Shelley (1990) reported that beginning flintworkers produce signifi-

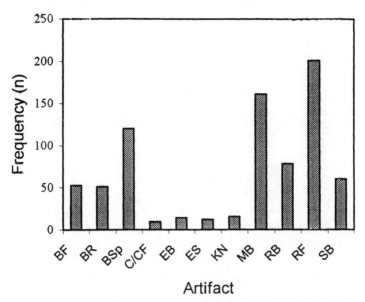

Figure 7.3. Tool type frequency from Mosquito Lake Denbigh localities (n = 773). BF = biface, BR = burin, BSp = burin spall, C/CF = core/core fragments, EB = endblades, ES = endscrapers, KN = knives, MB = microblades, RB = retouch blades; RF = retouch flakes, SB = sideblades.

cantly more hinge and step fractures than those with experience. However, his experiment was controlled by the use of high-quality silicates. It would be interesting to analyze the debitage created by experienced flintworkers utilizing poor-quality materials.

High-quality and nonlocal materials were expected to be reserved for formal tool production. In this analysis, formal tools are sideblades, endblades, microblades, blades, bifaces, burins, and burin spalls. Bifacially flaked, unhafted tools called flakeknives by Giddings (1964), scrapers, and retouched flakes are classified as expedient tools.

The complete assemblage from the Denbigh localities includes 773 formal and expedient tools (Figure 7.3). Microblades, retouched blades, and burin spalls account for the majority of the tool inventory, suggesting a primary emphasis on maximizing cutting edge per nodule via a blade and microblade technology. Endblades, sideblades, bifaces, and scrapers comprise relatively low frequencies. Cores are extremely rare in the assemblage, which is odd given its proximity to a lithic quarry.

Eighty percent of the formal tools were of high-quality material whereas 70 percent of expedient tools were made from low-quality material. As raw material quality decreases, so does the frequency of formal tools, as can be seen in Figure 7.4. A similar pattern emerges when formal and expedient tools are sorted by -

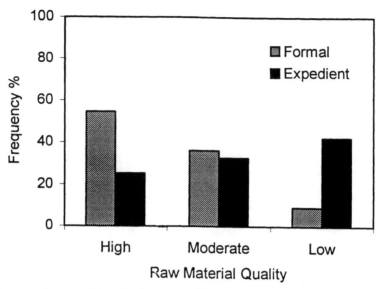

Figure 7.4. Raw material quality frequency of formal and expedient tools from the sampled localities (n=393).

local and nonlocal materials. The majority of nonlocal materials (98 percent) occur as formal tools on the site, suggesting maximization of high-quality materials for formal tool production.

It was expected that platform remnant type would provide information on maximizing strategies. While the majority of remnants were prepared (Figure 7.5), chi-square tests did not support a relationship between remnant preparation and quality. It is possible that other factors, such as raw material shape or technological considerations, may influence remnant type. It is interesting to note that the Mosquito Lake assemblage had a very high frequency of prepared platforms.

To summarize briefly, the Denbigh Flint Complex occupation of Mosquito Lake consists of a large lithic assemblage representative of a lithic workshop where late stage reduction was the primary activity. This is based on the high frequency of interior flakes and lack of cortical flakes, as well as the low frequency of cores. While there is a significant amount of locally available lithic material of adequate shape and size, the quality is variable. In addition, climatic data suggest a limited period of access to these materials, although there is no archaeological evidence to indicate seasonality of occupation. The Denbigh Flint occupants primarily utilized a microblade technology, a technique demonstrated to maximize cutting edge. It also appears that high-quality materials were low in quantity and reserved for the production of formal tools. While this research has not "proven"

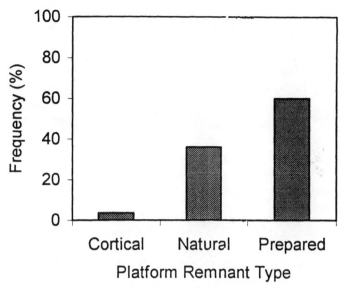

Figure 7.5. Frequency of platform remnant types in debitage sample (n=1,124).

that lithic raw material characteristics are the sole agents directing the organization of technology, it certainly has demonstrated that these characteristics influence the strategies employed by prehistoric toolmakers.

IMPLICATIONS

In a comparative study of blades from the Anangula site of southwest Alaska and Mosquito Lake microblades, Del Bene (1982:398) described the Denbigh Flint technological fingerprint as emphasizing labor input into manufacture and minimizing labor input for curation. He noted that there is an emphasis on high-quality materials, which suggested a mobile economy where raw materials are scarce.

Linda Owen (1988) conducted a most detailed analysis of blade and microblade technology on two continents. She documented and compared variation in blade, microblade, and core attributes through time from 72 sites in the North American Arctic and the Upper Paleolithic of southwest Germany. Her examination of microblades from several Denbigh Flint Complex sites, including Mosquito Lake, provided some interesting insight into the influence of raw material.

In general, Owen (1988:178) found a clear separation between raw materials used for microblade production and those used for flake and bifacial tool production. Owen's results concur with the findings of this research. Cryptocrystalline high-quality materials were favored for microblade production, with

obsidian becoming the primary raw material type in Denbigh Flint Complex assemblages. In fact, Denbigh Flint Complex obsidian microblades were retouched
twice as often as those manufactured from chert (Owen 1988:75).

Owen (1988:178–184) also found that later Denbigh Flint Complex assemblages are characterized by an increasing diversity of core form and use of locally
available raw materials. Also, battered platform preparation is prevalent throughout the Denbigh Flint sample. As discussed above, the majority of platforms at
the Mosquito Lake site were prepared, although this did not seem to correlate
with raw material quality. Owen (1988) concludes that Denbigh flintworkers organized their technology to use a greater variety of nodules and pebbles and to
maximize raw materials.

In comparing the entire sample of blades and microblades from all 72 sites,
Owen (1988:192) could not identify a universal criterion for differentiating
blades and microblades. This is a very significant finding, as Arctic archaeologists
have often used microblade width and length for temporal and cultural classifications. In fact, North American Arctic microblades were smaller than those
from the Old World. Owen (1988:192) attributes this to the limited availability
and size of materials in the region.

Owen's results concur with those of Del Bene (1982) and this research. The
Denbigh Flint Complex represents a technological organization focused on the
maximization of high-quality raw materials in a mobile economy. In a region
where most resources are time-stressed, lithic material acquisition can be viewed
in the same way as caribou or fuel sources. When the ground is frozen for a large
portion of the year, prehistoric peoples would have to schedule activities not only
around the availability of caribou but also the brief season during which lithic
raw materials were readily accessible and easily located.

FINAL REMARKS

> This is what we have to do. We have to look beyond the horizon because when
> you look into the horizon, you think that is the end—but it is not. You walk to
> that horizon again and there is another horizon. . . . You can go all the way
> around the world in this manner. If we can look at it that way, we will be better
> off. Otherwise, we will get too caught up in one simple thing, or one matter, or
> one problem. We have got to look at it from all angles. Robert Mulluk, Iñupiaq,
> cited in Chance (1990:13)

The results of this research are not the final horizon by any means. Rather, they
serve as a pathway to further questions and analyses. Lithic analysts have been
criticized (Jeske 1996) for not progressing beyond the comfort zones of mobility
and settlement studies. While these issues certainly deserve attention and contin-

uous research, it is also necessary to expand the scope of lithic analyses. Frameworks that emphasize the examination of variability of objects, whether at the attribute, typological, or mass aggregate scale, are productive means to study archaeological assemblages.

Perhaps the selective interplay of lithic raw material characteristics, climatic variation, and availability of other resources influenced the selection of objects that were small. The interplay of all of these resources and environmental variables might be the answer to the questions of what put the "small" in the Arctic Small Tool tradition. In an area with freezing temperatures throughout most of the year and limited economic options, strategies that maximized materials of any kind were advantageous. Caribou provided not only meat but also hide for clothing and tents, and bone and antler for tools (Dumond 1977). It appears that the people of the Denbigh Flint Complex also maximized the lithic raw materials available to them, selecting for properties that made small tools superior in the harsh Arctic environment. The property of smallness thus became a fixed "trait" that lasted throughout the extensive span of the Arctic Small Tool tradition.

Such adjustments to limited availability of raw materials are not surprising. The successful utilization of scarce resources often leads to survival in human systems and it follows that survival leads to persistence and increased frequency in the archaeological record. It is, after all, understanding the persistence of continuity and change in the archaeological record that will lead to a better understanding of the past.

ACKNOWLEDGMENTS

The authors would like to thank Michael L. Kunz, archaeologist, and the Northern District Office of the Bureau of Land Management, Fairbanks, Alaska, for their support of this project. Additional thanks are due Dr. Michael Lewis and the University of Alaska Fairbanks Museum for providing access to the Mosquito Lake collections.

III

DETAILING SOURCES OF DEBITAGE VARIABILITY

8

Flake Debris Analysis, Levels of Production, and the Organization of Technology

PHILIP J. CARR AND ANDREW P. BRADBURY

Knowledge of the amount of stone tool production activities conducted at a site can provide significant information concerning past human behavior. Determining the percentages of core reduction versus tool production has been problematic for lithic analysts. In this paper, we use data derived from a number of flintknapping experiments to develop a method to determine the percentages of core versus tool debris. It is shown that attributes commonly recorded in lithic analyses can be used to make these inferences. A standard measure of production, analytic core units, is presented that allows for accurate comparisons between different sites, components, raw materials, etc. These types of comparisons are critical when adopting an organization of technology approach and attempting to understand prehistoric behavior.

Over a decade ago, David Hurst Thomas (1986:247) suggested that the volume *Stones*, the companion volume to *Bones* by Lewis Binford (1981), was a long way from being written. While we are not ready to suggest that *Stones* will be published anytime soon, there have been major advances in method and theory associated with lithic analysis during the past 13 years. Flake debris analysis and the development of an organization of technology approach are two areas where significant progress has been, and continues to be, made. However, no generally accepted method exists for determining the composition of a lithic assemblage with regard to the relative amounts of core reduction, biface production, and uniface production. We address the question of lithic assemblage composition as well as investigating the amount of core reduction represented in an assemblage.

Today, it goes without saying that flake debris is an integral part of the study of chipped stone assemblages. With an understanding of curated and expedient technological strategies, it is clear that the tools recovered from a site may not necessarily have been produced there and that the study of flake debris provides some of the best evidence for understanding stone-tool production activities at any particular location. Integrating stone-tool and flake-debris data is essential for understanding lithic technologies and the role these technologies played in prehistoric lifeways. These types of investigations are only possible with the development of a means of classifying flake debris that allows for accurate inferences. The growing number of published or available experimental data sets is a key to such classification and inference making (i.e., Ahler 1989a; Bradbury and Carr 1995, 1999; Ingbar et al. 1989; Magne 1985; Odell 1989; Shott 1996a). Based on such experiments, significant advances have been made in the analysis of individual flakes (e.g., Hayden and Hutchings 1989; Magne 1985; Morrow 1997; Tomka 1989), determining which attributes to record (e.g., Bradbury and Carr 1995; Odell 1989; Shott 1994), characterizing batches of flakes (e.g., Ahler 1989a, 1989b; Patterson 1990; Shott 1994; Stahle and Dunn 1982, 1984), understanding fracture mechanics (e.g., Cotterell and Kamminga 1987; Pelcin 1997a, 1997b), and examining general approaches such as stage versus continuum (e.g., Bradbury and Carr 1999; Ingbar et al. 1989; Shott 1996a). The data resulting from these advances provide an important means to characterize prehistoric chipped stone assemblages and are one of the strengths of contemporary lithic analysis.

On the theoretical side, we would suggest that utilizing an organizational approach in the study of lithic technologies could provide new insights into prehistoric lifeways. There are several definitions of technological organization and all of these emphasize the dynamic role played by technology in adapting to the physical and social environments by a particular culture. Following Kelly (1988: 717), technological organization is defined as:

> the spatial and temporal juxtaposition of the manufacture of different tools within a cultural system, their use, reuse and discard, and their relation not only to tool function and raw material type, but also to behavioral variables which mediate the spatial and temporal relations among activity, manufacturing, and raw material loci.

Nelson (1991:59) has demonstrated this graphically in a framework for conducting studies using an organization of technology approach. She suggests that lithic analysts can use artifact form and artifact distribution to understand design and activity distribution respectively. In combination, these allow for an understanding of technological strategies, then social/economic strategies, and finally environmental conditions. With other means to reconstruct past environmental conditions at the top of Nelson's diagram, lithic analysts can work from both ends to understand past economic and social strategies.

One problem with operationalizing Nelson's diagram is that it is geared toward stone tool analysis and not flake debris. Going from flake debris to discussions of reliable, maintainable, or versatile tools is a difficult task. This points to something of a gap between lithic data and theoretical approaches. However, this is not limited to an organization of technology approach and flake debris, as such a gap is generally seen with other approaches and artifact classes.

DATA-THEORY GAP IN LITHIC ANALYSIS

Conducting middle range research has been suggested as one means to bridge the gap between certain types of data and theory. However, such a broad programmatic statement has little practical utility. Schiffer (1988:465) has discussed three realms of archaeological theory: social, reconstruction, and methodological. Each of these has certain domains. For example, methodological theory has three such domains: recovery, analytic, and inferential. Each domain is divided into high, middle, and low level theory. These realms, domains, and levels blend into one another so that the divisions are somewhat arbitrary. The utility is not in the correct classification of a study, but rather in providing a means to conceptualize the diversity and complexity of what archaeologists do in trying to understand the past. Based on a consideration of Schiffer's "theory framework," we would suggest that lithic analysts working with flake debris, ourselves included, have concentrated more on the "analysis" domain and less on "inference." This focus is one cause of the data-theory gap.

In analytic theory, one attempts "to understand variability in a particular artifact class, . . . arriving at low level inferences specific to the life history of those remains" (Schiffer 1988:475). An example is demonstrating that a particular flake was produced in the reduction of a blade core. The accurate understanding of the "life history" of a lithic tool or piece of debris is a major occupation of contemporary lithic analysts. Lithic analysts are also trying to go beyond these low-level inferences to making broader statements of prehistoric behavior. The development of inferential theory, "the process of assessing and synthesizing diverse lines of evidence to produce well-founded statements about the past" (Schiffer 1988: 477), has great potential to aid lithic analysts in this endeavor.

Our research can serve as an example. Based on flintknapping experiments we have built a methodological framework that employs multiple lines of evidence (Bradbury 1998; Bradbury and Carr 1995, 1999; Carr 1995). Following Schiffer (1988), we are building analytic theory in order to make low-level inferences concerning the life history of flake debris. Our methodological framework involves the combination of distinct methods of flake debris analysis to provide separate lines of evidence to accurately classify flakes. For example, individual flake analysis, as developed by Magne (1985), is used to assign flakes to a reduction stage. The results of this method are then checked against other lines of evidence. Mass analysis, as developed by Ahler (1989a, 1989b), provides general trends involving the number of cortical flakes in certain size grades and the count and weight of flakes in specific grades that serve as additional lines of evidence. Also, the amount of shatter, as defined by Sullivan and Rozen (1985), is used as a line of evidence. While different flintknapping experiments have produced a variety of results with regard to the efficacy of the Sullivan and Rozen method (e.g., Amick and Mauldin 1997; Bradbury and Carr 1995; Prentiss and Romanski 1989; Prentiss 1998, this volume), the association of a high percentage of shatter with core reduction holds throughout different experiments and bipolar technologies can be recognized by an extremely high rate of shatter (Kuitj et al. 1995; but see Amick and Mauldin 1997).

Employing multiple lines of evidence strengthens inferences or reveals ambiguities. If all lines of evidence suggest the same pattern of reduction for the flake debris, then inferences are strengthened, and therefore conclusions based on these data are much more likely to be correct. If ambiguities are revealed, however, something is also learned. The analyst can go back to the methods and try to determine if our understanding of these methods is flawed. The assemblage is re-examined to determine if there is something special about it that would produce the ambiguous results. By investigating ambiguities, new insights are gained.

Other researchers are also advocating that a variety of flake attributes be recorded (i.e., Morrow 1997; Shott 1994) and more methods for accurately classifying flake debris are being introduced. Often these data are used to make a variety of behavioral inferences about the past. However, the focus on accurately classifying flake debris as per experiments, while important, has potentially taken us away from making accurate interpretations of past behaviors, hence the data-theory gap. That is, we have low-level inferences of flake debris life history, but may not have the means to make broader inferences because of weakly developed inferential theory.

Returning to our methodological framework, if individual flake analysis indicates that 75 percent of the flakes are early stage, 15 percent middle, and 10 percent late and the other lines of evidence support a focus on core reduction, can we infer that three times as much core reduction took place than tool production/maintenance? Or, does this mean three times as many cores were reduced as tools? Should we simply say that the main activity at the site was core reduction? How can we accurately characterize the amount of core reduction as compared with the amount of tool production and maintenance? What does this indicate about site function? Trying to use data generated by this analytic theory to make behavioral inferences forced us to recognize that understanding the kind and level of production represented by an assemblage is critical for interpretation, especially when using an organization of technology approach.

TABLE 8.1.
Experimental Coding Format

---

1) Experiment Number
2) Event Number
3) Raw Material:
01: river gravel   .0: parent
02: river gravel, tabular   .1: flake
03: primary deposit   .2: Bifacial core
04: primary deposit, tabular
05: residual cobble

4) Type of Reduction:
01: unifacial   06: haft
02: bifacial   07: bipolar
03: core   08: unidirectional core
04: platform preparation
05: bifacial core

5) Percussor:
01: large hammerstone   06: pressure flaker
02: small hammerstone   07: abrader
03: large billet   08: 339 g hammerstone
04: medium billet
05: small billet

6) Size Grade:
1: ⅛ inch
2: ¼ inch   5: 1 inch
3: ½ inch   6: 2 inch
4: ¾ inch

7) Weight (in grams to nearest 0.1 g)
8) Count
9) Portion:
01: complete   05: blocky
02: broken, PRB   06: split
03: broken, medial   07: fragment (non-PRB)
04: broken, distal

10) Platform:
01: present, intact   99: N/A
02: present, broken

11) Platform Configuration:
01: crushed   05: cortical
02: non-lipped   99: N/A
03: lipped

TABLE 8.1. continued
Experimental Coding Format

---

12) Platform Facet Count (99 = N/A)
13) Dorsal Configuration:

00: no cortex	04: platform only
01: less than 50% dorsal	99: N/A
02: greater than 50% dorsal	
03: 100% dorsal	

14) Dorsal Scar Count: (99 = N/A)
15) Pulled for Further Reduction:
0: no
1: yes

EXPERIMENTS

Here, we employ data from flintknapping experiments conducted as part of an ongoing program to examine the level of production and related issues. For consistency and control, all knapping was conducted by one of us and the raw material utilized was Fort Payne chert from both primary and secondary sources. All experiments were conducted over a drop cloth with flakes larger than ¼ inch collected after each blow with a percussor and numbered sequentially. Flakes smaller than ¼ inch were collected together after a change in percussor such as switching from a hard hammer to an antler billet, but only flakes larger than ¼ inch are addressed here. These flakes were assigned an event number representing the order in which the flake was removed. To overcome potential problems associated with analyst bias, collecting the experimental data only began after a 95 percent correspondence was obtained for all attributes recorded. In addition, both authors analyzed an equal amount of flake debris from each experiment. A wide range of attributes was recorded for each flake (Table 8.1). Our experimental program is ongoing. For this study we have completed the analysis of 3,194 flakes from 25 experiments. As some experiments had multiple reduction types—for example, the experiment began with the reduction of a bifacial core and then the piece was made into a hafted biface—a total of 28 reductions are represented in the database. The reduction types examined here consist of six freehand core, three bipolar core, four bifacial core, six unifacial tools, and nine bifacial tools (generalized biface, drill, hafted biface). Note that blade cores and other core technologies are not represented in these experiments and are not considered here.

While there are a number of potential questions that could be addressed with this database, our interest here is in the investigation of the amounts of different types of reduction represented in archaeological assemblages. We first explore the issue of the basic unit of analysis. There are legitimate reasons to not consider certain flake classes in any analysis, but it must be kept in mind that this will affect the final results and may not allow comparisons between different assemblages. Second, we attempt to develop a method to reliably infer levels of core reduction and tool production represented in an archaeological assemblage.

BASIC ANALYTICAL UNIT IN FLAKE DEBRIS ANALYSIS

When attempting to quantify core reduction or the number of tools produced, it becomes obvious that the basic unit of analysis can have a significant impact on such questions. In many traditional approaches, complete flakes were the unit of analysis because of a focus on recording the percentage of dorsal cortex. In breaking away from traditional approaches, some researchers (Ahler 1989b:85–86; Magne 1985:104; Sullivan and Rozen 1985:756–757) suggested that a focus on complete flakes ignores much of the variability within an assemblage and therefore potentially biases any results. However, a flake may break into several pieces during, or subsequent to, removal. If each fragment were considered in the analysis, this would inflate that particular flake removal event. The possibility exists for greatly skewing one type of reduction over another, especially when several different types of raw materials are represented. Using our experimental database, we have found some interesting patterns in flake breakage. In examining flakes larger than ¼ inch, 2.75 flakes were produced on average for each event (*sensu* Magne 1985) of core reduction, 1.57 in biface production, and 1.22 in unifacial tool production. A one-way ANOVA shows that these are significantly different (F: 16.029, p<0.0001, df 2.21). Also, significant differences are found between each pair, except uniface and biface, when using Fisher's LSD (p<0.001). If all flakes are counted, core reduction will be represented 1.75 times as much as biface reduction because of differential flake breakage. This patterning will of course differ across raw materials, but the same general trend is observed in data presented by Magne (1985:105) for basalt: core reduction events, 7.6 flakes; biface, 2.8 flakes; and uniface, 2.0 flakes. For further comparison, Shott (1996a, fig. 2) reports 2.1 flakes produced per biface reduction event using Wyandotte chert.

One solution to this problem would be to consider only those flakes that retain a platform. Using our experimental database, we found 79.9 percent of the core reduction events produced a flake greater than ¼ inch with a platform, while 66.0 percent of the biface and 66.1 percent of the uniface events did so. Again, a one-way ANOVA shows that these are significantly different (F: 7.017, p=0.003, df 2.21) and using Fisher's LSD shows significant differences between each pair (p<0.001), except uniface and biface. It is important to note that there are 1.2 times as many core flakes as biface or uniface. Also, a core reduction event often produces more than one flake with a platform, while a tool production event rarely does.

If one is using Magne's (1985) method of individual flake analysis, these data present additional problems. Our previous experiments have shown that platform facet count is a conservative measure of reduction stage (Bradbury and Carr 1995, 1999). That is, flakes resulting from tool production are more likely to be misclassified by platform facet count than by dorsal scar count. The opposite is true for core reduction. If only platform-bearing flakes are utilized, then an alternate means of assigning flakes to a reduction stage would be necessary. We are exploring several ratio attributes that may facilitate more accurate classification. One of the most promising is dorsal scar/grams. This entails dividing the number of dorsal scars by flake weight. This, in essence, combines two separate aspects of stone tool reduction into one attribute. As reduction continues, flakes, on average, become smaller and there is an increase in the number of dorsal scars. This attribute was shown to be useful in conjunction with others when using a continuum-based model (Bradbury and Carr 1999). While many core reduction flakes exhibit multiple dorsal scars, the increased weight of these flakes means that they exhibit a lower ratio of dorsal scars to weight than those produced during tool production activities.

What to consider as the unit of analysis remains an issue that deserves further examination and one that is beyond the scope of this paper, but for further discussion see Steffen et al. (1998). In general, it appears that core reduction will be overemphasized by most analytical techniques. Additionally, many core flakes will be used as blanks for tool production and more flakes will be generally produced in biface manufacture than in the reduction of a core, which can further confuse the issue. Finally, differences in the organization of technology from one group to another and post-depositional processes may influence flake breakage, which further complicates the task of the analyst.

INFERRING LEVELS OF PRODUCTION WITH FLAKE DEBRIS

The experimental database discussed here provides the opportunity to develop methods for determining the amount of core reduction, biface production, and uniface production represented in an assemblage. We do consider the question of the basic unit of analysis to still be unresolved, but in this part of the study, complete and platform remnant-bearing flakes are used. While flakes in these categories with an incomplete platform are included, flakes classified as "split" are not. Our goal is to provide a model that is applicable to a wide range of data sets. For this reason, flakes larger than ¼ inch and smaller than ¾ inch were used in the analysis. Flakes smaller than ¼ inch are excluded in order to follow standard archaeological field recovery methods. Including only flakes in the ¼ inch and ½ inch size grades is a means to negate having to *guess* which of the "large" flakes would have been used for further reduction in prehistory. This is an important issue, as a flake that might be considered usable by one group may be totally unacceptable to another. For example, consider the difference between a Paleoindian and a late Prehistoric lithic technology or between a raw-material rich and a raw-material poor area.

Based on our experiments, no single attribute can reliably classify all the individual flakes in an assemblage as to reduction type. However, certain attributes occur more commonly with one type than in others. For example, while all types of reduction produce flakes with 0 or 1 platform facet, such flakes are more frequently produced in core reduction. In addition, flake mass decreases with continued reduction, as does the number of flakes retained in the smaller size grades. The general relationships between platform facets and reduction (e.g., Bradbury and Carr 1995; Magne 1985), mass and reduction (e.g., Ahler 1989a, 1989b; Shott 1994), and others have been substantiated by a number of researchers. Given these general relationships, examining data at the assemblage level rather than the individual flake for making inferences has promise. By assemblage level, we mean that batches of flakes, be they all flakes from a site, subsets of a site, specific raw material, etc., are taken as the focus of analysis (e.g., Ahler 1989a, 1989b; Stahle and Dunn 1982; Patterson 1990). Here, the proportions of flakes within a batch that retain certain individual attributes are used to determine the composition of the assemblage (i.e., core or tool). In essence, we are combining an aggregate and individual analysis approach (Andrefsky, this volume). Such data could be used in a discriminant function analysis to separate batches of flakes into their corresponding reduction type. However, as most archaeological assemblages are the product of multiple reduction types, perhaps a better solution is to partition an assemblage into its constituent parts.

PERCENT REDUCTION TYPE

Accurately partitioning an assemblage into its constituent reduction types (i.e., percent of tool production versus percent core reduction) is an important step in providing insight into prehistoric lithic activities, because the percentages of each reduction type are comparable. If it is determined that the assemblage contains 80 percent bifacial tool production and 20 percent core reduction, then there are four times as many bifacial tool production flakes than core reduction flakes. This, however, does not give specific information on the level of production. The second stage in the analysis is to derive meaning from these percentages in terms of numbers of tools and cores actually produced and reduced on site.

In an effort to determine the percentage of an archaeological assemblage that is represented by a specific reduction type, a series of regression analyses were undertaken using the experimental data as the baseline. We created simulated assemblages by combining a number of flintknapping experiments into one group. The percentages of flakes that exhibited 0 platform facets, 1 platform facet, 2 or more platform facets, 0–1 dorsal scars, 2 dorsal scars, 3 or more dorsal scars, average dorsal scar/grams, average weight of flakes in size grade 2 (¼ inch), and the percentage by count and weight of flakes retained in size 2 were calculated for each of these simulated assemblages along with the percentage of flakes produced during each experimental type (core reduction, biface production, and uniface production). Core reduction included both bifacial cores and amorphous cores. Bipolar reduction was dropped from consideration as few flakes produced during the bipolar experiments retained an intact platform. Bipolar technology is perhaps best identified at the assemblage level using other methods (e.g., Kuitj et al. 1995). A total of 80 simulated assemblages was constructed that had a mix of core, biface, and unifacial tools represented. Separate analyses were conducted to model the percentage of biface production, core reduction, and unifacial tool production.

In regression analyses, a number of different models can yield an acceptable equation when judged only by the resulting R^2. For this reason, several criteria were used in selecting the "best" model: R^2, slope, standard error of the estimate, and residuals. The R^2 is a measure of the proportion of variability in the dependent variable (i.e., percent of reduction type) accounted for by the independent variables (i.e., percent of flakes with 1 platform facet, percent with 3 dorsal scars, etc.). The higher the R^2, the greater the amount of variation accounted for by the model and, therefore, the better the predictive power. However, as suggested by Ingbar et al. (1989:125), a high value of R^2 indicates an accurate relationship, but not necessarily a useful one. A further test is regressing the percent of each reduction type on the predicted percent to determine the slope of the model. A perfectly accurate model would yield a slope of 1.0 and a good model will have a slope close to 1.0. Models with slopes less than 1.0 indicate that the predicted values exhibit a lower range than the actual ones while the opposite is true of slopes greater than 1.0. The standard error of the estimate gives an indication of the amount of error associated with the regression equation. A low standard error indicates a model with high predictive power. In addition, the standard error of the estimate can be used to calculate confidence intervals for archaeological samples. Finally, the residuals are the difference between the predicted value and the actual one. In this case, the residuals give an indication of how well the regression equation predicts the actual percent of each reduction type. We also note that any simulated assemblage that exhibited a residual of three standard deviations or greater was considered an outlier and was dropped from that particular analysis. The combination of these criteria was used in assessing the various models under investigation.

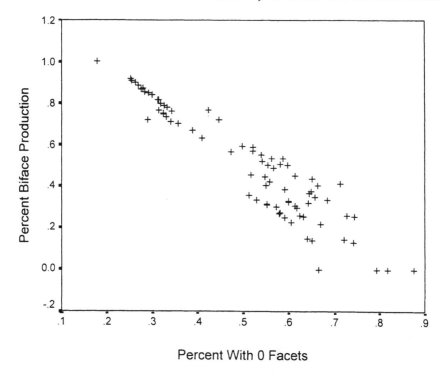

Figure 8.1. Scatter plot showing relationship between the percentage of biface production and the percentage of flakes with 0 platform facets.

As an initial examination of the data, scatter plots of each variable by the percentage of reduction were made for the three experimental types. These indicated good relationships between certain variables and a specific reduction type (Figures 8.1, 8.2, and 8.3). We should also note that the scatter plot for percentage of flakes with 0 platform facets shows less dispersion when high levels of biface production are in the assemblage. Similar patterns were not observed with the other variables. The reasons for this pattern are unclear at this time. Possibly this is the result of the greater numbers of flakes produced during biface production, relative to the other reduction types. To obtain simulated assemblages with low percentages of biface production, only one or two biface experiments could be included. An examination of the percentages of flakes with 0 platform facets for all experiments within a reduction type, showed that biface production (17.9 percent with 0 platform facets) is distinct from the other reduction types (uniface production: 81.8 percent; amorphous core reduction: 79.2 percent; bifacial and amorphous core reduction: 66.4 percent with 0 platform facets).

The analysis began by regressing each individual variable on the percent of reduction represented (i.e., 1 platform facet on percent biface, 2 platform facets on percent biface, etc.). As no single variable provided an acceptable model, a num-

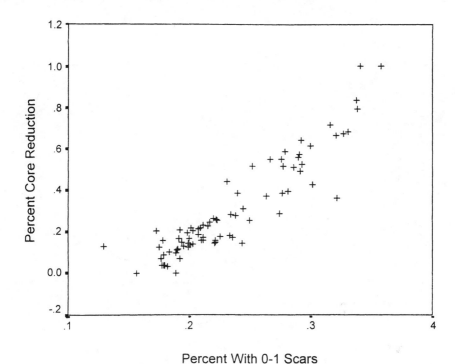

Figure 8.2. Scatter plot showing relationship between the percentage of core reduction and the percentage of flakes with 0 or 1 dorsal scars.

ber of multiple regression analyses were conducted. Separate regression analyses were undertaken for each of the three reduction types considered (core, biface, uniface). Transformation of several variables to their natural logarithm was accomplished to provide linear representation of the data. Quadratic terms were also examined in some cases. Rather than discuss all the analyses, the results pertaining to the "best" models are summarized for each reduction type.

For biface production, the percentage of flakes with 0 platform facets, 2 dorsal scars, percentage by count of ¼-inch flakes, and the percentage by weight of ¼-inch flakes (four separate variables) produced the best model. R^2 for the equation is 0.961 with a standard error of 0.0514. The slope is 0.992 and indicates that the model very slightly underestimates the actual amount of biface production. The range for the residuals is -0.15 to 0.1 (negative values are overestimates of the actual amounts, positive underestimates) with a standard deviation of 0.0501. The equation developed for the percentage of biface production is:

Percent biface production = (1.431 × percent count ¼ inch) + (1.438 × percent with 2 dorsal scars) − (0.447 × percent weight ¼ inch) − (percent with 0 platform facets) − 0.393.

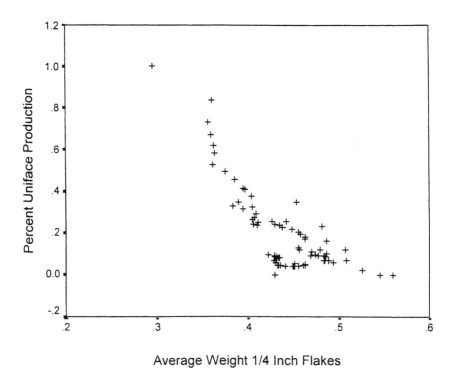

Average Weight 1/4 Inch Flakes

Figure 8.3. Scatter plot showing relationship between the percentage of uniface production and the average weight of ¼-inch flakes with 0 platform facets.

In the regression analysis of core reduction, the percentage of flakes with 0–1
dorsal scars, log percent count ¼ inch, percent weight ¼ inch, percent 2 dorsal
scars produced the best model. R^2 for the equation is 0.961, while the standard error is 0.0446 and slope is 0.986. The residuals show a range from -0.0972 to
0.111. These results compare favorably with those obtained for biface production.
The core reduction formula is as follows:

Percent of core reduction = (2.275 × percent with 0 or 1 dorsal scars) + (0.329
× percent weight ¼ inch) – (1.558 × log percent count ¼ inch) – (1.427 × percent with 2 dorsal scars) – 0.214.

For unifacial tool production, the percentage of flakes with 0 platform facets
squared, percent count size 2 (¼ inch), percent count size 2 squared, average
weight of size 2, and average weight of size 2 squared produced the best model. R^2
for the equation was 0.98 and the standard error of the estimate was 0.0288. The
residuals ranged between -0.0549 and 0.057 with a slope for the model of 0.969.
This regression formula produced the best predictive values. The resulting equation is:

Percent of uniface reduction = 1.193 – (10.163 × average weight size 2) + (9.192 × average weight of size 2 squared) + (0.661 × percentage with 0 platform facets) + (3.293 × percent by count size 2) – (1.731 × percent by count size 2 squared).

The vast majority of the differences between the actual percentage of a specific reduction type and the predicted percentage are in the range of 1 percent to 5 percent with a limited number of errors up to 15 percent. It is unclear why these larger errors occur, but this could be determined through more experimentation and attempting to isolate certain assemblage characteristics through controlling combinations of reduction types in simulated assemblages.

To further investigate the utility of the approach, biface and uniface reduction debris were combined into a single "tool" class for regression analysis. This follows a previously developed continuum-based approach where flakes were first divided into core reduction and tool production (Bradbury and Carr 1999). The analysis conducted here proved successful with a R^2 of 0.969. The standard error of the estimate is 0.0406 while the residuals range from -0.0869 to 0.0904 with a slope for the model of 0.997. The resulting equation is:

Percent tool reduction = (3.131 × percent with 2 dorsal scars) + (2.056 × percent with 3 or more dorsal scars) + (0.034 × log percent with 2 platform facets) + (1.725 × log percent by count size 2) – (0.346 × percent by weight size 2) – 0.648.

As a final check of the regression equations for each of the three reduction types, 10 additional simulated assemblages were created and analyzed to determine the percentage of core, biface, and nonbifacial tool experiment types represented. None of the experiment combinations in these assemblages were used in constructing the regression equations. For the most part, all equations predicted the composition of the simulated assemblages quite accurately (Table 8.2). Of note is one assemblage where all predicted values were off by nearly 10 percent or greater. The majority of the errors for each reduction type are below 5 percent (18 of 30) and none are greater than 14 percent.

These regression equations can be used to help determine the composition of a flake debris assemblage. The use of such equations provides more meaning to the analysis, as the percentages of each reduction type are comparable. While the method appears promising, we do not advocate blindly applying it to archaeological samples. Statistical formulae are never a substitute for common sense. For example, the regression equations will sometimes show less than 0 percent of a certain reduction type. Obviously, this is not possible and is merely an artifact of the regression method. In application, any percentage below zero should be

TABLE 8.2.
Results of Regression Equations When Applied to Ten Additional Simulated Assemblages

Assem-blage	Predicted				Actual			Difference			Tool	Actual	Differ-ence	Core+Tool
	Biface*	Core	Uniface	Total	Biface	Core	Uniface	Biface	Core	Uniface				
1	0.50804	0.376997	-0.01322	0.871815	0.429395	0.45245	0.118156	-0.07864	0.075453	0.131379	0.604354	0.547551	-0.0568	0.981351
2	0.492549	0.356094	0.17919	1.027833	0.539286	0.314286	0.146429	0.046737	-0.04181	-0.03276	0.661248	0.685715	0.024467	1.017341
3	0.793411	0.197804	0.141184	1.1324	0.765579	0.11276	0.12662	-0.02783	-0.08504	-0.01456	0.792731	0.892199	0.099468	0.990536
4	0.641953	0.230624	0.088784	0.96136	0.695015	0.167155	0.134897	0.053062	-0.06347	0.046113	0.76675	0.829912	0.063162	0.997374
5	0.706595	0.211886	0.070605	0.989087	0.729977	0.201373	0.06865	0.023382	-0.01051	-0.00195	0.793748	0.798627	0.004879	1.005635
6	0.737223	0.199734	0.054102	0.991059	0.668067	0.245798	0.086134	-0.06916	0.046064	0.032032	0.788645	0.754201	-0.03444	0.988379
7	0.499982	0.353025	-0.00977	0.843237	0.609467	0.260355	0.130178	0.109485	-0.09267	0.139948	0.618121	0.739645	0.121524	0.971146
8	0.721021	0.064915	0.148571	0.934508	0.703927	0.151057	0.145015	-0.01709	0.086142	-0.00356	0.933821	0.848942	-0.08488	0.998736
9	0.598018	0.176699	0.158738	0.933455	0.665761	0.168478	0.165761	0.067743	-0.00822	0.007023	0.821733	0.831522	0.009789	0.998432
10	0.573858	0.247823	0.1594	0.981081	0.616129	0.2	0.183871	0.042271	-0.04782	0.024471	0.753772	0.8	0.046228	1.001594

* multiply by 100 to obtain percentages

treated as zero. One also has to be aware of other pitfalls and should never accept predicted percentages without question. Again, this is an argument for the use of multiple methods. One must assess results of any equation in conjunction with other lines of evidence. For example, if it is determined that an assemblage consists of 33 percent core reduction flakes, but no other indications of core reduction are recovered (cores, hammerstones), then the core reduction equation may be suspect. Ambiguous results such as this would encourage further investigation of both the method and the particular assemblage in question.

The equations themselves can be used as multiple lines of evidence. The application of all four equations to a single archaeological assemblage will either mutually reinforce the results if the total percentages for the individual reduction types are close to 100 (+5 percent to -5 percent) or be equivocal if the percentages do not. Likewise, in using the tool production and core reduction equations, the total should be close to 100 percent. The total predicted values of the percentage of biface, core, and uniface debris in half of the 10 additional simulated assemblages were between 95 and 105 (Table 8.2). Of these, the majority of the errors for each reduction type are within 5 percent of the actual value (12 of 15) and none over 7 percent. The total predicted value for two of the remaining five assemblages is 93 percent and the results for these would be generally acceptable as only one error for each was greater than 5 percent and neither was over 9 percent. The remaining three simulated assemblages all produced percentages that totaled more than 10 percent above or below 100 percent. This would cause one to question the results of the individual equations and prevent larger errors from being accepted. The use of the tool production and core reduction equations can be used in a similar manner. In most of the cases listed in Table 8.2, the use of the tool production equation produced acceptable results (i.e., low error rates). This equation could also be used in conjunction with the bifacial and unifacial equations as a check of the inferred amount of core reduction.

NUMBERS OF CORES AND TOOLS

Given that the regression equations allow for the partitioning of an archaeological assemblage into reduction types, it is of interest to determine how many specific items were produced. Others who have investigated this question have focused on biface production (e.g., Bradbury 1998; Cassedy 1986; Root 1997; Sassaman 1994b; Shott 1997). We explore a new avenue of research using the percentage of a reduction type as determined by our regression equations. While determinations for each of the tool types or cores is likely possible, the focus is on core reduction here.

A variety of formulae could be developed that would estimate the number of cores necessary to account for the amount of flake debris determined to be from core reduction in an assemblage. An example would be to determine the average (using count or weight) of different types of flake debris produced from a single core and then simply dividing the amount in the assemblage to get at cores reduced. However, in applying this to archaeological samples, one has to assume that all cores were of the same size as used in the formula, that differences between the raw materials represented do not affect the flake attribute(s) examined, and that all cores were reduced the same amount. These assumptions are likely invalid for most archaeological assemblages. As there is a wide range of sizes for most raw materials that could be used for cores, there is a corresponding range of error in predicting the number of cores reduced. Additionally, one has to consider the situation where two cores are completely reduced at one site while on another site ten cores are partially reduced. A usable method must accommodate these issues, while still producing accurate results that allow for reliable inferences to be made.

A standardized measure of reduction is used here to refer to the difference in the weight of the starting and the ending point of core reduction (i.e., raw nodule weight minus exhausted core weight). If a relationship between the difference in weight and other flake attributes can be determined, then a standardized measure of reduction, or analytical core unit (ACU), can be formulated. While the weight of the corresponding flake debris is an obvious variable to consider, there are several problems that make it a poor choice. As a core is further reduced, the maximum size, and therefore weight, of the corresponding flake debris becomes smaller. If weight were used, then two cores completely reduced at a site could be equivalent to ten partially reduced at another. To overcome this problem, we focused on the count of platform-bearing flakes. Theoretically, as the levels of production increase, there is an increase in the numbers of platform-bearing flakes. Also, the use of count variables should overcome problems associated with differences in weight between cores, differences in raw material breakage patterns, and differences in the rates of reduction. For reasons previously mentioned, only flakes retained in the ½-inch and ¼-inch screens (i.e., flakes in the ¾- and 1-inch screens were excluded) were used in this analysis.

The difference in weight for all cores from our experiments was calculated. In addition, to increase the sample size, other experimental data sets (Bradbury 1995, 1996; Bradbury and Carr 1995; Bradbury and Franklin 2000) were added to the database. This resulted in the inclusion of 26 core reduction experiments for this part of the study. The inclusion of these additional experiments also meant that several raw materials with varying characteristics were included in the analysis (e.g., Ste. Genevieve, Kanawha Black, Fort Payne fibrous variety). The difference in starting and ending weights ranged from 41.7 to 1,231.1 g so that a wide range of variability is represented.

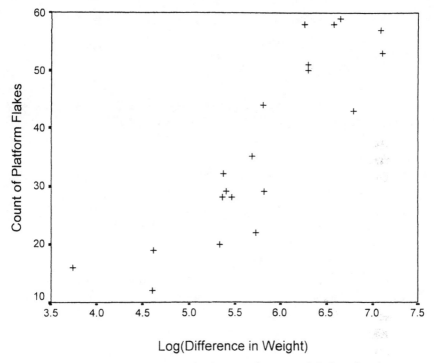

Figure 8.4. Scatter plot showing relationship between the count of platform-bearing flakes and the log (difference in weight).

Preliminary plots of the data indicated a nonlinear relationship between the count of platform flakes and the difference in weight. To create a more linear relationship, natural logarithms were taken for difference in weight (Figure 8.4). Regressing log (difference in weight) on the count of platform flakes produced a good relationship (Figure 8.2; R2: 0.921, slope: 0.96, standard error of the estimate: 6.2) and the following equation:

Count platform flakes (½ inch and ¼ inch) = log (difference in weight) × 3.601.

This formula can be used to provide a standardized measurement of core reduction. For example, setting the difference in weight to 500 g and plugging into the formula indicates that 22.38 platform flakes would be expected in the ½-inch and ¼-inch size grades for each ACU. If 300 platform-bearing flakes representing core reduction were recovered from an assemblage, we would infer 13.4 ACU of reduction (i.e., 300/22.38). This could be used to compare between sites, site components, different raw materials, etc. In archaeological applications, a core size would be used that best represents the available raw materials utilized at a given site. Sampling the available geologic sources in the area to find the average weight of the starting point and taking the average weight of cores at the site would provide these data. The difference between the two would represent the ACU for the site under investigation. If no cores were found or it is thought those recovered do not adequately represent the reduction that took place at the site, a reasonable estimate could be used. In either case, one has a standardized measure that can be used for comparison between archaeological assemblages.

There are a number of questions that could potentially be addressed with such an analytical unit. These range from those involving settlement patterns to investigating craft specialization. In all cases, it is suggested that the ACU be used in conjunction with the regression data on percentages of biface and core production and other lines of evidence.

Inferring the amount of production based on analytical units provides a new line of evidence for understanding past technological, economic, and social strategies from an organizational perspective. Nelson (1991) has diagramed studies of technological organization, but this diagram is geared toward stone tool analysis, not flake debris. The ACU developed here, and the potential to derive various tool analytical units, makes flake debris studies of greater relevance for making behavioral inferences. The use of a standard measure allows for quantification and comparison within and between lithic assemblages. For example, comparing the inferred number of ACUs with the actual number of cores recovered at a site has implications for understanding production and curation.

In examining settlement models, one can suggest that differing levels of core use should represent different types of sites in a given raw material environment. For example, consider the numbers of cores reduced at a quarry versus those reduced at a limited activity location or a large residential base. The ACU allows us to make comparisons not only between the number of cores recovered at these locations, but also between the number of ACUs determined by the flake debris. This has the potential to lead to new insights as sites formerly seen as dissimilar based on number of cores may have an identical number of ACUs and the opposite scenario is also possible. The ACU provides a new tool for understanding of how prehistoric peoples were utilizing their landscape.

Related to settlement patterns, information concerning mobility could be revealed by levels of production. For example, Parry and Kelly (1987) suggest that an increased use of expedient flake tools and, by extension, cores should be seen with an increase in sedentism. Again, the ACU potentially allows a greater understanding of the importance of core reduction in an assemblage other than that simply based on the number of cores recovered. Also, the examination of ACUs per raw material could provide information concerning residential, logistical, and minimum range of mobility. The relationships between mobility/sedentism and technological strategies are variable depending on a number of factors, including raw material distributions. Utilizing ACUs as part of a research strategy provides an additional line of evidence for exploring that relationship in a meaningful manner.

The ability to measure levels of production through analytical units will also allow an understanding of what is commonly found at sites of a given time period in a region and which are outliers. Those sites with extremely high levels of production may be interpreted in a number of ways such as workshops or special activity areas. Volume of production debris has been linked to craft specialization and production for exchange (Johnson 1996; Root 1997; Sassaman 1994b). The use of analytical units would arguably allow for more meaningful quantification for comparative purposes.

SUMMARY AND CONCLUSIONS

In order to answer questions concerning past stone-tool using societies, lithic analysts must continue to develop new methods and reexamine old ones. However, there is a data/theory gap that is related to a lack of inferential theory (*sensu* Schiffer 1988). Development of theory in other realms and domains is also needed in order to allow for the kinds of inferences sought in contemporary archaeology.

The lack of contemporary cultures that routinely use stone tools as a major part of their economy has been lamented because this robs lithic analysts of the opportunity to employ ethnographic analogies (Kelly 1992). On the other hand, given the tyranny of the ethnographic record (Isaac 1987), one may contend that lithic analysts are better off without such analogies. In any case, lithic analysts must take advantage of their creativity in developing a wide range of models for testing with the archaeological record.

Even for something investigated as often as prehistoric settlement/mobility patterns, lithic analysts have produced interpretations that are "subjective, intuitive, and sometimes contradictory" (Kelly 1992:56). However, models that link data and theory aid in illustrating essential concepts and making assumptions explicit. For example, Ingbar (1994) employed simple simulations to examine the relationship between raw materials and hunter-gatherer mobility. By varying certain parameters of the model, such as the number of tool using events or the size of the toolkit, it was demonstrated that raw material source proportions are "highly responsive to organizational patterns" (Ingbar 1994:50). In another case, Magne (1989, fig. 1) developed a chipped stone assemblage formation model that employs a flake debris to stone tool ratio and the percent of late stage flakes to characterize manufacture, maintenance, and conservation that occurred at a site. Additionally, the percent of late stage flakes is modeled with the stone tool diversity slope as a means of inferring site type (Magne 1989, fig. 7). These models link data and theory and are important steps for furthering our understanding of the dynamics of stone tool manufacture, use, and discard.

Here, we have developed another method for characterizing flake debris assemblages. This method was developed with the data-theory gap in mind as well as application of multiple lines of evidence. Multiple lines of evidence are important for insuring data quality. This is an important concern in archaeology (Beck and Jones 1989) and especially lithic analysis (Andrefsky 1998; Bradbury and Carr 1995, 1999; Jochim 1989; Kelly 1992; Odell 1989; Shott 1994; Sullivan and Rozen 1985). Percentages of core reduction, uniface production, and biface production are comparable across a wide range of contexts. Further, the concept of analytical core unit was introduced as a standardized unit for inferring the amount of core reduction in an assemblage (site, raw material type, etc.). With further work, analysts should also be capable of developing analytical uniface and biface units. Again, multiple lines of evidence should be used whenever possible. The various data generated by the regression equations developed here should be employed in models that can continue to bridge the data-theory gap.

ACKNOWLEDGMENTS

The authors thank Bill Andrefsky for the invitation to present a version of this paper in the 1999 SAA symposium and commenting on various drafts. He also deserves thanks for ensuring a successful transformation from presented papers to published volume. Discussions with Martin Magne and Michael Shott, as well as their specific comments, aided in fine-tuning the research presented here. Comments by an anonymous reviewer were also helpful in making this a better paper.

9

Reliability and Validity of a "Distinctive Assemblage" Typology: Integrating Flake Size and Completeness

William C. Prentiss

Recent research suggests that there are multiple sources of variation in debitage assemblages as measured with the flake-completeness typology of Sullivan and Rozen. Recognizing that rate and pattern of flake breakage may vary with flake size, a modified version of the typology incorporating size and completeness is presented and tested using experimental data. Results suggest that (1) random and systematic measurement error are similar to results obtained with the flake completeness-only typology; (2) percussor characteristics, platform preparation, and degree of applied force have significant and recognizable effects on modified typology patterning; and (3) continued reliability and validity studies will be important for further application of this technique.

The Sullivan and Rozen typology or SRT is an instrument for measuring variation in lithic debitage assemblages (Sullivan and Rozen 1985; Sullivan 1987). Variation in percentage representation of the five "completeness" related (Ingbar et al. 1989) flake types hypothetically provide information on technological agents responsible for the formation of the assemblage in question. Early studies attempted to recognize effects of "core" versus "tool" production in archaeological contexts (e.g., Sullivan and Rozen 1985). More recent experimental research has explored effects of a variety of reduction techniques including biface production (e.g., Amick and Mauldin 1997; Bradbury and Carr 1995; Ingbar et al. 1989; Morrow 1997; Prentiss 1998; Prentiss and Romanski 1989), scraper production (Baumler and Downum 1989; Prentiss et al. 1988), bipolar core reduction (Kuijt et al. 1995), and various other forms of core reduction (e.g., Bradbury and Carr 1995; Prentiss 1993, 1998; Prentiss and Romanski 1989; Tomka 1989). Other studies have assessed the effects of technological mixing (Austin 1998; Prentiss 1993), size sorting (Prentiss et al. 1988), trampling (Prentiss 1993; Prentiss and

Romanski 1989), and preferential flake removal or culling (Prentiss 1993) on typology patterning. Results of many studies suggest a significant degree of variability in sources of flake breakage patterning. My recent research (Prentiss 1998) suggests that ambiguity problems may stem significantly from application of the typology in absence of consideration of size variability (see also Shott 1994). I have presented experimental data suggesting that the performance of the SRT would be significantly improved with the inclusion of a series of size classes (small: .64 to 4 sq cm; medium 4 to 16 sq cm; large: 16 to 64 sq cm; and extra large: >64 sq cm) effectively bringing the typology from 5 to 20 flake types. In this paper, I present a formal reliability and validity test of this modified SRT or MSRT and an example of its archaeological application. I close with a discussion of implications for further archaeological application and experimental testing.

RELIABILITY AND VALIDITY TEST OF THE MSRT

The goal of reliability and validity testing is to identify the presence and degree of random and systematic error associated with the application of an instrument of measurement. Random error is a component of any measurement and results from both operator error and limits on instrument precision. Reliability analyses are conducted prior to validity tests to ensure random error does not attenuate validity results. An instrument can be concluded to be reliable if it provides the same or nearly the same results in repeated measurements on the same phenomena (Carmines and Zeller 1979; Nance 1987; Nance and Ball 1986). Validity analysis tests for the effects of systematic error or variation resulting not from the phenomenon of interest but from bias in instrument design or consistently patterned operator errors. Validity tests allow us to determine if the instrument provides accurate results. Stated differently, to achieve validity, the results must match up with theoretical expectations for appropriate instrument performance (Carmines and Zeller 1979; Nance 1987).

When applied to the MSRT, the goal of reliability assessment emphasizes consistency: does the typology provide consistently similar results when applied to assemblages with a common technological origin? An assessment of the SRT demonstrated an acceptably high degree of reliability (Prentiss 1998). A successful validity test of the MSRT depends on its ability to segregate the effects of "core" versus "tool" production. I have recently been critical of the use of the latter rather generalized concepts (Prentiss 1998:648). Thus, following from Crabtree (1972:30), I define core reduction as the production of flakes from a "nucleus," or "a mass of material . . . preformed by the worker to the desired shape to allow for the removal of a definite type of flake or blade." Cores used in this study include prepared and unprepared varieties, similar, respectively, to Callahan's (1979) block and spheroid cores with striking platforms in the range of 60 to 90 degrees. Tools in this study are other results of the lithic reduction/shaping process, which in this case include bifaces (approximating Callahan's stage 3 level of reduction) and unifacially modified flakes (edge angles 10–40 degrees).

The reliability test is accomplished with a principal components analysis (PCA) and coefficient theta (Carmines and Zeller 1979; Prentiss 1998). PCA allows an assessment of the degree of contribution of each variable to the overall problem solution. The fundamental assumption is that, if the instrument is reliable, the first factor will capture the largest portion of the total variance and that most or all variables will load on the first factor with comparatively high loadings than on other factors. Theta provides a direct measurement of reliability in a single internal consistency statistic. High correlations in the original correlation matrix and an associated high eigenvalue on the first factor in PCA result in high theta scores, indicating low random error and high degrees of reliability. PCA is also used in validity analysis, assuming that, if valid, correlations among the MSRT flake types correspond to actual variability in lithic reduction behavior (Prentiss 1998). Rotated factor loadings and plotted factor scores allow the contributions of both variables and cases to be assessed.

DATA COLLECTION

This study relies on the same debitage assemblages as described in Prentiss (1998). To briefly summarize, reliability data derive from 30 experimental biface reduction assemblages collapsed randomly into 10 analytical assemblages. Validity data were derived using different combinations of hard- and soft-hammer percussors, pressure flakers, varying flake production size goals, and flakes, bifaces, and prepared and unprepared cores for a total of 60 experimental reduction assemblages, collapsed into 20 analytical assemblages (Table 9.1). Collapsing of multiple reduction assemblages into a more limited array of analytical groupings was considered critical for minimization of error variance associated with factors such as idiosyncratic knapper behavior (Prentiss 1998).

DATA

All raw flake count data were converted to proportions for purposes of multivariate analysis. The purpose was to maintain consistency in data transformation with my previous analysis of the SRT (Prentiss 1998) and to avoid problems with differential sample size. As the MSRT includes size variation, the use of proportion data may cause structural correlations to occur in multivariate analysis. I suggest, however, that effects of structural correlation are likely minimal as an earlier study of these data using a rescaling technique, designed to avoid structural correlations, provided very similar results (Prentiss 1993). The original

TABLE 9.1.
Validity Study Analytical Assemblage Organization

Flake Size Goal	Flake	Biface	Unprepared Core	Prepared Core
Extra large (>64 cm²)			1. HH	2. HH
Large (16–64 cm²)		3. HH	5. HH	7. HH
		4. SH	6. SH	8. SH
Medium (4–16 cm²)	9. HH	12. HH	15. HH	18. HH
	10. SH	13. SH	16. SH	19. SH
	11. PR	14. PR	17. PR	20. PR

Note: HH = hard hammer; SH = soft hammer; PR = pressure; 1–20 = analytical assemblage numbers

rescaling technique required conversion of the highest flake count per analytical assemblage to an arbitrary score of 100 and rescaling all other counts in relation to that original count. This is the same approach applied by Binford (1978a) to faunal assemblages at Anaktuvuk Pass, Alaska, and elsewhere (e.g., Binford 1981). This data transformation strategy had advantages and drawbacks. On the positive side, it provided an effective method for avoiding potentially adverse effects of sample size problems and structural correlations. Unfortunately, however, small medial-distal fragments always scored 100 with a variance of zero and had to be dropped from the principal components analysis, thereby resulting in an incomplete assessment of reliability. The following is a description of the data to be used in reliability and validity assessment.

Biface reduction accomplished for the reliability analysis produced a distribution of size classes including small, medium, and large flakes (Table 9.2). The matrix illustrates a consistent pattern of numerous medial-distal fragments, reduced numbers of proximal fragments and low numbers of complete and split flakes in the medium and small size classes. Few large proximal or medial-distal fragments and no large complete or split flakes were produced. Complete flakes are more consistently produced in the small class than in the medium class. This may be the result of edge shaping and platform preparation resulting more often in small thicker flakes that are less susceptible to breakage during production. Large and medium flakes are primarily the result of biface thinning and are consequently thin and naturally more likely to be broken during the reduction process (Sullivan and Rozen 1985).

A wide range of variation in assemblages is represented in the validity data matrix (Tables 9.3 and 9.4) that are best described by size class. Only two assemblages have many extra-large size category flakes [1 and 2]. Two other assemblages have lesser numbers in this category (hard-hammer flake production, unprepared core [5] and soft-hammer flake production, prepared core [8]), in the

Table 9.2.
MSRT Reliability Analysis Flake Count and Proportion Data

	1	Prop.	2	Prop.	3	Prop.	4	Prop.	5	Prop.	6	Prop.	7	Prop.	8	Prop.	9	Prop.	10	Prop.
Large Flake																				
CF	0	.00	0	.00	0	.00	0	.00	0	.00	0	.00	0	.00	0	.00	0	.00	0	.00
PF	1	.01	2	.02	0	.00	1	.01	0	.00	2	.02	1	.01	1	.01	1	.01	1	.01
MDF	1	.01	0	.00	0	.00	1	.01	1	.01	0	.00	0	.00	0	.00	2	.02	1	.01
NF	0	.00	0	.00	0	.00	0	.00	0	.00	0	.00	0	.00	0	.00	0	.00	0	.00
SF	0	.00	0	.00	0	.00	0	.00	0	.00	0	.00	0	.00	0	.00	0	.00	0	.00
Medium Flake																				
CF	2	.03	3	.03	0	.00	1	.01	0	.00	1	.01	0	.00	0	.00	0	.00	0	.00
PF	10	.14	10	.10	5	.05	6	.06	14	.12	5	.04	5	.05	3	.02	7	.06	6	.05
MDF	6	.08	11	.11	17	.17	17	.17	13	.11	17	.15	19	.19	12	.09	14	.12	13	.11
NF	0	.00	0	.00	0	.00	0	.00	0	.00	0	.00	0	.00	0	.00	0	.00	0	.00
SF	0	.00	1	.01	0	.00	1	.01	2	.02	1	.01	1	.01	3	.02	1	.01	0	.00
Small Flake																				
CF	2	.03	4	.04	1	.01	2	.02	3	.03	2	.02	1	.01	2	.02	1	.01	1	.01
PF	17	.23	11	.11	14	.14	21	.21	15	.13	14	.12	14	.14	18	.14	21	.18	13	.11
MDF	32	.44	54	.54	61	.61	48	.48	71	.59	69	.61	60	.60	85	.67	68	.59	81	.68
NF	0	.00	0	.00	0	.00	0	.00	0	.00	0	.00	0	.00	0	.00	0	.00	0	.00
SF	2	.03	4	.04	3	.03	2	.02	1	.01	2	.02	1	.01	3	.02	1	.01	3	.03

Note: CF=complete flake; PF=proximal fragment; MDF=medial-distal fragment; NF= nonorientable fragment; SF=split flake.

Table 9.3.
MSRT Validity Analysis Flake Count Data

	HH UPC	HH PC	HH BF	SH BF	HH UPC	SH UPC	HH PC	SH PC	HH FL	SH FL	PR FL	HH BF	SH BF	PR BF	HH UPC	SH UPC	PR UPC	HH PC	SH PC	PR PC
	1	2	3	4	5	6	7	8	9	10	11	12	13	14	15	16	17	18	19	20
Extra-Large Flake																				
CF	4	11	0	0	1	0	0	1	0	0	0	0	0	0	0	0	0	0	0	0
PF	2	0	0	0	0	0	0	0	0	0	0	0	0	0	0	0	0	0	0	0
MDF	0	0	0	0	0	0	0	0	0	0	0	0	0	0	0	0	0	0	0	0
NF	0	0	0	0	0	0	0	0	0	0	0	0	0	0	0	0	0	0	0	0
SF	2	0	0	0	0	0	0	0	0	0	0	0	0	0	0	0	0	0	0	0
Large Flake																				
CF	2	2	1	1	7	4	11	4	0	0	0	1	0	0	3	3	0	4	1	0
PF	7	3	2	1	10	8	3	2	0	0	0	0	0	0	4	0	0	0	0	0
MDF	10	8	2	8	6	8	6	7	0	0	0	0	0	0	2	1	0	1	1	0
NF	0	0	0	0	0	0	0	0	0	0	0	0	0	0	0	0	0	0	0	0
SF	7	3	2	0	4	2	0	2	0	0	0	0	0	0	1	2	0	0	0	0
Medium Flake																				
CF	2	2	3	0	0	0	1	1	3	1	0	7	3	0	4	3	0	7	6	0
PF	3	4	10	5	1	3	3	7	0	2	0	2	1	0	4	3	0	10	3	0
MDF	31	17	21	23	12	22	18	22	0	0	0	5	6	0	14	10	0	6	24	0
NF	0	1	1	0	1	1	0	1	0	0	0	0	0	0	1	0	0	0	0	0
SF	2	2	3	3	2	3	7	2	1	0	0	0	0	0	3	2	0	1	1	0

TABLE 9.3. continued
MSRT Validity Analysis Flake Count Data

	HH UPC 1	HH PC 2	HH BF 3	SH BF 4	HH UPC 5	SH UPC 6	HH PC 7	SH PC 8	HH FL 9	SH FL 10	PR FL 11	HH BF 12	SH BF 13	PR BF 14	HH UPC 15	SH UPC 16	PR UPC 17	HH PC 18	SH PC 19	PR PC 20
Small Flake																				
CF	0	3	14	4	2	0	10	3	40	9	10	12	3	4	3	3	9	8	10	12
PF	3	21	10	16	3	3	28	12	3	16	23	10	10	10	6	7	36	6	15	22
MDF	93	69	91	83	56	63	103	77	39	44	19	33	39	34	63	67	32	49	47	30
NF	19	13	11	5	7	8	13	14	0	0	0	1	0	0	12	17	1	12	0	1
SF	4	6	8	4	3	16	7	10	13	5	19	4	6	10	6	9	9	3	6	20

Note: CF=complete flake; PF=proximal fragment; MDF=medial-distal fragment; NF=nonorientable fragment; SF=split flake; HH=hard hammer; SH=soft hammer; PR=pressure; UPC=unprepared core; PC=prepared core; BF=biface; FL=flake.

Table 9.4.
MSRT Validity Analysis Flake Proportion Data

	HH UPC 1	HH PC 2	HH BF 3	SH BF 4	HH UPC 5	SH UPC 6	HH PC 7	SH PC 8	HH FL 9	SH FL 10	PR FL 11	HH BF 12	SH BF 13	PR BF 14	HH UPC 15	SH UPC 16	PR UPC 17	HH PC 18	SH PC 19	PR PC 20
Extra-Large Flake																				
CF	.02	.07	.00	.00	.01	.00	.00	.01	.00	.00	.00	.00	.00	.00	.00	.00	.00	.00	.00	.00
PF	.01	.00	.00	.00	.00	.00	.00	.00	.00	.00	.01	.00	.00	.00	.00	.00	.00	.00	.00	.00
MDF	.00	.00	.00	.00	.00	.00	.00	.00	.00	.00	.00	.00	.00	.00	.00	.00	.00	.00	.00	.00
NF	.00	.00	.00	.00	.00	.00	.00	.00	.00	.00	.00	.00	.00	.00	.00	.00	.00	.00	.00	.00
SF	.01	.00	.00	.00	.00	.00	.00	.00	.00	.00	.00	.00	.00	.00	.00	.00	.00	.00	.00	.00
Large Flake																				
CF	.01	.01	.01	.01	.06	.03	.05	.02	.00	.00	.00	.01	.00	.00	.02	.02	.00	.04	.01	.00
PF	.04	.02	.01	.01	.09	.06	.01	.01	.00	.00	.00	.00	.00	.00	.03	.00	.00	.00	.00	.00
MDF	.05	.05	.01	.05	.05	.06	.03	.04	.00	.00	.00	.00	.00	.00	.02	.01	.00	.01	.01	.00
NF	.00	.00	.00	.00	.00	.00	.00	.00	.00	.00	.00	.00	.00	.00	.01	.00	.00	.00	.00	.00
SF	.04	.02	.01	.00	.03	.01	.00	.01	.01	.00	.00	.00	.02	.02	.01	.02	.00	.01	.00	.00
Medium Flake																				
CF	.00	.09	.04	.00	.03	.02	.00	.07	.05	.00	.01	.01	.02	.00	.00	.00	.01	.01	.03	.01
PF	.00	.03	.01	.00	.03	.02	.00	.09	.03	.00	.02	.02	.06	.03	.01	.02	.01	.04	.00	.03
MDF	.00	.07	.09	.00	.11	.08	.00	.06	.21	.00	.16	.10	.12	.15	.10	.16	.09	.13	.00	.03
NF	.00	.00	.00	.00	.01	.00	.00	.00	.00	.00	.00	.01	.01	.00	.01	.01	.00	.01	.00	.00
SF	.00	.00	.00	.00	.02	.02	.00	.01	.01	.00	.01	.01	.02	.02	.02	.02	.03	.01	.01	.00

TABLE 9.4. continued
MSRT Validity Analysis Flake Proportion Data

	HH UPC 1	HH PC 2	HH BF 3	SH BF 4	HH UPC 5	SH UPC 6	HH PC 7	SH PC 8	HH FL 9	SH FL 10	PR FL 11	HH BF 12	SH BF 13	PR BF 14	HH UPC 15	SH UPC 16	PR UPC 17	HH PC 18	SH PC 19	PR PC 20
Small Flake																				
CF	.12	.16	.04	.07	.02	.02	.10	.07	.09	.14	.00	.02	.08	.03	.02	.00	.05	.02	.40	.12
PF	.28	.13	.15	.17	.05	.06	.41	.06	.13	.26	.04	.13	.06	.10	.03	.02	.14	.07	.03	.21
MDF	.23	.44	.57	.59	.50	.54	.37	.46	.42	.35	.49	.42	.51	.54	.48	.45	.51	.47	.39	.59
NF	.00	.01	.00	.00	.09	.14	.01	.11	.00	.01	.10	.08	.06	.03	.06	.06	.06	.09	.00	.00
SF	.23	.05	.09	.17	.05	.07	.10	.03	.05	.24	.02	.04	.04	.03	.03	.11	.03	.06	.13	.07

Note: CF=complete flake; PF=proximal fragment; MDF=medial-distal fragment; NF=nonorientable fragment; SF=split flake; HH=hard hammer; SH=soft hammer; PR=pressure; UPC=unprepared core; PC=prepared core; BF=biface; FL=flake.

form of one complete flake each. The unprepared core assemblage contains fewer complete flakes and more numerous proximal fragments and split flakes than the prepared core assemblage, dominated by complete flakes. This is a demonstration of the importance of platform shaping and grinding allowing more consistent complete flake removal in the desired size range.

All soft- and hard-hammer core reduction and large-flake production biface assemblages contribute to the large flake category. Two patterns are notable in the matrix. First, complete flakes are most common in hard-hammer core reduction, and second, the medium-flake production cores contribute only small numbers of flakes to the large category either as overshots by the knapper aiming at slightly smaller flake production or as a consequence of large flakes removed to clear a new face for further reduction. There appears to be little difference between all large-flake core reduction assemblages in the complete flake category. However, unprepared hard-hammer cores produced more numerous proximal and medial-distal fragments than did the prepared hard-hammer cores.

All assemblages excepting those resulting from pressure flaking contribute to the medium flake category. The primary source of variability across the matrix appears to be the result of flake size goal differences. All extra-large–and large-flake goal assemblages produce high numbers of medium-sized flakes, each with numerous medial-distal fragments, reduced proximal fragments, and split flakes and very few complete flakes or nonorientable fragments. The majority of these flakes are the result of breakage of originally larger class flakes. They are not generally produced during platform preparation.

Patterning in the medium-flake goal assemblages is variable and appears to be linked to platform preparation and hammer type. As noted in the large size class, platform preparation produces assemblages with high numbers of complete flakes and reduced split flakes. Representation of proximal and medial-distal fragments varies highly and appears to be conditioned to a greater degree by hammer type.

The small flake category is patterned similarly to those described above. All core reduction assemblages with platform preparation contain higher numbers of proximal fragments and increased numbers of complete flakes. These are the result of small blows of force aimed at removing small, relatively thick flakes to shape platforms. A fair number of these flakes retain platforms and may be identified as proximal or complete.

A major source of variation in the matrix is those assemblages resulting from pressure flaking and hard-hammer reduction of a flake edge. Results of these reduction tactics include very few medium-sized flakes and more typically distributions only within the small size class. This is in contrast to situations such as prepared core reduction, where platform preparation and large flake removal

TABLE 9.5.
Reliability Analysis Correlation Matrix

	LP	LMD	MC	MP	MD	MS	SC	SP	SMD	SS
LP	1.000									
LMD	−.238	1.000								
MC	.542	−.103	1.000							
MP	−.131	.317	.635	1.000						
MMD	−.089	−.297	−.362	−.436	1.000					
MS	.000	−.086	−.269	−.122	−.121	1.000				
SC	.316	−.151	.772	.691	−.507	.286	1.000			
SP	−.160	.510	.307	.357	−.078	−.213	.025	1.000		
SMD	−.110	−.243	−.737	−.692	.035	.221	−.515	−.766	1.000	
SS	.323	−.339	.648	.203	−.288	−.554	.408	−.134	−.187	1.000

Note: LP=large proximal fragment; LMD=large medial-distal fragment; MC=medium complete flake; MP=medium proximal fragment; MMD=medium medial-distal fragment; MS=medium split flake; SC=small complete flake; SP=small proximal fragment; SMD= small medial-distal fragment; SS=small split flake.

promotes a three-tiered situation of primary flakes or those which were intended to be removed; residual fragments of those primary flakes resulting from poorly designed, executed flake removals, or raw material flaws; and residue from platform preparation. The technological origins of single size class assemblages are least likely to be masked by flake completeness typologies lacking size as a critical variable.

RELIABILITY ANALYSIS

A principal components analysis was conducted using the SPSS (Version 7.5) statistical package. A correlation matrix (Table 9.5) was first produced from the reliability proportion data (Table 9.2). Four factors were then extracted with an eigenvalue criterion of 1.0 and a significant loadings criterion of .3 (Carmines and Zeller 1979). Initial statistics and the unrotated loadings matrix are presented in Tables 9.6 and 9.7. As noted by Carmines and Zeller (1979:60), reliability assessment using PCA is accomplished in two ways. First, the first factor should account for a significant proportion of the variance (>40 percent) and most variables should also load on that factor. Second, a single summary statistic, known as coefficient theta, can be produced as a reliability coefficient using the first factor eigenvalue score.

Principal components analysis results suggest that some random error is present since the first eigenvalue is 37.678 and only five of the ten variables have significant positive loadings on the first factor. Coefficient theta, however, provides

TABLE 9.6.
Reliability Principal Components Analysis Initial Statistics

Factors	Eigenvalues (>1.0)	Percentage of Total Variance Explained
1	3.768	37.678
2	2.213	22.132
3	1.569	15.594
4	1.077	10.772

TABLE 9.7.
Reliability Principal Components Analysis Factor Loading Matrix

	Factor 1	Factor 2	Factor 3	Factor 4
LP	.313	.594	−.038	.325
LMD	.135	−.790	.094	−.295
MC	.947	.258	−.105	.129
MP	.807	−.297	.200	−.134
MMD	−.491	−.022	−.498	.609
MS	−.238	.029	.885	.358
SC	.796	.286	.478	.103
SP	.454	−.728	−.234	.234
SMD	−.814	.371	.186	−.393
SS	.550	.577	−.399	−.363

Note: LP=large proximal fragment; LMD=large medial-distal fragments; MC=medium complete flake; MP=medium proximal fragment; MMD=medium medial-distal fragment; MS=medium split flake; SC=small complete flake; SP=small proximal fragment; SMD= small medial-distal fragment; SS=small split flake.

a reliability coefficient of .82, indicating minimally acceptable reliability. Given this result, I conclude that the MSRT, like the SRT (Prentiss 1998), is indeed reliable and acceptable for further analysis focusing on validity.

VALIDITY ANALYSIS

A second principal components analysis was conducted, first deriving a correlation matrix (Table 9.8) from the validity proportion data (Table 9.4). Five varimax-rotated factors were extracted under the same significance parameters as in the reliability analysis (Tables 9.9 and 9.10). Factor one contains high positive loadings on large complete flakes, large proximal fragments, large medial-distal fragments, large split flakes, medium medial-distal fragments, medium nonorientable fragments, and medium split flakes. High negative loadings are present for small proximal fragments and small split flakes. Factor two contains

TABLE 9.8.
Validity Analysis Correlation Matrix

	ELP	ELS	LMD	LS	MC	MMD	MN	MS	SC	SMD	ELC	LC	LP	MP	SP	SN	SS
ELP	1.000																
ELS	1.000	1.000															
LMD	.325	.325	1.000														
LS	.657	.657	.629	1.000													
MC	-.093	-.093	-.366	-.250	1.000												
MMD	.288	.288	.662	.413	.125	1.000											
MN	-.150	-.150	.572	.433	-.221	.394	1.000										
MS	-.012	-.012	.606	.347	-.154	.555	.439	1.000									
SC	-.207	-.207	-.580	-.464	.248	-.559	-.389	-.348	1.000								
SMD	.064	.064	.139	.133	.040	.283	.043	.274	-.374	1.000							
ELC	.213	.213	.483	.500	-.155	.175	.398	.016	-.251	-.095	1.000						
LC	-.067	-.067	.533	.346	.035	.346	.381	.711	-.402	.163	.009	1.000					
LP	.253	.253	.743	.693	-.318	.414	.630	.475	-.423	.075	.225	.631	1.000				
MP	-.026	-.026	.098	.005	.518	.385	.224	.242	-.234	.250	-.026	.299	-.068	1.000			
SP	-.203	-.203	-.522	-.480	-.238	-.585	-.444	-.630	.151	-.399	-.098	-.495	-.480	-.428	1.000		
SN	.285	.285	.510	.640	.018	.395	.415	.600	-.547	.223	.298	.554	.337	.486	-.569	1.000	
SS	-.225	-.225	-.483	-.404	-.329	-.661	-.270	-.551	.395	-.520	-.248	-.501	-.301	-.563	.530	-.523	1.000

Note: LP=large proximal fragment; LMD=large medial-distal fragment; MC=medium complete flake; MP=medium proximal fragment; MMD=medium medial-distal fragment; MS=medium split flake; SC=small complete flake; SP=small proximal fragment; SMD= small medial-distal fragment; SS=small split flake; ELP=extra-large proximal fragment; ELS=extra-large split flake; LS=large split flake; MN=medium nonorientable fragment; ELC=extra-large complete flake; LC=large complete flake.

TABLE 9.9.
Validity Principal Components Analysis Initial Statistics

Factors	Eigenvalues (>1.0)	Percentage of Total Variance Explained
1	4.391	25.830
2	2.829	16.639
3	2.256	13.269
4	2.090	12.294
5	2.003	11.784

TABLE 9.10.
Validity Principal Components Analysis Rotated Factor Loading Matrix

	Factor 1	Factor 2	Factor 3	Factor 4	Factor 5
ELP	.015	.985	−.007	.049	.078
ELS	.015	.985	−.007	.049	.078
LMD	.668	.268	−.147	.471	.270
LS	.482	.660	−.081	.430	.104
MC	−.126	−.047	.878	−.195	−.150
MMD	.475	.241	.298	.224	.449
MN	.584	−.222	−.021	.621	.051
MS	.840	−.053	.072	−.027	.279
SC	−.274	−.112	.113	−.404	−.722
SMD	.116	.038	.143	−.216	.814
ELC	−.008	.200	.016	.883	−.025
LC	.842	−.098	.120	−.007	.131
LP	.788	.233	−.282	.256	.019
MP	.169	−.093	.806	.112	.266
SP	−.719	−.214	−.429	−.005	−.106
SN	.534	.247	.318	.331	.272
SS	−.417	−.188	−.548	−.163	−.495

Note: LP=large proximal fragment; LMD=large medial-distal fragment; MC=medium complete flake; MP=medium proximal fragment; MMD=medium medial-distal fragment; MS=medium split flake; SC=small complete flake; SP=small proximal fragment; SMD= small medial-distal fragment; SS=small split flake; ELP=extra-large proximal fragment; ELS=extra-large split flake; LS=large split flake; MN=medium nonorientable fragment; ELC=extra-large complete flake; LC=large complete flake.

high positive loadings on extra-large proximal fragments, extra-large split flakes, and large split flakes. Factor three features significantly high positive loadings on medium complete flakes and medium proximal fragments and high negative loadings on small split flakes. Factor four exhibits high positive loadings on large medial-distal fragments, medium nonorientable fragments, and extra-large complete flakes, while significant negative loadings only occur on small complete

TABLE 9.11.

Validity Principal Components Analysis Factor Score Matrix

Case	Assemblage Type	Factor 1	Factor 2	Factor 3	Factor 4	Factor 5
1	ELF,Hh, PC	.066	4.184	−.029	.209	.331
2	ELF, Hh, UPC	−.448	−.254	.181	3.600	−.200
3	LF, Hh, B	.357	−.480	.880	.236	.398
4	LF, Hh, B	.157	−.261	−.322	−.441	1.484
5	LF, Hh, UPC	2.460	−.069	−1.043	.234	−.430
6	LF, Sh, UPC	1.697	−.359	−.875	.230	−.003
7	LF, Hh, PC	1.090	−.425	−.463	−1.150	.714
8	LF, Sh, PC	.298	−.424	.316	1.077	.419
9	MF, Hh, F	.274	.169	.329	−1.264	−2.602
10	MF, SH, F	−1.194	−.260	−.162	−.480	1.008
11	MF, Pr, F	−.806	−.190	−1.155	.158	−1.774
12	MF, Hh, F	−.649	−.021	1.728	−.411	−.891
13	MF, Sh, B	−1.107	−.152	.055	−.465	1.021
14	MF, Pr, B	−1.067	−.241	−1.188	−.672	.872
15	MF, Hh, UPC	.854	−.397	.355	.170	.274
16	MF, Sh, UPC	.361	.117	.211	−.471	.791
17	MF, Pr, UPC	−1.330	−.297	−1.097	.164	−.155
18	MF, Hh, PC	.177	.331	2.510	−.252	−.190
19	MF, Sh, PC	.335	.117	.968	−.312	.079
20	MF, Pr, PC	−.853	−.191	−1.200	−.159	−1.147

Note: ELF=extra-large flake production goal; LF=large flake production goal; MF=medium flake production goal; Hh= hard hammer; Sh=soft hammer; Pr=pressure; UPC=unprepared core; PC=prepared core; B=biface; F=flake.

flakes. Factor five has high positive loadings on medium and small medial-distal fragments and high negative loading on small split flakes. I interpret the results of this matrix in reference to the contribution of individual cases through plotted factor scores (Table 9.11, Figures 9.1–9.3).

With its high loadings on most large and several medium flake types, emphasizing complete, nonorientable, and split flakes in particular, factor one segregates large flake core reduction from other techniques (Figure 9.1). Most critically, large flake core reduction (assemblages 5, 6, and 7) is separated from large flake biface reduction (assemblages 3 and 4) and extra-large flake core reduction (assemblages 1 and 2) in that each of these contains relatively low numbers of large complete flakes and medium nonorientable fragments and split flakes while these flake types are increased in the large flake core reduction assemblages.

Factor two isolates extra-large flake unprepared core reduction from all other techniques (Figure 9.2). This is because this form of core reduction routinely results in relatively frequent very large split flakes and proximal fragments that range from very infrequent to impossible in other techniques.

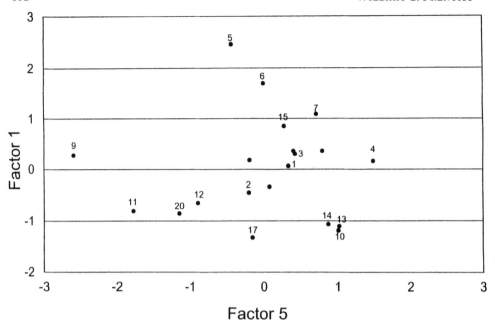

Figure 9.1. Validity principal components analysis factor scores plot (factors one and five).

In a continuum of variability, factor three segregates pressure flaking assemblages (assemblages 11, 14, 17, and 20) from hard-hammer biface (assemblage 12) and hard- and soft-hammer, medium flake goal, core reduction (assemblages 18 and 19) assemblages (Figure 9.2). The biface and medium flake core reduction assemblages contain flake distributions centering heavily on medium-size flake categories as well as relatively high numbers of small medial-distal and nonorientable fragments. They contain relatively few split flakes and variable numbers of proximal fragments depending on the presence and degree of platform preparation. In contrast, pressure flake assemblages contain no medium-size flakes and numerous small split flakes and proximal fragments. The large flake goal, unprepared core reduction assemblage is also included within the cluster of pressure flake assemblages due to extremely low flake counts in the medium size class.

Factor four delineates the extra-large flake goal, prepared core reduction assemblage (#1) from all other assemblages types (Figure 9.3). This assemblage is unique with comparatively high frequencies of extra-large complete flakes.

Factor five identifies soft-hammer tool production with extremely high positive factor scores on soft-hammer biface and flake reduction (Figure 9.1). Interestingly, these assemblages are marked by exceptionally high, small medial-distal fragment counts.

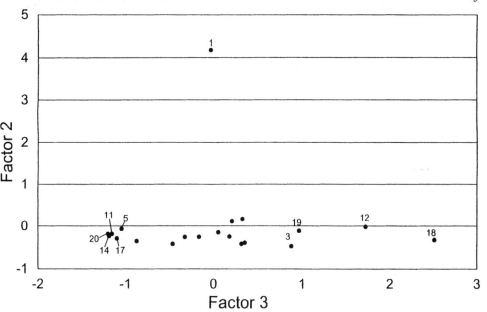

Figure 9.2. Validity principal components analysis factor scores plot (factors two and three).

DISCUSSION

I highlight five major implications of the validity analysis. First, tool and core re-duction are identified as relatively unique contributors to assemblage content and thus, all things equal, the MSRT appears to be valid for recognizing distinc-tions between tool versus core reduction as defined in this study. All forms of core reduction are segregated in this analysis. Factor three identifies medium flake cores, factor one isolates large flake cores, and factors two and four identify the extra-large flake cores. Tool production is designated in two ways: pressure flake assemblages are identified on factor three, and biface and flake edge reduction as-semblages are isolated on factor five.

Second, there are indicators that percussor type will affect overall MSRT dis-tributions. Indeed, hard-hammer biface production is recognized on factor three as similar to hard-hammer prepared core reduction. Factors three and five iden-tify distinctions between hard- and soft-hammer biface production assemblages. Hammer type does not appear to significantly affect the identification of core re-duction.

Third, flake size goal is extremely important. All factor results are affected to some degree by size distributions. In particular, factor one separates large flake goal core reduction from other forms and factors two and four identify extra-large flake core reduction. Flake size goal appears less significant in tool produc-tion contexts.

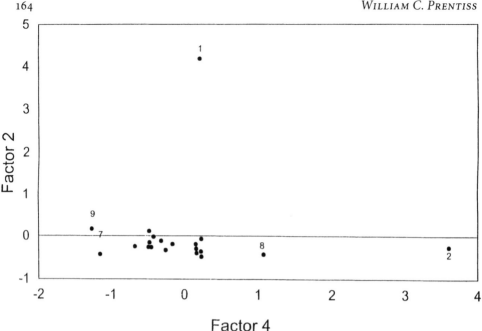

Figure 9.3. Validity principal components analysis factor scores plot (factors two and four).

Fourth, strategy and degree of platform preparation is an important conditioner of assemblage variation. The strong loading of small proximal fragments and small split flakes in the negative dimension of factors one and three marks the significant effects of platform preparation, edge shaping, and general flake removal tactics requiring pressure flaking or light percussion to core/blank margins.

Finally, the solution has produced some data ambiguities requiring further investigation. Two obvious examples include the linking of hard-hammer unprepared core reduction with pressure flake assemblages on factor three and the pairing of soft-hammer prepared core reduction and hard-hammer flake reduction on factors one and five. In the former case, the linkage was made due primarily to the low-scoring medium proximal and complete flakes in the core reduction assemblage, despite little resemblance in the small size class. In the latter example, soft-hammer prepared core reduction and hard-hammer flake retouch are linked due to similarly low scores for small and medium medial-distal, and small proximal fragment.

ARCHAEOLOGICAL APPLICATION

I emphasize that the MSRT represents only one instrument among many for characterizing variation in the archaeological record. As demonstrated by Sulli-

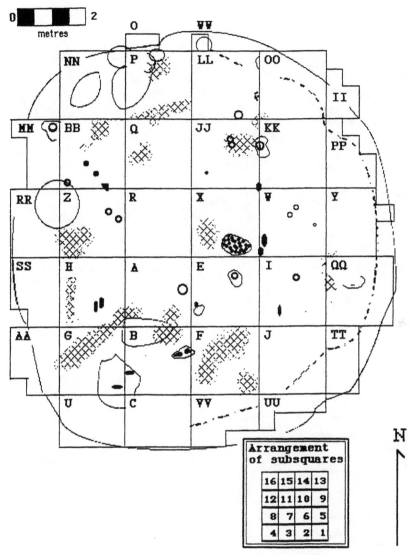

Figure 9.4. Excavation plan map of Housepit 7, Keatley Creek site, British Columbia.

van and Rozen (1985), the flake completeness approach is most profitably applied in contexts of other debitage analyses. I explored the archaeological applicability of the MSRT in an analysis of debitage from a large late prehistoric housepit floor at the Keatley Creek site in British Columbia (Prentiss 1993, 2000). The entire floor of Housepit 7 at Keatley Creek (see Hayden 1997) was excavated in 50-sq-cm quadrats (organization of 50-cm quadrats within larger 2 by 2 m units in lower right corner of Figure 9.4). Debitage was distributed throughout the floor, often in relatively high quantities. The MSRT was applied in tandem with other

TABLE 9.12.

Select Vitreous Trachydacite Assemblage Data from Housepit 7,
Keatley Creek Site, British Columbia

	Edge Retouch		Biface		Prepared Core		Bipolar and Prepared Core	
	N	Proportion	N	Proportion	N	Proportion	N	Proportion
Large Flake								
CF	0	.00	0	.00	0	.00	0	.00
PF	0	.00	1	.02	1	.01	0	.00
MDF	0	.00	0	.00	0	.00	0	.00
Medium Flake								
CF	0	.00	0	.00	5	.04	3	.06
PF	0	.00	1	.02	8	.06	1	.02
MDF	1	.06	9	.15	6	.05	6	.13
NF	0	.00	0	.00	0	.00	2	.04
SF	0	.00	0	.00	0	.00	0	.00
Small Flake								
CF	0	.00	8	.13	11	.08	4	.08
PF	8	.53	19	.30	26	.20	10	.21
MDF	5	.33	22	.35	59	.46	16	.33
NF	0	.00	0	.00	8	.06	3	.06
SF	1	.06	2	.03	4	.03	3	.06

Note: CF=complete flake; PF=proximal flake; MDF=medial-distal fragment; NF=nonorientable fragment; SF=split flake.

instruments for a comprehensive assessment of technological and taphonomic variation. Results of MSRT (Prentiss 1993, 2000) and the more traditional flake-type (Spafford 1991) technological analyses were strongly congruent. MSRT analyses focused only on vitreous trachydacite, a form of basalt, with several interesting results (Table 9.12). Interpretation of assemblage patterning was facilitated by prior experimentation with obsidian and vitreous trachydacite reported in this paper and in Prentiss (1993, 2000). Tool edge retouch/resharpening was recognized consistently adjacent to hearths (Figure 9.5). Biface reduction also clustered around hearth features and, more broadly, on the west side of the house floor (Figure 9.6). Core reduction debris was found throughout the housepit floor (Figure 9.7). Finally, bipolar reduction was identified in two restricted contexts on the west and northeast sides of the house (Figure 9.8). Additional MSRT studies moved beyond technological identification in an effort to determine

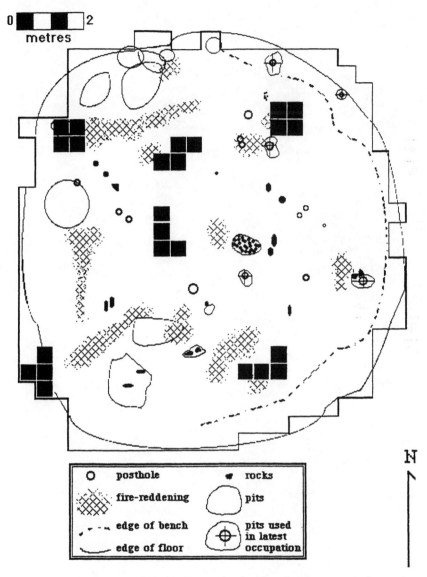

Figure 9.5. Housepit 7 analytical units associated with tool maintenance/resharpening.

effects of trampling and flake culling. These studies are described in depth else-where (Prentiss 1993, 2000).

These results supported and expanded upon additional lithic, faunal, and flo-ral studies (described in Hayden 1997) indicating consistent hearth-centered patterning around the housepit floor, likely reflecting activities of multiple

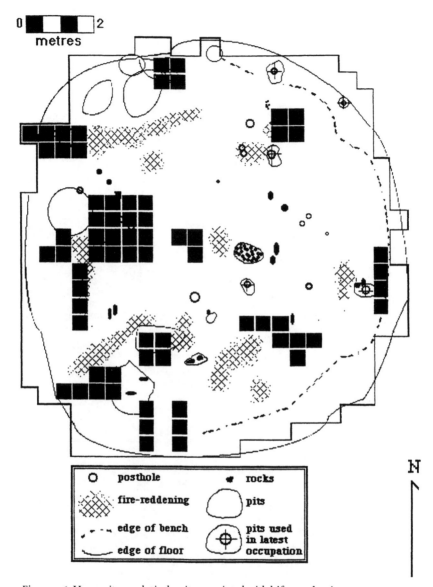

Figure 9.6. Housepit 7 analytical units associated with biface reduction.

domestic units living within the house. For example, lithic tool maintenance/re-sharpening activities and biface reduction occurred redundantly associated with hearth features around the perimeter of the Housepit 7 floor. The recognition of fine retouch activities adjacent to hearth features and trampling and culling patterns throughout the housepit floor (Prentiss 1993, 2000) were a unique contribution of the MSRT analysis. This paralleled similar patterning in fire-cracked

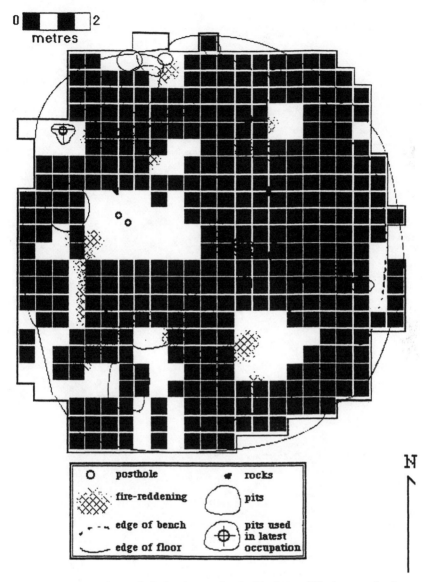

Figure 9.7. Housepit 7 analytical units associated with prepared block core reduction.

rock, and faunal and floral remains (Hayden 1997; Lepofsky et al. 1996). The results of the MSRT analysis also corroborated Hayden et al. (1996) and Spafford
(1991) suggesting that the most frequent form of lithic reduction on house floors
appears to have been reduction of small block cores, followed to a lowered degree
by biface reduction, tool maintenance, and bipolar reduction. As the vitreous trachydacite raw material does not occur locally, it was most likely transported to

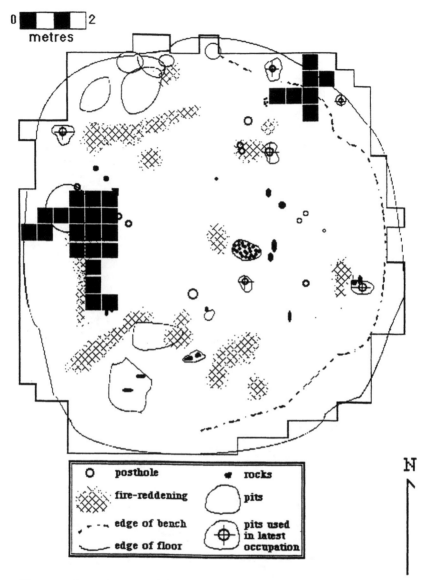

Figure 9.8. Housepit 7 analytical units associated with bipolar core reduction.

the housepit village through lithic procurement strategies embedded into spring
or fall deer hunting and root collection forays (e.g., Alexander 1992). The transported cores likely served as raw material sources through the long winter for the
sedentary population at the village (Hayden et al. 1996). Bipolar reduction appears to have been typically applied to exhausted cores and bifaces during late

winter as suggested by comparatively little trampling damage to bipolar artifacts as compared to others (Prentiss 1993, 2000).

Despite these apparent successes, the analytical result was confounded to some degree by ambiguities. Technological conclusions were typically drawn from assessment of patterning in the small size class, as the larger size classes were heavily affected by a variety of nontechnological agents, particularly trampling and flake culling. Proximal and nonorientable fragments were the best markers of different reduction strategies. In many cases, patterning was clear—high numbers of nonorientable fragments coupled with lowered proximal fragments marked core reduction while low nonorientable fragment counts and high numbers of proximal fragments marked different forms of tool production. Ambiguity occurred when both proximal and nonorientable fragment counts were at intermediate levels (Prentiss 1993). In retrospect, I suggest that assessment of patterning in additional size classes below the small size cutoff (4 sq cm) would likely have increased the clarity of the overall result.

CONCLUSIONS

I have recently argued (Prentiss 1998) that the major problem with application of the SRT is the fact that variability in debitage assemblages is typically partitioned by flake size. To demonstrate this, I provided data suggesting that some variation in reduction technique could be recognized using the SRT in combination with size classes. This paper has provided a quantitative test of this contention through a reliability and validity analysis of the MSRT. Results suggest that application of size classes to the SRT does not change reliability as the score was essentially the same (Prentiss 1998). Size classes do appear to make a big difference in validity analysis. Core and tool reduction resulted in distinctively different debitage distributions. Core reduction assemblages tended to produce more numerous larger, complete, proximal and split flakes, in addition to medium medial-distal and nonorientable fragments and small nonorientable fragments. Tool production assemblages resulted in more frequent small medial-distal and proximal fragments and very few to no nonorientable fragments. Variability within each group was conditioned by percussor/pressure-flaker use and flake size goals.

Application of the MSRT to debitage from Housepit 7 at the Keatley Creek site has been insightful from several standpoints. First, it allowed an important independent test of conclusions drawn from more standard debitage analyses. Second, new technological patterns were recognized that were less easy to see in previous studies, particularly fine, small clusters of tool resharpening/maintenance debris. Third, though not detailed in the paper, the MSRT analysis allowed an assessment of different taphonomic factors affecting debitage found on the housepit floor (Prentiss 2000).

Experimentation remains a critical research strategy in lithic technology (e.g., Andrefsky 1998, this volume; Bradbury and Carr 1999; Carr and Bradbury, this volume; Patterson, this volume; Pelcin 1997a; Prentiss 1998 Prentiss 1998). Thus, I offer several recommendations for future research:

(1) Reliability studies. The next experiments need to explore the effects of knapper variation in reliability assessment. Will different knappers, producing the same tools, also produce consistently similar debitage assemblages, as measured by the SRT and MSRT? It is also clear that we need more direct tests of inter-observer error variation. Amick and Mauldin (1997) provide data suggesting that inter-observer error may be significant in the flake completeness approach.

(2) Validity studies. Though I suggest that this analysis implies a substantial degree of validity for use of the MSRT in technological studies of debitage, some ambiguities were noted. In addition, other experiments (Prentiss 1993; Prentiss et al. 1988) suggest that nontechnological agents will modify MSRT patterns particularly in the larger size classes so that data in these tiers are not always directly reflective of technological input. Baumler and Downum (1989) demonstrate that extremely small sized debitage may be useful as markers of reduction technique. These artifacts are also least susceptible to nontechnological modification (e.g., Fladmark 1982). An important set of future experiments will be to explore the use of even greater size variation in the MSRT. I expect this will provide even more distinct markers of technological behavior and will ultimately allow us to more clearly recognize interactive effects of a wide range of cultural and noncultural site formation processes.

ACKNOWLEDGMENTS

I thank Bill Andrefsky for the invitation to participate in the symposium in Chicago. Brian Hayden provided permission and encouragement to study Housepit 7 lithics from Keatley Creek. This research has benefitted from earlier comment and criticism from Harold Dibble, Knut Fladmark, Brian Hayden, Ian Kuijt, Jack Nance, and Jim Spafford. Tom Foor reminded me of the issue of structural correlations. Jim Spafford produced the Keatley Creek Housepit 7 graphics. Partial funding for the experimental studies was provided by a dissertation research fellowship from Simon Fraser University.

10

Chipped Stone Tool Production Strategies and Lithic Debitage Patterns

Albert M. Pecora

In this paper I examine how the organization of prehistoric stone tool production may have affected lithic assemblage formation. Simplified models of production are constructed to illustrate how raw material may be prepared and transported. Data collected from experimental flintknapping indicate that subtle differences in manufacturing organization have a significant effect on the quantity and quality of debris produced. Assuming that prehistoric tool manufacturing strategies were patterned, it is expected that the distribution, density, and diversity of debris would be patterned accordingly. This research is significant in that it examines the fundamental source of lithic assemblage formation.

As a formation process, the organization of prehistoric stone tool production is a fundamental source of lithic assemblage variability. For the purposes of this essay, the organization of tool production refers to the manner in which stone-working people procured, prepared, transported, and used lithic material. I am particularly interested in how lithic material was prepared and transported. The preparation of lithic material for transport may be organized in terms of reduction junctures, where lithic material is partially reduced to a particular point or juncture within the longer reduction trajectory (Binford 1979; Ozbun 1987). Reduction junctures are defined as terminations or pauses in the reduction process, at which point partially reduced lithic material is transported away from places of preparation and reduced into usable tools elsewhere. For the purposes of this paper I subdivided an established model of chipped stone tool production (Collins 1975) to illustrate potential reduction junctures. Each consecutive subdivision represents the termination of the reduction process (juncture) at a different stage and marks the stage at which the reduction process would be resumed. Following this subdivided reduction model, experimental flintknapping episodes were conducted to examine how debris production rates vary for each consecutive juncture. Data collected from the experiments indicate that subtle differences in reduction junctures would have a significant impact on the quantity and quality of debris produced, and hence influence the formation of lithic assemblages. Early stage reduction junctures, for example, are expected to result in the production of substantial lithic artifact deposits, whereas later reduction junctures are expected to result in the formation of less substantial lithic concentrations. In sum, lithic assemblages are more likely to reflect the process of manufacture from a particular reduction juncture than site function and occupation intensity. This is illustrated with the lithic assemblage from the Martin Justice site (15PI92) in southeastern Kentucky, where an extremely sparse lithic assemblage was identified despite other evidence for more substantial prehistoric residential occupations (Kerr and Creasman 1995).

BACKGROUND

Over the last 30 years, there has been a growing interest in modeling chipped stone tool manufacturing systems. Many of these attempts have focused on the placement of flakes within reduction trajectories, or systemic context characterization (Ahler 1989b; Callahan 1979; Johnson 1987b). Much of this research has focused on the identification of site types based on the presence of lithics representing a particular stage of reduction (following Binford 1979, 1980). For example, simple distinctions between extraction locations and maintenance locations have been attempted (Johnson 1987b:2). Theoretically, given the reductive nature of chipped stone tool manufacture, it might be expected that extraction locations would contain what Johnson (1987b) has defined as short trajectory lithic assemblages, in contrast to what he refers to as long trajectory lithic assemblages at maintenance activity sites. The premise behind Johnson's short- and long-term reduction trajectory model is that, at special purpose activity locations, a smaller range of flake types reflecting short reduction trajectories would be expected. Flakes types reflecting longer trajectories would be expected at long-term habitation sites, where tool manufacture and maintenance might be expected. In other words, the length of a chipped stone tool manufacturing trajectory within a location is thought to reflect the range of prehistoric activities carried out, as well as the intensity of occupation at the location. In general, the ultimate goals of such analyses are to develop an understanding of how chipped stone tool manufacturing systems were organized and how they "functioned" within prehistoric living systems.

Given these goals, it is understandable why archaeologists might be interested in modeling chipped stone tool manufacturing systems and developing methods for recognizing prehistoric behaviors that cause or influence lithic artifact patterning. Unfortunately, different tool manufacturing systems, or the organization of such, may not be a function of site activities or even mobility strategies.

That is, the organization of manufacturing trajectories may be variable regardless of site function and settlement. The following discussion examines the manufacturing process, and how the organization of this process may have influenced the characteristic of prehistoric lithic assemblages regardless of site activities or settlement organization.

LITHIC TRANSPORT JUNCTURES

Following Collins's (1975) model, all stone-working people employed a manufacturing process that begins with some level of stone procurement and ends with the production, use, and discard of tools. It is generally understood that this process did not occur at a single location. Instead, the process was organized into junctures, where the reduction process was terminated prior to the completion of finished objects. The termination of the reduction process at a particular point or juncture within the longer reduction process is necessary to facilitate the transport of lithic materials. That is, rock is partially reduced into a transportable form. The transported material is in a form that represents the termination of the reduction process prior to transport and the beginning point (juncture) at which the manufacturing process is resumed after transport. If the preparation of lithic material for transport is culturally patterned, it is expected that this pattern varies over time and space.

For example, Binford (1979) observed that the Nunamiut referred to "carrying cores," where lithic material was reduced to a point where enough waste was removed to facilitate transport, but not reduced too much to limit the range of things that could be done with the cores. The Nunamiut "core" is an example of a reduction juncture. Ozbun (1987) identified similar reduction junctures at the Buttonhole Rockshelter/Quarry site, New Mexico, where the lithic assemblage reflected an emphasis of the production of flake blanks that were then exported from the site.

The Nunamiut and Buttonhole examples illustrate two different reduction junctures. The Nunamiut employed an earlier juncture (core), whereas the Buttonhole inhabitants employed a slightly later juncture (flake blanks). In each case, lithic materials were reduced to a particular point in the manufacturing process and transported for further reduction elsewhere. Because each example is a different reduction juncture, lithic deposits generated from the resumption of the manufacturing process would be different. All things being equal, Nunamiut sites would contain higher lithic debris densities, whereas the sites produced by the Buttonhole inhabitants would contain lower densities of lithic debris. This is because the Buttonhole reduction juncture is further along in the reduction process than is the Nunamiut example. More waste was removed prior to transport.

As the above examples illustrate, lithic material was transported in partially reduced forms, each representing a different reduction juncture (i.e., cores and flake blanks). Because each reduction juncture represents the resumption of the manufacturing process at different stages (after transport), the respective form in which the stone is transported and introduced to a location is likely to have a profound impact on the formation of lithic assemblages. Thus, in order to understand interassemblage variability across time or space, it is important to address how different reduction junctures influence lithic assemblage formation. Traditionally, artifact patterning, in terms of density, diversity, and distribution, is treated as a reflection of site function (Binford 1973, 1977, 1978a, 1978b, 1979, 1980). Similarly, a group's lithic technology or organization of technology is often treated as a reflection of settlement systems and mobility (e.g., curated versus expedient, core versus biface technologies) (Bleed 1986; Nash 1996; Roth and Dibble 1998; Shott 1986).

While most of these studies acknowledge that lithic materials were transported in a prepared from, few have examined the relationship between how lithic material is prepared for transport and the formation of lithic assemblages after transport. Although certainly more complex than presented here, artifact patterning and technological organization may merely reflect the use of different reduction junctures, rather than site function or mobility. While it may be true that different reduction junctures facilitate different levels of mobility, subtle differences in how stone is prepared for transport may have considerable impact on lithic assemblage formation. In other words, the differences are not great enough to affect transport feasibility (for example), but are great enough to affect the characteristics of the lithic assemblage produced at a given location.

Bamforth (1986) argued that the organization of technology, in terms of curated and expedient technologies, is a reflection of raw material availability. This is a very important argument since stone-working people were capable of altering raw material availability. In fact, raw material availability is greatly affected by how the stone is prepared prior to transport. Cores, for example, provide more lithic material and manufacturing flexibility than do blanks or finished tools. Different reduction junctures affect raw material availability, and thus have an effect on lithic assemblage formation. Different reduction junctures, then, produce distinct archaeological patterns.

LITHIC REDUCTION MODEL AND TRANSPORT JUNCTURE MODELS

Following the principles laid out by Collins (1975), lithic tool production is a reductive process beginning with the selection of unaltered raw material and ending with the discard of exhausted lithic material (Figure 10.1). The top row of

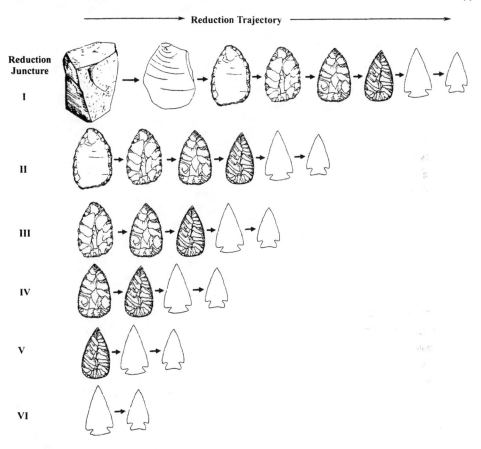

Figure 10.1. Schematic representation of lithic reduction model (top row), with each proposed reduction juncture.

Figure 10.1 illustrates a complete lithic reduction process. Exhausted lithic material refers to all lithic material that, for some reason, is no longer suitable to further reduction or use. Each consecutive row illustrates a particular transport juncture and illustrates a partial reduction trajectory that begins with a partially reduced or altered piece of lithic material. Each juncture represents the reduction trajectory that would be employed at a given location after the transport of the lithic material. Two axioms presented below reflect how different junctures are thought to influence lithic assemblage composition and serve as a basis for developing the juncture models provided below.

(1) Lithic assemblage density (artifact quantity) is not directly related to occupation intensity, but is instead dependent on the point or juncture of manufacture within a geographical space. In other words, all things being equal, it is

TABLE 10.1.
Reduction Juncture Models

I	Unaltered raw material through the discard of exhausted material
II	Prepared core through the discard of exhausted material
III	Prepared flake blank through the discard of exhausted material
IV	Prepared biface blank through the discard of exhausted material
V	Prepared biface preform through the discard of exhausted material
VI	Serviceable tool through the discard of exhausted materials

expected that artifact density is proportionate to the reduction juncture. Earlier reduction junctures will generate higher density assemblages in comparison to later reduction junctures.

(2) The organization of manufacture is a major limiting factor in determining artifact variability/diversity. It is expected that because earlier reduction junctures provide greater lithic material availability, a greater variety of artifacts would be produced. Later reduction junctures limit the range of artifact types and increase the likelihood of lithic material recycling and resharpening.

I have created a series of reduction juncture models based on the segmentation of general lithic reduction model presented above (Table 10.1). These junctures are arbitrarily defined, but represent the point at which the manufacturing process may be terminated at one location and resumed at another location. These are not meant to reflect all of the possible reduction systems and the organization of these systems employed in prehistory. Instead, these models reflect a single system of stone procurement, use, and discard for the purpose of illustrating general trends that might be reflected by the segmentation of all lithic reduction systems.

The proposed reduction juncture models presented in Table 10.1 and Figure 10.1 reflect how lithic reduction processes might be organized in terms of prepared lithic materials for transport. Juncture I, however, reflects the entire manufacturing process through the use and discard of implements, without interruption. On the other end of the continuum, Juncture VI reflects only the final stages of manufacture through use and discard. With this latter juncture, finished, serviceable tools mark the point at which the manufacturing process resumes after transport. The reduction activities involved in Juncture VI include resharpening, rejuvenation, and recycling. The middle reduction junctures reflect the resumption of the manufacturing process at various stages, including prepared flake blanks, biface blanks, and preforms, for example.

Following these reduction juncture models and the two axioms presented above, it is possible to suggest correlating lithic assemblage profiles for debris density and artifact diversity (Table 10.2). Assemblages generated from reduction

TABLE 10.2.
Expected Lithic Assemblage Profiles for Each of the Reduction Juncture Models

Juncture	Debris Density	Artifact Diversity
I	High	High
II	Medium	High/limited
III	Moderately low	Moderate/limited
IV	Low	Low/limited
V	Low	Very low
VI	Very low	Extremely low

Juncture I would be expected to have high artifact density and high artifact diversity because this juncture involves the entire lithic reduction process. This would naturally result in the production of greater quantities of debris, and offer greater flexibility in the range of objects that could be produced. Juncture VI, on the other hand, involves the further reduction of finished, serviceable tools. Debris production would be minimal, the range of objects that can be produced is greatly limited, and implement and debris recycling is likely. In sum, debris production and formed artifact variability is greatly reduced from Juncture I through Juncture VI. This is simply due to the fact that each juncture imposes greater limitations on the quality and quantity of lithic material available for reduction.

EXPERIMENTAL FLINTKNAPPING REDUCTION JUNCTURE DATA

Following the system of manufacture presented above, I conducted a series of 32 successful experimental flintknapping episodes. The purpose of this exercise was to illustrate waste production trends under controlled conditions. Although different skill levels, raw material characteristics, techniques used, and other variables influence the results of experimental flintknapping, the general trends represented are useful for illustrative purposes.

In the experiment, the quantity and size of debris generated during each arbitrarily defined reduction stage and corresponding reduction juncture was controlled. The complete reduction process was terminated at each reduction juncture defined earlier. The debris at each juncture was collected, counted, and passed through a series of nested screens. Figure 10.2 presents the average quantity of experimental debris per objective piece by size grade (>1 inch, 1 inch >½ inch, ½ inch >¼ inch, ¼ inch >⅛ inch) following Ahler (1987), for each reduction stage.

The experimental data indicate that on average 16 percent of the debris generated during the experiments was from core reduction, or Stage 1. Of particular

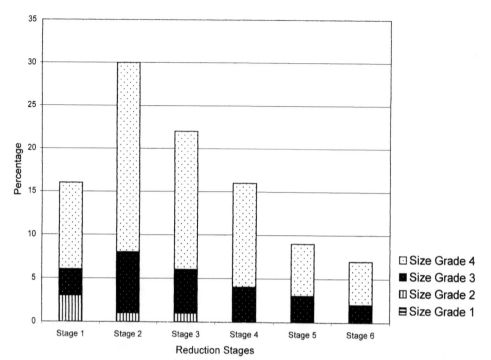

Figure 10.2. Average percentage of debitage generated per experimental reduction stage per objective piece produced.

interest here is that the most archaeologically visible debris (>¼ inch) is generated during the earlier stages. And even more importantly, although larger-sized debris tends to be generated during the earliest stages, most of the small debris is also generated during the earlier stages. This observation is of analytical importance and illustrates how size is an extremely poor indicator of technology or reduction stage. That is, as the reduction process might impose restrictions on how large a flake can be from a core, there are no restrictions imposed by the reduction process in terms of how small a flake can be.

The experimental data are transformed to represent the reduction junctures defined earlier (Figure 10.3). One hundred percent of the debris produced is generated through Juncture 1. This should be obvious because Juncture I represents the entire manufacturing process uninterrupted. For each consecutive reduction juncture, the proportion of debris produced per objective piece decreases significantly. For example, fifteen times more debris is produced in Juncture I than is produced in Juncture VI. Similarly, the debitage production rate for Juncture II is 2.5 times higher than it is for Juncture V. The point is these data reflect a substantial decrease in debris production with each consecutive juncture. While the experimental data support the expected assemblage profiles provided in Table 10.2

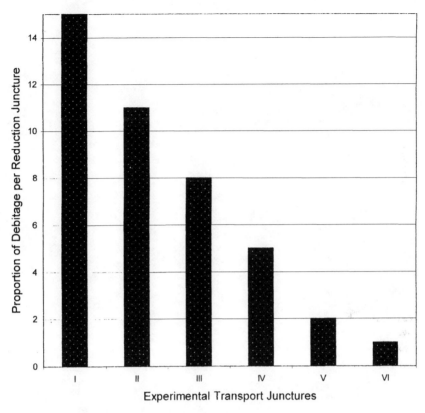

Figure 10.3. Experimental reduction data transformed to reflect reduction junctures.

in terms of artifact (debris) quantity, the experimental data reflect little concerning artifact diversity, specifically tool diversity.

THE MARTIN JUSTICE SITE

Because the focus of this paper is to develop a framework for understanding lithic assemblage formation, it is useful to test the proposed models against archaeological data. The Martin Justice site (15PI92) represents a series of prehistoric occupations located on a low toe-ridge situated in the upper reaches of Island Creek of the Levisa Fork in the rugged region of Pike County, Kentucky (Figure 10.4) (Kerr and Creasman 1995).

The Martin Justice site was chosen as a case study for this paper because it has been interpreted as containing a series of residential camps containing a variety of archaeological features associated with chipped stone artifacts, pitted stones, and pottery (Kerr and Creasman 1995; after Binford 1983). This site is represented by a complex arrangement of archaeological features (n=33), interpreted

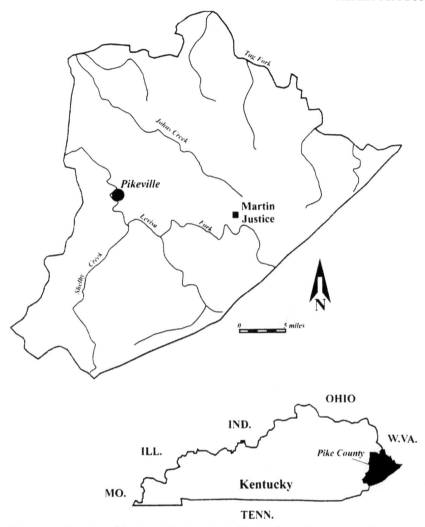

Figure 10.4. Location of the Martin Justice site (15PI92). Adapted from Kerr and Creasman (1995).

as hearths (n=14), shallow basins (n=15), earth ovens (n=3), and a possible burial (n=1) (Figure 10.5). In addition, an approximately 5.5 m diameter ring of post-molds (n=11) is interpreted as a Middle Woodland house location with an associated external feature cluster. Artifacts recovered from this site include chipped stone debris (n=2,723); formed chipped stone artifacts (n=76), including a "cache" of large stemmed bifaces (n=11); pitted (nutting) stones (n=23); pottery sherds (n=217); and a variety of botanical and fauna remains.

A suite of six radiocarbon ages obtained from wood and nutshell charcoal

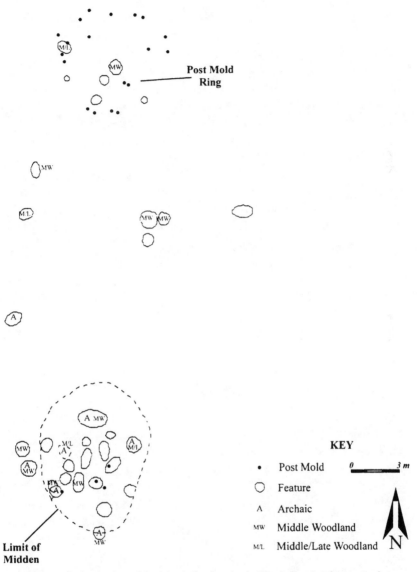

Figure 10.5. Schematic plan of the Martin Justice site (15PI92) showing feature and post mold locations. Highlighted features produced diagnostic artifacts and radiocarbon dates that correspond with the Middle Woodland period. Adapted from Kerr and Creasman (1995).

collected from features was used to date the archaeological sequence at this site (Kerr and Creasman 1995:148). Radiocarbon ages ranged from 1,870 to 5,400 B.P. These radiocarbon ages, coupled with what are thought to be temporally sensitive artifacts, represent Middle Archaic, Late Archaic, Early Woodland, Middle Woodland, and Late Woodland occupations at this location.

These functional interpretations were determined based on the site structure and the artifact assemblage. Site structure at Martin Justice is rather complex and represents numerous occupations spanning several millennia. Following Binford's (1980) forager/collector dichotomy, the Martin Justice site is interpreted as representing several residential bases, with varied lengths of occupation, during the Middle Archaic, Late Archaic, Early Woodland, late Middle Woodland, and early Late Woodland periods (Kerr and Creasman 1995). The Middle Woodland component is thought to represent the most substantial occupation at this site based on its association with the circular post structure and two feature clusters (or external activity loci). This interpretation is supported with evidence of maintenance and cleaning around the Middle Woodland feature clusters and structure. Although the presence of features and structures alone is not a priori evidence for a residential base camp, since field camps also contain such facilities (Fisher and Strickland 1991; Griffin 1974), the Martin Justice site clearly represents substantial occupations.

CHIPPED STONE ARTIFACTS FROM MARTIN JUSTICE

The Martin Justice lithic assemblage is interesting because it does not have the characteristics generally thought to reflect intensive prehistoric occupations. Of the 2,723 pieces of debris recovered, only 442 (or 16 percent) were recovered with the use of ¼-inch screens for 70 1-by-1-m units and 33 features. The remaining lithic debris (or 84 percent) was recovered from controlled volume samples. Each controlled volume sample was passed through a flotation device. The controlled volume samples served as a means for collecting artifacts smaller than ¼ inch in size. The Martin Justice lithic assemblage is very sparse, with few artifacts larger than ¼ inch. Thus, the archaeological visibility of the lithic assemblage from Martin Justice is very low, despite other evidence suggesting a series of intensive occupations.

The formed artifacts from the Martin Justice site are defined as modified pieces of lithic debris, or "stone objects" from which flakes were removed in some systematic fashion. Overall, in terms of functional artifact properties, the Martin Justice site has very low artifact variability. Of the formed chipped stone artifacts (n=76), most were classified as tools (n=52), followed by nontool-formed artifacts (n=24) (Pecora et al. 1995). As a measure of activities at the site, formed tools are the most important since they have utilitarian attributes, defined by Pecora et al. (1995). Of the 52 tools identified, three "utilitarian" tool types were identified. The majority was classified as "projectile points" (n=47, 90 percent) "unifacial scrapers" (n=4, 8 percent), and a drill (n=1, 2 percent). Overall, this "utilitarian" assemblage reflected an emphasis on hunting tools or weaponry. The unifacial scrapers and drill may represent limited processing and manufacturing activities. Two of the unifacial tools were actually recycled projectile points, or hafted endscrapers. Additional artifacts include ground stone artifacts consisting of a hammerstone (n=1) and nutting stones (n=23), and a variety of ceramics.

DISCUSSION AND INTERPRETATION OF MARTIN JUSTICE LITHIC ASSEMBLAGE

How might the low quantity, low diversity, and small artifact size be explained for Martin Justice in light of what appears to be a site that was generated over relatively long term and repeated residential occupations? I would like to offer three potential explanations for the lithic artifact patterning represented at this site.

(1) Despite apparent substantial occupations at this site over several millennia, stone working at the Martin Justice site was not an important activity. This explanation would suggest that stone tool manufacture, use, and discard are not always important activities at substantially occupied sites, where a broad range of activities are expected to occur. This potential explanation is important because it questions the usefulness of lithic remains as indicators of site function and occupation intensity.

(2) Stone working occurred at a substantial level at this site but the evidence for this has since been removed. This second explanation suggests that the Martin Justice site was somehow depleted of more intensive stone-working evidence. Considering the topographic location of this site, it is entirely possible that the majority of the waste generated may have been removed (culturally or by erosion, or both) to secondary or tertiary deposits (following Schiffer 1983, 1985). If the inhabitants of this site practiced site maintenance, it is not unlikely that most of the larger lithic debitage (artifacts) would have been removed from the living space, dumped elsewhere, such as into the creek. Erosion is an unlikely explanation because larger debris is expected to remain in place.

(3) The Martin Justice inhabitants used a late lithic reduction juncture. The resulting lithic assemblage fits the profile for what might be expected from a late reduction juncture. The third explanation suggests that the lithic assemblage generated at the Martin Justice site is a product of a late reduction juncture. As presented earlier, reduction junctures (as a reflection of how manufacturing

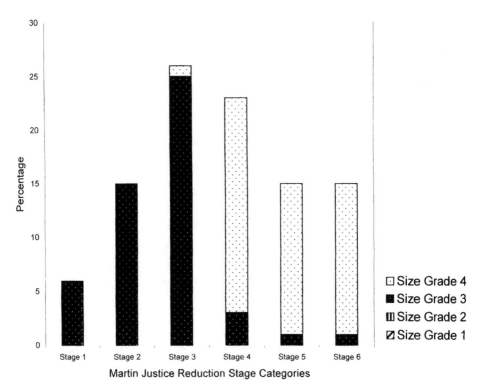

Figure 10.6. Percentage of debitage per technological class and size from the Martin Justice site (15PI92).

processes are organized) have a considerable impact on artifact quantity, size, and diversity. This is especially true for manufacturing debris size and quantity, as is supported by the experimental data presented above.

A technological analysis of the Martin Justice lithic assemblage best supports the third explanation presented here. Of the 2,723 pieces of chipped stone flaking debris recovered from the Martin Justice site, 936 artifacts (34 percent) exhibit characteristics considered to be technologically diagnostic of reduction stages (Pecora et al. 1995). Such technological characteristics are thought to reflect how and when flakes were detached (produced) during the reduction process. The remaining 1,787 artifacts (66 percent) are biface edge preparation flakes (which could not be associated with a particular technological category), flake fragments, or shatter, which are excluded from further discussion. Technologically diagnostic debris categories were adapted from definitions constructed by Crabtree (1972) and Flenniken (1987b). These include flakes detached from nonbiface stone objects, or nonbiface core reduction debris (n=62, 7 percent); percussion flakes detached to form a biface edge and rough bifaces, alternate flakes and early

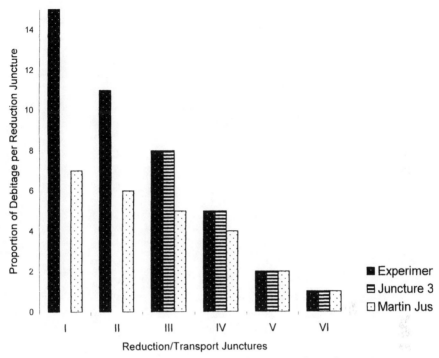

Figure 10.7. Martin Justice site debitage data transformed to reflect reduction junctures.

biface thinning flakes (n=139, 14 percent); percussion flakes detached from bifaces, or late biface thinning flakes (n=239, 26 percent); early pressure flakes detached from bifaces (n=217, 23 percent); and late pressure flakes detached from bifaces (n=279, 30 percent). These data represent reduction stages illustrated in Figure 10.6. It is clear that the technologically diagnostic debris from this site is dominated by the later reduction stages. Stages V and VI include all late pressure flakes, divided evenly between the two stages since it is difficult if not impossible to distinguish late pressure flakes from tool finishing, and pressure flakes from resharpening and rejuvenation.

The Martin Justice lithic assemblage data converted to reflect reduction juncture exhibits an interesting pattern that may be anticipated by the reduction stage data (Figure 10.7). While it is evident that the earliest stages of lithic reduction occurred at Martin Justice, such activities occurred very rarely. According to the data presented in Figure 10.7, Junctures IV–VI account for most of the debitage. Thus, compared to what might be expected from the experimental data, it is evident that the manufacturing process at Martin Justice began with the "pre-biface" form at the earliest (Juncture III), but more commonly at later biface stages (Junctures IV–VI). In other words, lithic material most frequently entered

Martin Justice in the form of biface blanks and preforms, and finished tools as illustrated in Figure 10.1. These forms were then further reduced, used, and discarded, contributing to the Martin Justice lithic assemblage.

As mentioned above, tool diversity is low in the Martin Justice assemblages. In the chipped stone assemblage, projectile points (n=47) dominate over unifacial scrapers (n=4) and a drill (n=1). This implies that the lithic production trajectory was oriented toward the production of projectile points, which might be expected where access to raw material is limited and where later reduction juncture is employed. This is supported by the presence of heavily reworked projectile points (n=35, of 46) and two scrapers that had been recycled from exhausted projectile points (Pecora et al. 1995:90). The two remaining unifaces were made from small flakes.

In sum, the Martin Justice lithic assemblage is rather sparse, consists mostly of small debris (<¼ inch, n=2,281, 84 percent of 2,723), and contains relatively low tool diversity (n=47 projectile points of 52 tools). Considering the lithic assemblage alone, this site might be thought of as a low intensity, short-term occupation. Site structure, however, indicates rather substantial occupations of various lengths during the Middle Archaic, Late Archaic, Early Woodland, late Middle Woodland, and early Late Woodland periods (Kerr and Creasman 1995). Substantial occupations are supported by feature diversity, the presence of circular structure remains, midden deposits, and one potential burial.

Although the Martin Justice assemblage may have been depleted through cultural and noncultural processes (i.e., discard and erosion), technological attributes suggest that the Martin Justice inhabitants used a late reduction juncture. As predicted earlier, and supported with experimental data, later reduction junctures result in the production of relatively low quantities of small debris. Similarly, because late reduction junctures limit lithic reduction flexibility and material availability, artifact (tool) diversity is expected to be low.

CONCLUSIONS

As a formation process, lithic tool manufacture is a fundamental source of lithic artifact variability prior to any other cultural or noncultural formation process. The understanding of how chipped stone industries were organized in terms of raw material procurement, use, and discard is essential for understanding how assemblages are formed. In this paper I have illustrated that lithic tool production can be organized into reduction junctures. Earlier reduction junctures result in the production of substantially more waste, but offer greater flexibility in the range of tools that can be produced. Later reduction junctures do just the opposite.

Of particular interest is that lithic debris patterns are the result of different reduction junctures and appear to be poor indicators of site function (or range of activities manifested at a given location). Because of this, without an understanding of assemblage formation in terms of how stone was procured and transported, lithic assemblages reflect little in terms of settlement organization and mobility. This point is fairly well supported by data collected from the Martin Justice site. Despite apparently substantial residential occupation episodes over several millennia, especially during the Middle Woodland Period, the lithic assemblage is represented by a relatively low quantity of debris and formed artifacts. In fact, only 442 pieces of debris and 76 chipped stone formed artifacts larger than ¼ inch were recovered during the entire excavation of this site. The remaining lithic assemblage consists of debris (n=2,281) smaller than ¼ inch, collected from controlled volume samples.

The technological attributes represented in this assemblage suggest that the Martin Justice inhabitants employed late reduction junctures. Based on technological attributes, it appears the lithic material was introduced to the site most frequently in the form of biface blanks, preforms, and finished tools (Junctures IV–VI). In addition, tool diversity is low, consisting mostly of projectile points. As is expected by such late reduction junctures, debris production and tool diversity is minimal.

This research is important for at least two reasons. First, archaeological surveys and other levels of investigation often rely on lithic debitage densities for site identification and evaluation. Low debitage density sites are often considered as ephemeral, short-term occupations representing minor components of more complex settlement systems. Sites like Martin Justice are frequently overlooked or ignored, despite the fact that they may represent more substantial occupations. For example, I would suggest that the Middle Woodland component of Martin Justice represents one of many Middle Woodland homesteads located in the rugged, secondary and tertiary drainageways of southeastern Kentucky. Unfortunately, such sites are poorly represented in the literature, or are at best labeled as "sparse, ephemeral lithic scatters."

A second area of research importance is that, although it was not possible to segregate reduction junctures according to temporal components from the Martin Justice assemblage, it was evident that several different (yet late) reduction junctures are represented. Though the differences in technological organization represented by these junctures are subtle, each would greatly impact artifact patterning within sites. If tool manufacturing strategies are patterned behaviors, there may be cultural (and temporal) differences in reduction junctures. If true, reduction junctures are important sources of assemblage variation that should be identified in the course of site function and larger settlement studies. More substantial replicative studies, along the lines of those presented by Jeff Flenniken (1981), are essential for such research.

ACKNOWLEDGMENTS

I would like to thank Jennifer Pederson, Jarrod Burks, Andrew Bradbury, Richard Yerkes, Jeff McKee, Kristen Gremillion, and the anonymous reviewers for their comments. I am responsible for all errors and failures. I would also like to thank Cultural Resource Analysts, Inc., Lexington, Kentucky, for providing access to data and for the support of my research.

IV

ALTERNATIVE PERSPECTIVES TO DEBITAGE VARIABILITY

11

Holmes's Principle and Beyond: The Case for Renewing Americanist Debitage Analysis

ALAN P. SULLIVAN III

Inspired largely by William H. Holmes, twentieth-century Americanist debitage studies have employed units of analysis, such as object- or stage-of-reduction based taxa or alleged diagnostic attributes that presuppose the origins of individual debitage artifacts. In addition, confirmation strategies have relied on attribute-matching or expectation-matching methods and on assertions about the meaning of inter-taxa variation to infer the origins of debitage assemblages. In this chapter, I explore the theoretical and methodological consequences of these features of conventional Americanist debitage analysis, particularly from the viewpoint of how they have constrained the development of inferences. To release the interpretive potential of debitage, I illustrate how the analysis of complete-flake relative thickness and weight may be used profitably to understand the sources of variation among lithic assemblages. The chapter concludes with some suggestions for reformulating taxa and confirmation protocols to ensure that debitage analysis contributes to the expansion of an independent analytical theory in American archaeology.

Gone are those innocent days when a few experts dominated the study of untouched lithic artifacts with positive percussion features—debitage. Most archaeologists today are familiar with "lithic" basics and routinely perform debitage analyses. Anyone who tries to keep abreast of the literature realizes, however, that new "approaches" to debitage analysis seem to emerge seasonally. Lost in the rush for analytical hegemony has been an examination of the history, theory, and method of debitage analysis itself. In this paper, I begin to rectify this situation by presenting a brief overview of the emergence of Americanist debitage analysis, by highlighting some of its historically derived and distinctive features, and by discussing some of the conceptual problems that currently afflict the study of debitage. My goal is to suggest a way to renew the study of these bothersome artifacts that clutter up our labs, repositories, and, indirectly, the literature. I offer no new approach but present instead some arguments and analyses to illustrate how the interpretive potential of debitage assemblages can be unlocked so that we may pursue the field's urgent problems.

THE EMERGENCE OF AMERICANIST DEBITAGE ANALYSIS

Nearly two decades ago, Kenneth A. Honea (1983) published an annotated bibliography of works related to lithic technology that had appeared between 1725 and 1980. Although the kinds of problems that archaeologists address with lithic assemblages have expanded somewhat since then (Shott 1994), the bibliography makes fascinating reading because it causes one to consider the theoretical and methodological challenges of inferring aspects of prehistoric lithic technology by examining variation in archaeological samples of lithic artifacts.

For instance, Honea includes two references to the writings of John Wesley Powell, the peripatetic naturalist and consummate bureaucrat (Pyne 1982; Stegner 1954), which were published in 1895. Reflecting on aspects of his widely acclaimed, heroic expeditions to the Colorado River and its canyons (Euler 1969), Major Powell remarked that tribes in central and eastern Utah had taken full advantage of lithic material outcrops there and that, consequently, "the chips of these workshops pave the valleys" (Powell 1895a:79). In his other publication for 1895, with the provocative title "Stone Art in America" (Powell 1895b), the Major contributed to the then-raging Paleolithic Debate, coincidentally assisting the cause of his good friend and colleague William Henry Holmes, by offering an explanation for why such "chips" were omnipresent continent-wide. With direct observations on assemblages from Ohio and the West, Powell asserted that "All forms of 'paleolithic' and 'neolithic' implements were found to be made at the same time and by people in the same stage of culture, adapting their work to the materials found, while the chips and rejects . . . were produced in great abundance."

William Henry Holmes's (1894, 1897) famous studies of aboriginal American lithic technology are equally edifying with regard to inferences about lithic assemblage origins (Cantwell 1980). Holmes's "implement" (i.e., tool) taxa and his concept of "stages of manufacture" seem astonishingly modern (or, perhaps, "modern" analysis is astonishingly archaic) (Ingbar et al. 1989; Shott 1996a), as is his acknowledgment of the confounding effects of equifinality on inferring the actual "progressive steps" of tool manufacture (Meltzer and Dunnell 1992:xxxii). Moreover, Holmes is responsible for introducing the key assumption—here termed Holmes's Principle—that underlies Americanist debitage studies. From the study of percussion and pressure "flakage," which "produces fragments, flakes, and chips broken from the specimens shaped and cast aside as waste," Holmes argued, "much is learned about the nature of the work done" (Holmes 1894:134).

By any measure, both Holmes and Powell were men ahead of their time and were engaged in controversies with profound consequences—in these cases, determining the antiquity and cultural attribution of stone tools in North America (Jackson and Thacker 1992; Meltzer 1985). In view of the impact of Holmes's and Powell's synergistic thinking on these matters, it is somewhat surprising to realize that "flakage" analysis was largely neglected for decades (Andrefsky, this volume). In fact, by the time archaeologists routinely began to analyze nontool lithic artifacts systematically, which seems to have occurred during the late 1950s or early 1960s, American archaeology was fatally embraced in the clutches of the late stages of the culture-history paradigm (Lyman et al. 1997). Consequently, analytical theory was dependent upon methodological and interpretive protocols inherited from American cultural anthropology (Dunnell 1982). Not unexpectedly, debitage types, like Holmes's tool types, were designed to carry meaning, that is, they were presumed to have interpretive content, although opinions differed dramatically regarding which sources of variability (Sullivan 1987) were responsible for interassemblage differences (Cross 1983).

A weighty consequence of this embryonic time in the history of Americanist debitage analysis is that variation among nontool lithic artifacts was attributable, using Holmes's Principle, to variation in the type of implement being manufactured or to its stage of manufacture (Flenniken 1984:191). So compelling was the strength of this reasoning that, as archaeologists began to explore the interpretive potential of debitage, scant attention was focused on the units of analysis themselves (Steffen et al. 1998). Debitage categories proliferated as additional aspects of artifact form, such as curvature (Andrefsky 1986), platform lipping (Crabtree 1972), and flake-scar number and pattern (Tomka 1989), were suspected of providing ever-more penetrating insights into the circumstances influencing artifact origins (Fitting 1967:240; Honea 1965:29; Jelinek 1966). Lamentably, many such ostensively defined units were not mutually exclusive, were frequently undefined (e.g., "shatter"), were based on unreliable variables (e.g., cortex percent), and incorporated attributes whose expressions are imperfectly understood (e.g., the forces and circumstances that produce platform "lipping"). Of course, these kinds of conceptual problems afflicted analytical approaches, spawned during the era of culture history, for investigating the sources of ceramic variation (Zedeño 1994) and the origins of archaeological landscapes (Wandsnider 1998), among others. Such problems, however, have become particularly entrenched and, moreover, difficult to eradicate in Americanist debitage studies (e.g., Clark 1990).

An additional difficulty is the moribund attention to confirmation, which refers to procedures for assessing the reliability of inferences (Kelley and Hanen 1988:233–256; Salmon 1973), particularly with respect to evaluating alternative or competing inferences that are supported by the same data (Connor and Simberloff 1986). Americanist debitage analyses largely have been characterized by "attribute matching" or "expectation matching" methodologies (e.g., Carr 1994). That is, inferences about an artifact's origins were based on how closely its attributes matched the criteria of an analytical taxon. Problems arose, of course, when a conflict emerged among allegedly "diagnostic" attributes. A flake may possess the characteristics of a flake of bifacial retouch, for example, but because of its problematic size be classified into a different taxon (Ahler 1989a:210).

Additionally, with the exception of refitting projects (Cahen et al. 1979), few studies have attempted to ascertain whether debitage artifacts were produced in circumstances other than those stipulated by the categories themselves (Young 1994). Exploration of hypotheses related to the origins of debitage often ceased when a match was secured between the properties of a debitage artifact and the expectations associated with a "reduction trajectory" model (Johnson 1989), for example. Such methods dramatically increase the likelihood of affirming the consequent, which is an invalid inductive argument (Salmon 1984:28), and of committing a Type II Error (failure to reject a false hypothesis) (Connor and Simberloff 1986:158). For instance, a flake expressing properties that correspond to those stipulated by the flake of bifacial retouch (FBR) taxon is often considered indicative of biface reduction or bifacial-tool manufacture. Yet, it is well known that not all flakes produced by bifacial reduction meet FBR criteria and that many flakes not produced by bifacial reduction express FBR characteristics (Andrefsky 1998:118). As noted earlier, Holmes (1897:81; see also Binford and Papworth 1963:93) acknowledged but dodged the substantial interpretive problems that arise if the same type of tool can be produced by different methods that yield different by-products (Grayson 1986).

BEYOND HOLMES'S PRINCIPLE

Contemporary Americanist debitage analyses largely reflect a mix of Holmes's Principle and the analytical theory of the culture-history paradigm (Dunnell 1986). It is generally assumed, therefore, that variation among units of debitage analysis—typological variation—can be used to infer reliably the sources of assemblage composition and variation. As Andrefsky (1998:110–126) notes, however, little overlap exists among three common typological approaches—Triple Cortex, Application Load, and Free Standing (a.k.a. the SR [Sullivan and Rozen 1985] approach)—with respect to their constituent units of analysis. Disagreement persists, as well, as to how debitage taxa variation should be interpreted

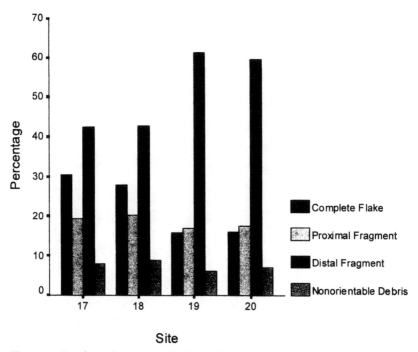

Site

Figure 11.1. Bar charts showing typological variation among four debitage categories. Note that the assemblages from Sites 17 and 18 have higher percentages of complete flakes and lower percentages of distal flake fragments than the assemblages from Sites 19 and 20. It is inferred that such patterned differences are attributable to variation in core reduction (prevalent at Sites 17 and 18) and tool manufacture (intensive at Sites 19 and 20).

(Amick and Mauldin 1989). For example, I consider the interassemblage variation in Figure 11.1 compelling evidence of differing emphases on core reduction (prevalent at Sites 17 and 18 [Sullivan 1986:55, 207]) and tool manufacture (prevalent at Sites 19 [Sullivan 1995] and 20 [Sullivan 1986:288]). These inferences are problematic, though, if one suspects that the protocols associated with the SR approach are invalid, that is, that core reduction is not implied by comparatively high frequencies of complete flakes, and that tool manufacture is not implied by comparatively high frequencies of distal fragments. Although experimentally confirmed (Geib 1992; also Kvamme 1998; but see Prentiss and Romanski 1989), these empirical generalizations between debitage taxa variation and assemblage origins inexplicably continue to attract profound skepticism (e.g., Prentiss 1998). To my knowledge, however, neither experiments (Magne and Pokotylo 1981:37) nor archaeological studies (Teltser 1991) invalidate these typologically based interpretive postulates of the SR approach.

Nonetheless, these approaches, and others as well (Bradbury and Carr 1999),

TABLE 11.1.
Comparison of Two Formulae for Computing Complete-Flake
Relative Thickness

Measurements (mm)			Relative Thickness	
Length	Width	Thickness	Formula 1	Formula 2
10	5	1	15	50
20	10	2	15	100

Formula 1: Relative Thickness = (Length + Width)/Thickness
Formula 2: Relative Thickness = (Length × Width)/Thickness

are unified by one characteristic that applies to the basic unit of observation in debitage analyses: individual debitage artifacts are ambiguous with respect to their origins. Hence, deep uncertainty exists as to whether taxa-tinkering (Prentiss 1998) can ever sustain the principal assumption in Americanist debitage analysis—variation among debitage taxa is attributable to variation in lithic artifact production (core reduction, tool manufacture, or some combination thereof).

To surmount these problems, I explore the interpretive potential of a single meaning-free (interpretation-neutral) debitage taxon—complete flake. All methods of lithic-artifact production yield complete flakes in varying quantities (Fish 1981:375). Alternatively, there is no method of lithic reduction that does not yield complete flakes. By themselves, complete flakes are thus wonderfully ambiguous with respect to the objects from which they originated (Rozen and Sullivan 1989a:179) but, as the following analyses illustrate, can be unexpectedly informative about the factors that influence debitage assemblage variability.

INVESTIGATING VARIATION IN COMPLETE FLAKE FORM

A complete flake is a debitage artifact whose length, width, and thickness can be measured accurately (Sullivan and Rozen 1985). Thus, a complete flake does not necessarily have to be entirely intact, only intact enough so that no break or flaw interferes with the measuring of form variables (Rozen and Sullivan 1989b:170). For my purposes, complete flake length is the distance between the point of impact of the detaching blow and the termination of the flaking axis; width is the distance between lateral margins measured perpendicularly at the midpoint of length; and thickness is the distance between the interior and exterior surfaces measured at the intersection of length and width (Sullivan 1995:54). These three form variables are the basis for a composite, nondimensional (i.e., it carries no

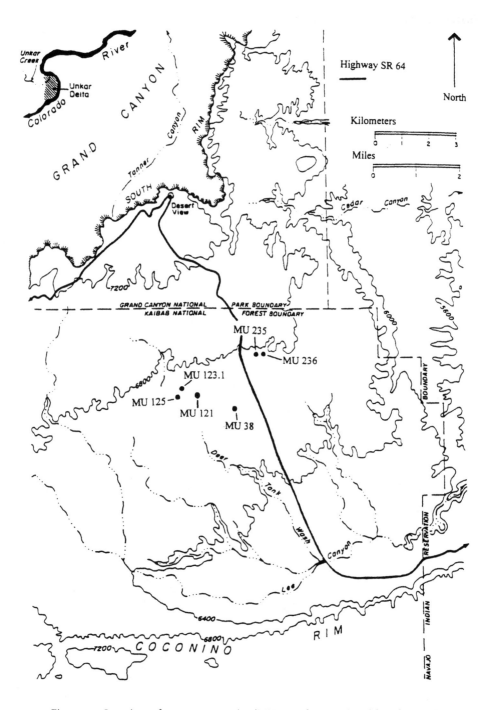

Figure 11.2. Locations of two masonry ruins (MU 38 and MU 125) and four fire-cracked rock pile sites (MU 121, MU 123.1, MU 235, and MU 236), excavated by the Upper Basin Archaeological Research Project (UBARP) in Kaibab National Forest, northern Arizona, whose lithic assemblages are the focus of this study.

TABLE 11.2.
Properties of Six Archaeological Sites in the Upper Basin, Northern Arizona

Site	Number of Structures	Number of Rooms	Date A.D.	Occupation		Accumulation History	Cultural Affiliation
				Mode	Pattern		
MU 38	1	1	1080–1120	Seasonal	Discontinuous	Metachronous	Grand Canyon Anasazi
MU 121	0	0	950–1140	Subseasonal	Continuous	Synchronous	Grand Canyon Cohonina
MU 123.1	0	0	1060–1200	Subseasonal	Discontinuous	Metachronous	Grand Canyon Anasazi
	0	0	1250–1625	Subseasonal	Discontinuous	Metachronous	Protohistoric Hopi
MU 125	2	5	1070–1080	Perennial	Continuous	Synchronous	Grand Canyon Anasazi
MU 235	0	0	900–1200	Subseasonal	Discontinuous	Metachronous	Grand Canyon Anasazi
	0	0	1300–1625	Subseasonal	Discontinuous	Metachronous	Cerbat, Protohistoric Hopi
MU 236	0	0	775–900	Subseasonal	Discontinuous	Metachronous	Grand Canyon Anasazi
	0	0	1090–1285	Subseasonal	Discontinuous	Metachronous	Grand Canyon Anasazi
	0	0	1375–1625	Subseasonal	Discontinuous	Metachronous	Protohistoric Hopi, Pai

TABLE 11.3.

Aspects of Six Lithic Assemblages from the Upper Basin, Northern Arizona

Site	Debitage[a]	Tools[a,b]		Cores[a,b]
		Unifaces	Bifaces	
MU 38	561	17	31	9
MU 121	394	2	3	2
MU 123.1	560	7	12	4
MU 125	1419	50	62	39
MU 235	5409	49	195	44
MU 236	1669	12	57	12

[a] Definitions from Rozen and Sullivan (1989a:181).

[b] Includes complete and fragmentary specimens (see Purtill 1995, appendix A).

units) variable called relative thickness (RT), which, as its name implies, measures variation in flake thickness by controlling for length and width (Sullivan and Rozen 1985:764). The basic idea is that as reduction proceeds, flakes become not only absolutely thinner but also relatively thinner as well, in comparison to length and width. Of the two common formulae for calculating relative thickness (Table 11.1), I prefer Formula 1 because, unlike Formula 2, it does not respond to variation in absolute flake size. High RT values indicate that a flake is relatively thin in view of its length and width, whereas low RT values are associated with a flake that is relatively thick in view of its length and width measurements (Rozen 1981:188; cf. Jelinek 1977:95).

To demonstrate their interpretive potential, analysis focuses on complete flakes recovered from surface and subsurface contexts at two masonry ruins (MU 38 and MU 125) and four fire-cracked rock (FCR) pile sites (MU 121, MU 123.1, MU 235, and MU 236) located in the Upper Basin near Grand Canyon National Park in northern Arizona (Figure 11.2). Inspection of Table 11.2 reveals that these six cases differ in terms of occupation mode, occupation pattern, accumulation history, and other variables. In addition, they all have large lithic assemblages (Table 11.3).

Scattergrams of complete-flake relative thickness and weight (Figure 11.3) illustrate visually that these two variables are basically uncorrelated (Table 11.4). It would be risky, consequently, to predict which assemblage arose from core reduction (intensive or otherwise), tool manufacture (unifacial, bifacial, or some mixture thereof), or various combinations of these methods of lithic artifact production (Newcomer 1971; Stahle and Dunn 1982). Hence, it can only be assumed that these debitage assemblages are mixed with regards to the by-products of objects that sustained lithic reduction (flakes, cores, or tools).

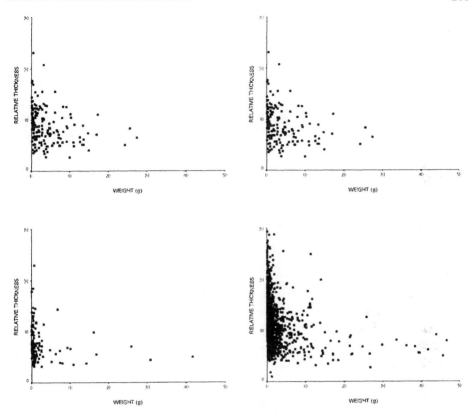

Figure 11.3. Scattergrams of weight (g) and relative thickness values for complete flakes recovered from a single-room masonry ruin (MU 38, top left), an artifact scatter associated with a small fire-cracked rock pile (MU 121, bottom left), a five-room masonry ruin (MU 125, top right), and an artifact scatter associated with a large fire-cracked rock pile (MU 235, bottom right).

EXPLORING THE ORIGINS OF MIXED DEBITAGE ASSEMBLAGES

Whether mean or median values for relative thickness and weight are considered (Figure 11.4), the six samples of complete flakes are patterned with respect to site type and site size. MU 235 and MU 236, two large, multicomponent, FCR piles that are not associated with masonry structures, form a tight cluster based on high relative thickness and low weight values for complete flakes. These two assemblages are both characterized by low percentages of complete flakes and high biface/uniface ratios (Table 11.5). A second, looser cluster is represented by MU 121, a single-component FCR-pile site not associated with a structure, and MU 123.1, a dual-component FCR-pile site (one of its occupational episodes may have been affiliated with a nearby one-room structure, MU 123.0). Both of these

TABLE 11.4.

Sample Sizes (n), Pearson Correlation Coefficients (r), R^2 Values, and
Significance Levels (p) for Relative Thickness for Six Complete-Flake Assemblages from the Upper Basin, Northern Arizona

Site	n	r	r^2	p
MU 38	164	−.267	.071	.001
MU 121	116	−.156	.024	.094
MU 123.1	199	−.149	.022	.036
MU 125	521	−.245	.060	.000
MU 235	1070	−.221	.049	.000
MU 236	380	−.175	.031	.001

relatively small FCR-pile sites, notably, have high debitage/tool ratios in common, although that of MU 121 seems abnormally high (Table 11.5). Finally, the complete-flake assemblages from MU 38 and MU 125, both of which are masonry ruins unaccompanied by FCR-piles, differ dramatically from the two aforementioned clusters and, to a large extent, from each other. Yet, they both have low and virtually identical debitage/tool ratios and coefficient of variation values for weight (Table 11.5).

These interassemblage patterns are attributable to the vastly different constraints conferred on the design and use of lithic-technological systems by variation in production and consumption activities (Sullivan 1996). For example, the FCR-pile sites were used episodically but intensively for very short periods of time when edible resources were processed in bulk quantities for transport and storage elsewhere; no evidence of ceramic production has been found at these sites (Sullivan 1992). In the absence of storage facilities and architecture, therefore, complete-flake assemblage properties of FCR-pile sites vary depending on the intensity of biface manufacture (high at MU 235 and MU 236, low at MU 121 and MU 123.1) and the extent of FCR-pile reuse (frequent at MU 235 and MU 236, infrequent at MU 123.1, nonexistent at MU 121) (Sullivan et al. 2001). In contrast, with evidence of ceramic production (Becher and Sullivan 1994) but not of bulk edible-resource processing (Sullivan 1997) or of intensive biface manufacture at MU 125 and MU 38 (Purtill 1995), the complete-flake assemblage properties of these two masonry ruins vary depending on mode of occupation (perennial versus seasonal, respectively) and the availability of storage facilities (present at MU 125, absent at MU 38).

Taking these results a step further, I would argue that, no matter how many times the FCR-pile sites had been re-used (Cook 1995), it is unlikely that their complete-flake assemblages ever would have assumed the characteristics of those of either architectural site. Similarly, unless MU 38 or MU 125 had experienced

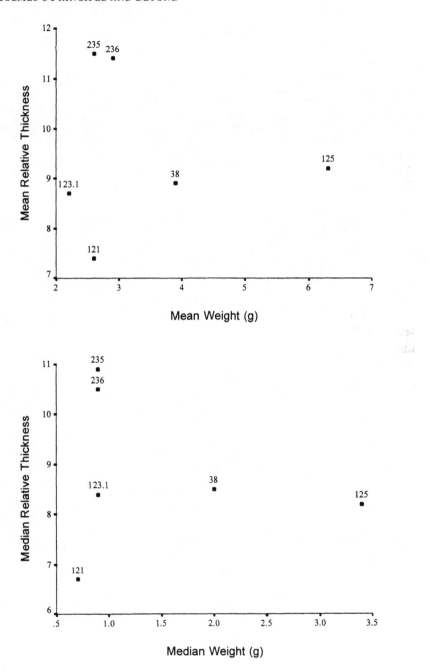

Figure 11.4. Scattergrams of mean (top) and median (bottom) weight (g) and relative thickness values for complete flakes recovered from a single-room masonry ruin (MU 38), a five-room masonry ruin (MU 125), and artifact scatters associated with four fire-cracked rock piles (MU 121, MU 123.1, MU 235, and MU 236).

TABLE 11.5.
Descriptive Statistics of Complete Flake Relative Thickness and Weight, Debitage/Tool Ratios, and Biface/Uniface Ratios for Six Upper Basin Sites

| Site | Complete Flakes | | Relative Thickness | | | | Weight (g) | | | | Debitage/ Tool Ratio | Biface–Uniface Ratio |
	N	Percent	Mean	Standard Deviation	Median	C.V.*	Mean	Standard Deviation	Median	C.V.*		
MU 38	164	29.2	8.9	3.5	8.5	.39	3.9	4.9	2.0	1.26	11.7	1.8
MU 121	116	29.4	7.4	3.5	6.7	.47	2.6	5.9	0.7	2.27	78.8	1.5
MU 123.1	199	35.5	8.7	3.3	8.4	.38	2.2	4.2	0.9	1.91	29.5	1.7
MU 125	521	36.7	9.2	3.7	8.2	.40	6.3	7.6	3.4	1.21	12.7	1.2
MU 235	1071	19.8	11.5	4.6	10.9	.40	2.6	6.2	0.9	2.39	22.2	4.0
MU 236	380	22.8	11.4	5.2	10.5	.46	2.9	8.6	0.9	2.97	24.2	4.8

* C.V. = Coefficient of Variation (Standard Deviation/Mean).

profound changes in their occupation modes, the intensity of biface manufacture at both sites would have remained stable and, hence, their complete-flake assemblage characteristics would not have migrated statistically toward those of the FCR-pile sites. The spatial mosaic created by such technological dependencies, moreover, was a principal contributing factor in the evolution of the Upper Basin's distinctive archaeological landscape (Mink 1999).

RENEWAL IN AMERICANIST DEBITAGE ANALYSIS

In surveying the contemporary panorama of Americanist debitage studies, the concept of "renewal," which has several meanings, seems pertinent. One meaning, of course, is "to start over." In debitage studies, starting over is indeed germane with respect to eradicating the inappropriate use of biological nomenclature, such as dorsal and ventral for exterior and interior surfaces, respectively (Jelinek et al. 1971). Another meaning of renewal is "to take up again," which seems particularly appropriate because the time is long overdue to scrutinize the usefulness of the widely held assumption that analytical units should carry meaning. This atavistic protocol in debitage analysis reflects American archaeology's historic intellectual and pedagogical dependence on sociocultural anthropology for analytical theory—there is some question as to whether this dependence has served us well, if at all (Dunnell 1982; Lamberg-Karlovsky 1970). One point of this chapter, which I hope persists as long as the controversy over the SR approach, is that strong inferences about debitage assemblage origins can be developed with interpretation-neutral units of analysis. It seems reasonable to add, furthermore, that, freed of the burden of ruminating endlessly about the meaning of intertaxa variation, debitage analysts can focus their attention on investigating how different causal factors (Salmon 1992), such as technological dependencies, promote variability in lithic assemblages.

The challenge of renewal for Americanist debitage analysis may not be to debate, often hotly and contemptuously, the merits of different approaches or typologies—an activity that has proven largely unproductive in advancing the field. Perhaps traces of prehistoric economic organization, technological organization, adaptive diversity, and social agency do indeed lurk in samples of debitage, but we will never know until we have parsed the ambiguity that arises from the equifinal results of lithic artifact production. Like those relentlessly aggressive, welt-producing piñon gnats that appear in biblical quantities during late spring and early summer on the Colorado Plateaus, debitage analysis is something to be endured so that we can investigate vital problems in American archaeology, such as understanding the formation of regional archaeological records (Powell 1895a; Sullivan 1998). Moving beyond Holmes's Principle is a positive step in that direction.

ACKNOWLEDGMENTS

I thank Michael J. Shott (University of Northern Iowa) for his lengthy and penetrating comments that caused me to sharpen my arguments and to broaden their
scope. Archaeological investigations of the sites mentioned in this chapter were
made possible by grants from the USDA Forest Service (Kaibab National Forest),
the Center for Field Research, the C. P. Taft Memorial Fund (University of
Cincinnati), McMicken College of Arts and Sciences (University of Cincinnati),
and the University Research Council (University of Cincinnati). I appreciate especially the support and encouragement of Dr. John A. Hanson (Kaibab National
Forest) and Dr. Robert C. Euler (SWCA, Inc.).

12

The Effect of Processing Requirements on Reduction Strategies and Tool Form: A New Perspective

Steve A. Tomka

It has been commonly assumed that among highly mobile hunter-gatherers, toolkit portability rather than the functional requirements of the tools condition their form and the reduction strategies employed in their manufacture. This paper diverges from this premise by suggesting that tool form is conditioned by processing requirements, rather than mobility. To support this proposition, it is argued that formal tools are more effective than expedient variants in the performance of lengthy and repetitive tasks. In addition, examples are brought forth to show that the design of toolkits among some late prehistoric, protohistoric, and historic Southern Plains groups may not have been related to either decreased mobility or raw material availability. Finally, diachronic trends in tool forms and reduction strategies are discussed, using central and west-central Texas examples, to suggest that variability in the relative proportions of expedient and formal tools and bifacial and multidirectional core reduction strategies may be related to changes in processing requirements.

Various researchers have noted a general decrease in biface manufacture debitage and bifacial tool use between the Archaic and late prehistoric periods throughout North America (Hester and Shafer 1975; Koldehoff 1987:155; Odell 1985; Sullivan and Rozen 1985). A similar trend also appears to characterize the manufacture and use of formal unifacial tool classes such as end and side scrapers. As systematic bifacial and core reduction strategies (e.g., biface and blade manufacture) declined, they were replaced by multidirectional core reduction and the use of expedient tool forms.

In an influential paper, Parry and Kelly attribute this technological shift to decreased mobility (1987:285; see Abbott et al. 1998 for an ultimate explanation).

They argue that expedient tools and toolkits have some significant advantages over formal ones, including sharp working edges, low manufacture costs, and lesser dependence on high-quality raw materials. In contrast, bifacial tools are more expensive to make, use, and maintain, and are less effective. Nonetheless, because they are multifunctional and multiuse implements, bifacial tools have overall lower transportation costs compared to toolkits composed of expedient tools. Therefore, highly mobile hunter-gatherers should be equipped with toolkits dominated by bifacial tools, particularly in raw-material–poor regions. Concomitantly, bifacial reduction debitage should be most common on sites occupied within a mobile land-use strategy, while debitage derived from multidirectional core reduction should reflect increasingly more sedentary strategies.

Underlying Parry and Kelly's (1987) explanation is the assumption that highly mobile land-use strategies favor formal and/or standardized toolkits produced through standardized reduction strategies, while semisedentary and sedentary strategies encourage the use of expedient tools produced through less systematic means. The belief that mobility and not the functional requirements of a tool condition its form also is echoed by Nelson (1991:76), and many others believe that toolkit portability is either the single most or one of the most significant concerns for mobile hunter-gatherers (Gould 1969:76; Shott 1986:19–34; Torrence 1983:13).

Based on the examination of the Late Archaic through the protohistoric archaeological record in central Texas and selected portions of the Southern Plains, I propose an alternative explanation for the diachronic variability in tool forms and raw material reduction strategies. I suggest that the choice between formalized and expedient tools is conditioned by processing requirements rather than degree of mobility. Specifically, tool-using contexts that require the processing of large quantities of resources in a relatively limited time favor the use of formal hafted tools. On the other hand, tasks and/or activities that involve the processing of smaller quantities of resources favor the utilization of expedient technologies. This is not to say that other factors, such as reliability and maintainability, are not important considerations in tool design (Bleed 1986).

Often, one of the goals of debitage analysis is to reconstruct reduction strategies, define the products of manufacture processes, and relate the two to broad systemic factors conditioning land-use strategies. While this discussion concerns primarily finished tools, it is clear that defining the factors that condition tool forms and reduction strategies has significant implications for understanding variability in debitage assemblages. Understanding the factors that condition tool forms and reduction strategies may improve our abilities to relate variability in debitage characteristics to broad systemic factors.

Definition of Terms and Concepts

Because of the lack of standardization in lithic analyses and terminology, it is necessary to define a number of terms. In using the terms *expedient* and *formal* to describe tool form, I place the emphasis strictly on the amount of effort invested in tool manufacture because I believe that tool manufacture/replacement costs are significant components of lithic technological organization (Bousman 1993). I also agree with Shott (1996b), however, that the differences between expedient and formal tools might simply be viewed as differences in maximum (i.e., built-in) utility.

Overall, I see tool manufacture as varying along a continuum from expedient to formal. Expedient tools represent flake/blade blanks that have not been altered prior to their use in the performance of a task (e.g., the use of an unmodified flake as a knife or scraper). The working edges of expedient tools exhibit only use-related wear such as damage scars, but often this wear may be limited to polish and striations. In contrast, formal tools are made by sufficient flaking to significantly change the outline of the original blank (i.e., a bifacial knife, a unifacial end scraper with retouch along the distal end and margins).

Standardization refers to similarity in manufacture techniques and processes as well as formal similarity in the final products. The assembly of the components of a composite tool often requires matching the stem portion of a working bit to a preexisting haft. Fitting the working bit to the haft often requires some formal modifications of the haft element. However, a high degree of formal standardization during blank manufacture can significantly reduce the need for significant shaping. Therefore, a blank can often be hafted following minimal retouch if the specimen is produced close to its finished form (see unifacially worked macroblade knives/projectile points from Colha [Hester 1994]). Similarly, the selection of flakes of suitable shapes and sizes also can reduce or potentially even eliminate the need for blank shaping prior to hafting and use (see Odell and Cowan 1986; L. Patterson 1992).

The existence of minimally retouched hafted implements is mentioned on the one hand to prevent the a priori association of these tool forms with the lack of hafting. Having said this, however, it is important to note that it is the formal standardization of these blanks, achieved through manufacture or selection, that facilitates or allows their hafting. The diachronic trends noted earlier refer to the increase in the proportion of expedient unstandardized tool forms, at the expense of formal and/or standardized variants, over time.

The following discussion contrasts the use of expedient tools representing unmodified flakes and formal tools representing heavily retouched blanks. I include both unifacial and bifacial tools in the discussion and contend that a broad range of functional types have both formal and expedient variants including scrapers, knives, perforators, gravers, and projectile points (see Yerkes [1987] for examples of expedient scrapers, knives, etc., and Odell and Cowan [1986] for expedient projectile points).

Two critical assumptions are made at the outset of the paper. I accept that some expedient tools consisting of standardized flake blanks may be hafted. However, I also assume that most formal tools tend to be hafted and therefore, at the minimum, their proximal ends (e.g., haft elements) are standardized in shape and form (e.g., shape, length, width, thickness) to fit specific hafts. Although an exhaustive review of the ethnographic literature on the use of stone tools would be necessary to support this contention, such an analysis is beyond the scope of this paper. The review of a few site reports summarizing archaeological finds from shelters and caves from the American Southwest and the lower Pecos region of Texas records a number of hafted knives and large bifaces but no hafted expedient tools. Ethnohistoric accounts and ethnographic studies among historic and modern stone-tool–using groups also suggest that hafted tools tend to fall in the formal category (Gallagher 1977; Niessen and Dittemore 1974) while most unretouched tool forms are not hafted.

Even if this relationship is correct, it raises yet another assumption underlying the paper. Given the nature of broad theoretical statement, by necessity, the argument put forth here also assumes to some degree that similarity in form reflects similarity in function. For instance, it is assumed that distally beveled unifaces that are similar in morphology and working edge attributes to Southern Plains hide scrapers were probably employed as scrapers even if the materials being worked may not have been hides. These assumptions are made due to the breadth of the theoretical statements, but the author is aware of their pitfalls (Siegel 1984) and the need to empirically document these patterns on individual assemblages.

PROCESSING REQUIREMENTS AND TOOL FORM

To support the proposition that tool form is conditioned by processing requirements rather than mobility, first I argue for the comparative effectiveness and superiority of formal hafted tools over expedient tools in the performance of lengthy and repetitive tasks. Next, I present a number of examples of semisedentary late prehistoric and protohistoric groups with toolkits containing formalized hafted tools. Thirdly, I cite an example of late prehistoric lithic assemblages rich in formal tools in a lithic raw-material–rich region. And finally, I discuss the trends in Late Archaic to historic period tool use and reduction strategies showing that a strong relationship exists between the intensification of hunting and the increase of specialized processing tools in many assemblages.

Over the years, archaeologists have butchered many deer and other medium and small mammalian species using replicas of prehistoric tools (Brose 1975; Elliott and Anderson 1974; Hester et al. 1976; Jones 1980; Odell 1980; L. Patterson 1975). In general, these experiments indicate that unmodified flake edges are more effective than bifacially retouched edges particularly in cutting muscle (Walker 1978:7110). Furthermore, based on Odell's (1980) review of butchering experiments with stone tools, a deer or other medium-sized ungulate, can be butchered with as few as one to three flakes (Odell 1980:43; see also L. Patterson 1975).

While these types of replication studies are indispensable for understanding the formation of use wear, they cannot accurately replicate the full range of prehistoric tool-using circumstances. With few exceptions (Callahan 1994; Frison 1978:316–328), the butchering experiments involve a single or a small number of prey, or small to medium-sized animals. These limitations imposed by prey quantity or size leave one to question the applicability of the results to prehistoric contexts involving the processing of a large number of prey or large-bodied prey.

Despite the advantages mentioned above, expedient tools appear to have two major draw backs: (1) loss of tool control at higher pressures, and (2) discomfort and strain on fingers holding and manipulating the tools. Butchering experiments indicate that tool users experience some loss of control of small expedient and bifacial cutting tools (Elliott and Anderson 1974:5; Jobson 1986:15, 17; Jones 1980:153–165; Odell 1980:41) under increased pressure. The path of movement of small tools held between the fingers is more difficult to control when pressure is increased upon small tools. For instance, Walker and Long (1977:613) report that the most comfortable load at which hand-held obsidian flake tools could be used was 4 kg, and as the load increased to the maximum of 7 kg the tool became very difficult to control (Walker and Long 1977:611). An additional aspect common to most butchering experiments is the discomfort experienced in using a small expedient tool held between the fingers in the performance of lengthy tasks. The discomfort stems from the fact that much of the work of holding and stabilizing the tool is done by a range of very small muscles that are not normally relied upon to this degree.

In contrast to the majority of the expedient tools used in both cutting and scraping tasks, unifacial and bifacial hafted tools can be used at higher load rates and with greater control than their expedient counterparts (see also Keeley 1982:799; Morrow 1996:586). Walker and Long (1977:613) report that hafted cutting tools (e.g., knives) could be used at loads of up to 12 kg without affecting tool control. Morrow (1996:587) found that hafted tools reduced the energy expended in cutting by 50 percent compared to unhafted equivalents. Finally, hafted tools provide easier ways of grasping a tool and therefore transfer the strain from the smaller muscle groups of the fingers to the larger and stronger muscles of the forearm, thereby reducing strain and fatigue.

Although some prehistoric hafting methods may not have been as secure as modern rivets (see Keeley 1982:799–800), hafted tools should still have allowed greater loading stresses to be exerted compared to the use of expedient flakes. It is likely that higher loading translates into higher cutting/scraping power. This relationship suggests that the greater efficiency of expedient flake tools may be overcome by the use of unifacial and bifacial hafted functional equivalents. I suggest that the greater leverage and reduced hand strain provided by hafted tools translate into significant advantages when the tool user is faced with the performance of lengthy or physically stressful tasks such as the butchering of large-bodied animals (Callahan 1994:38–39) or a large number of butchering events. Therefore, while a small number of flakes may be adequate to butcher a single deer or a small number of animals, the processing of large numbers of medium- to large-bodied prey, such as antelope, deer or bison, would be approached not with expedient tools but with formal bifacially flaked hafted tools. Similarly, while a rabbit or deer hide may be processed without difficulty using an unmodified flake, the processing of a mountain of bison hides obtained during the summer bison hunt would scarcely be possible without hafted end scrapers.

Parry and Kelly (1987:297) and Parry (1987:226–227) suggest that under decreased or restricted residential mobility, manifested in less frequent and shorter distance moves, tool assemblages should be dominated by expedient tools. They cite late prehistoric Puebloan and Plains village groups as examples of the shift from formal to expedient technologies through time (Parry and Kelly 1987:289–293). A look at the toolkits of some late prehistoric Puebloan and Plains village horticultural groups involved in seasonal bison hunting provides further insights into the factors that may condition their technological organization.

Studies of stable-isotope ratios of the Pecos Pueblo population (Spielmann et al. 1990) indicate that bison was part of the diet throughout the occupation. Kidder's (1932:196) description of the presence of bison bone throughout the middens also supports this interpretation. Mule deer, rabbits, and antelope made up the majority of the bone from the middens, and bison bone was relatively common only in the upper deposits dating to the later part of the fifteenth century. Bison bone was also present in the middens of Gran Quivira National Monument in New Mexico, a second border pueblo excavated by Hayes et al. (1981). Here, bison bones appear to increase in frequency in the late fifteenth- and early sixteenth-century middens (Spielmann et al. 1990:748). Spielmann et al. (1990) imply that much, if not all, of the bison at a number of the eastern-border trading pueblos derived from trade with hunter-gatherers of the Plains.

Excavations at both pueblos recovered a number of formal tools most likely associated with bison processing. For instance, in addition to a number of leaf-shaped bifacially flaked specimens that may have been knives, Kidder (1932:15, 30–34) recovered 50 two-edge beveled and 10 four-edge beveled knives. With the

Figure 12.1. Selected Late Prehistoric and protohistoric complexes and sites mentioned in the text.

possible exception of two specimens, the majority is made of Alibates dolomite. All but two of the specimens come from deposits dating between A.D. 1600 and 1750 (Glaze V and later). Based on the quantity of Alibates debitage found throughout the middens, Kidder (1932:31) believed that even though the knives were of imported raw material, they were made at Pecos Pueblo. In addition to the beveled knives, Kidder (1932:15) also recovered 185 "snub-nosed" end scrapers also made of Alibates dolomite. These specimens are heavily retouched (e.g., formal) and standardized (e.g., probably hafted), and are morphologically identical to hafted end scrapers used by Plains bison-hunting groups.

Excavations of Mound 7 at Gran Quivira yielded similar lithic assemblages.

Hayes et al. (1981:110) identified 54 projectile points that may have also been hafted knives, 7 specialized knives, and 110 unnotched knives. A number of these unnotched knives are described as having long, lanceolate to subrectangular blades with beveled edges (Hayes et al. 1981:110). In addition to the knives, 374 end scrapers also were recovered (Hayes et al. 1981:111). Unfortunately, the report lacks the necessary use-wear analysis, so it is not known at present how many of these "unhafted" unifaces were actually hafted.

Puebloan peoples who moved onto the western edge of the Llano Estacado between the thirteenth and sixteenth centuries also relied on agriculture and seasonal bison hunting (Collins 1968; Pearce 1936). Lithic assemblages from Ochoa phase sites on the Llano Estacado contain arrow points, formal beveled knives, and moderate to large numbers of end scrapers (Salt Cedar site, Collins 1968). Late prehistoric (A.D. 700–1540) Plains village groups of the Canadian and North Canadian river drainages in western Oklahoma and the Texas Panhandle (Figure 12.1) had a similar mixed economy (Brooks 1989; Habicht-Mauche et al. 1994; Lintz 1984). Beginning with the Custer phase (A.D. 800–1100; Hofman 1984a) and on to the Washita River (A.D. 1150–1375; Bell 1984a) and Antelope Creek phases (A.D. 1200–1450; Lintz 1984), the typical toolkits of horticultural groups consisted of a range of triangular arrow points, beveled knives, and standardized hafted end scrapers (41OL2, Landergin Mesa, Lintz 1990, appendix B; 41Hc-6, the Roper site, Lintz n.d.; Ruin No. 55, Studer 1934).

Even more significantly, some elements of this formal toolkit persist into the protohistoric period. For instance, Wheeler Complex (A.D. 1500–1750; Little Deer site, Hofman 1984b), protohistoric Wichita (A.D. 1600–1800; Bryson-Paddock, Deer Creek, Longest site, Bell 1984b; Pearson site, Duffield and Jelks 1961; Stansbury site, Stephenson 1970), and protohistoric Caddoan sites (A.D. 1700–1750; Womack site, Harris et al. 1965; Gilbert site, Jelks 1967) contain formal end scrapers and beveled knives. Similar tool assemblages are present in sixteenth- and seventeenth-century Great Bend Aspect sites in Kansas (Tobias, Thompson, Eliott, Larcom-Haggard; Wedel 1970:210–320, 347–351, 571–589). The number of beveled knives is relatively small and may in part reflect their replacement by metal trade knives. However, end scrapers persist in moderate to large numbers.

In addition to the composition of the toolkit, what makes some of these protohistoric examples even more interesting is that these formal tool forms persisted even after these groups began using horses. Horses were in use by A.D. 1650 and were being traded together with European items by people of the Edwards Complex (A.D. 1500–1650; Hofman 1984b:353). Since the availability of horses most likely resulted in a significant reduction in transportation costs (cf. Hanson 1986), one would expect toolkits to be dominated by expedient forms as pre-

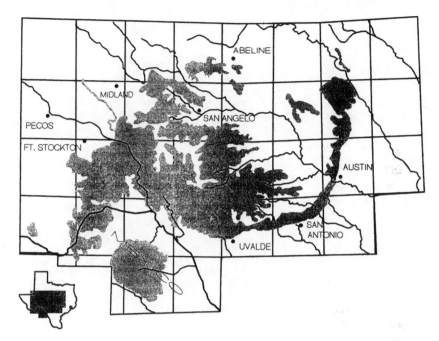

Figure 12.2. Distribution of chert-bearing Edwards Group Members in Texas and northern Mexico (after Fredersick et al. 1994).

dicted by Parry and Kelly (1987). Yet, formal cutting tools and scrapers continue in use well after horses became widely available on the Southern Plains.

Parry and Kelly (1987:300–301) suggest that one of the key factors conditioning the formal properties of tools is raw material availability. They assume that since bifacial tools represent a strategy employed to reduce transportation costs, highly mobile groups, in regions where raw materials are abundant, should use few formal tools. Given this assumption, one way to examine the nature of the interrelationship between mobility and tool form is to investigate the tool forms used by mobile hunter-gathers in raw-material–rich areas.

Many of the Edwards Group formations of the Edwards Plateau are rich in high-quality raw materials (Figure 12.2; Frederick et al. 1994, fig. 1.1; Frederick and Ringstaff 1994, fig. 6.2). In addition, both the eastern and southeastern margins of the plateau and the neighboring Blackland Prairie have been prime bison-hunting country during the later half of the late prehistoric and through the historic periods. The Toyah phase (Prewitt 1981) is one of the well-studied late prehistoric archaeological entities most directly associated with bison hunting. Although disagreements persist as to the origins of the adaptation and its appearance in Texas (Black 1986, 1989; Prewitt 1985), it is clear that between A.D.

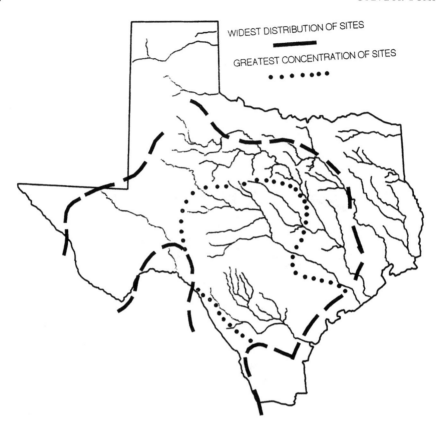

Figure 12.3. Distribution of Toyah components and sites in Texas (after Johnson 1994).

1200–1300 and 1500–1650 (Johnson 1994) human populations were engaged in bison hunting, at least on a seasonal basis, throughout much of the Southern Plains and the Blackland Prairie (Figure 12.3; Johnson 1994, fig. 105). Much of the range of Toyah groups overlaps the raw-material–rich Edwards Plateau region. Therefore, one would expect that Toyah toolkits would be dominated by expedient rather than formal tool forms.

An examination of Toyah components from various sites in central Texas and the surrounding regions (41TG91 [Creel 1990], 41KM16 [Johnson 1994], 41HI1 [Jelks 1962], 41TV42 [Suhm 1957], 41JW8 [Black 1986; Hester 1977], 41LK201 [Highley 1986], 41SS20 [Green and Hester 1973 (1975)], 41BX528 [Ahr 1998], 41TG346 [Quigg and Peck 1995], 41HY209T [Ricklis 1994], 41FY74 [Skelton 1977]) indicates that, although not the predominant tool types, most Toyah components consistently contain two- or four-beveled knives and end scrapers. These tools have for a long time been recognized as diagnostic elements of bison-hunting complexes throughout the Southern Plains and central Texas (Creel 1991; Poteet 1938). Although few of the beveled knives have been subjected to extensive use-wear analysis, the limited data available indicate that at least two-beveled knives were hafted (Shaller et al. 1997). The selected four-beveled knives examined by this author also show haft wear. My microscopic examination of a large number of "snub-nosed" end scrapers also indicates that Toyah period end scrapers were hafted. Examples of historic period Plains hide scraper hafts support this observation (Metcalf 1970; Wedel 1970). The abundance of these formal tool types in Toyah phase sites in raw-material–rich central Texas again suggests that factors other than raw material availability are responsible for the proportions of expedient and formal tools in these toolkits.

Finally, reconstructions of subsistence practices during the Late Archaic and the late prehistoric indicate that hunter-gatherer groups were, to a greater or lesser extent, engaged in bison procurement during portions of both periods. During the late Holocene, bison were present in central Texas at two times: (1) 2000 B.C.–A.D. 200 during the Late Archaic (Collins 1995, fig. 2; Dillehay 1974), and (2) A.D. 1250–1550 during the later part of the late prehistoric (Collins 1995, fig. 2; Dillehay 1974). Baugh's analysis suggests that at least in western Oklahoma bison also may have been present between A.D. 800 and 1300 but perhaps in smaller numbers (Baugh 1986).

I have already described the emphasis of Toyah hunter-gatherers on bison hunting during the later part of the late prehistoric period. During the Late Archaic, bison hunting appears to have flourished particularly between 1000 B.C. and A.D. 100. Archaeological sites containing Marcos, Montell, and Castroville projectile points, as well as Ensor, Ellis, Frio, and Fairland types (Turner and Hester 1993) commonly contain bison bones in addition to the bones of medium-sized ungulates. As in the case of the late prehistoric Toyah phase tool assemblages, two tool forms are consistently present in deposits containing these point types, bifacial knives and end scrapers. Unlike at any preceding time in prehistory, the manufacture and use of specialized hafted bifacial knives appears to have flourished during the Late Archaic. A number of specialized bifacial knives make their appearance including corner-tang knives, "short-stemmed" knives, and San Gabriel bifaces.

Corner-tang bifaces tend to occur in sites with Castroville, Marcos, Montell, Ensor, and Frio points (Saner and Tomka 1998) and have been recovered in burial contexts in association with Marcos points (Hall 1981; Mitchell et al. 1984). In central Texas they are found throughout the raw-material–rich Edwards Plateau and along the Blackland Prairie (Figure 12.4). Their distribution extends outside of Texas and tends to follow the Central Plains region (Patterson 1937:38). Edwards Plateau specimens examined by the author clearly retain

Figure 12.4. Distribution of corner-tang knives (adapted from J. T. Patterson 1936, fig. 3, 1937:38).

haft wear, sometimes in combination with probable mastic residue (Saner and Tomka 1998).

A second bifacial knife that tends to occur in Late Archaic sites is a large triangular biface with a short stem (Hester 1995; Hester and Green 1972). As in the case of the corner-tang knives, wear analysis of these specimens shows that they were used as hafted knives (Hester and Green 1972:345). These hafted knives, and other large, well made, and very thin triangular bifaces are consistently found in Late Archaic components (Hester 1995). Although the triangular unstemmed specimens may represent "trade blanks" (Hester and Barber 1990), some of the specimens exhibit considerable use wear, such as the heavily edge-polished specimen recovered from a Late Archaic burial in Wilson County, Texas (Labadie 1988). Although use-wear analyses of these specimens have not been performed, the degree of wear exhibited by many of these triangular specimens would have developed only if these knives were hafted while in use. Finally, while these specimens are found primarily in south and south-central Texas, an additional triangular form, the San Gabriel biface (Prewitt 1982), was common in central Texas during the Late Archaic. These triangular, well-thinned bifaces occur in association with Late Archaic Ensor points.

The bifacial knives and the hafted end scrapers mentioned above are associated with periods of bison presence in central Texas. However, the composition of historic period Caddoan tool assemblages from northeast Texas supports the contention that the manufacture and use of bifacial hafted knives and formal end scrapers is not restricted to bison exploitation but is related more broadly to increased processing requirements. Red River Caddoan tribes began participating in the French Louisiana fur trade in the early eighteenth century. By the mid-eighteenth century Caddoan involvement in the fur trade was well established. In 1744, for instance, a total of 100,000 deer skins were shipped to France from New Orleans, a large proportion of them obtained from Red River Caddoan groups (Perttula 1994:76). Deer were hunted by solitary stalking and group surrounds (Swanton 1942). The bow and arrow was the preferred hunting weapon until about 1700. Guns were adopted in the early eighteenth century and trade goods such as powder and shot, axes, and knives became widely traded to Caddoan groups after 1740 (Perttula 1994:87). Although trade goods changed the material culture of these Caddoan groups, they also allowed them greater involvement in the fur trade (Perttula 1994:44). This greater involvement led to increased processing requirements. Although metal knives already were replacing specialized stone knives, hafted stone end scrapers continued to be used long after. For instance, excavations at the Womack site, occupied by Caddoan-speaking groups around 1700–1720, yielded six four-beveled knives and a total of 620 snub-nosed end scrapers (Harris et al. 1965). The Gilbert site, occupied circa 1750, yielded a similar assemblage composed of 27 knives and 418 end scrapers (Allen et al. 1967:197–206). White tail deer dominated the faunal assemblage at the site (minimum number of individuals = 127), with only 4 bison identified (Lorrain 1967: 225–248).

The lithic assemblages of protohistoric Caddoan groups involved in the eighteenth-century fur trade contrast significantly with other contemporaneous and earlier Caddoan groups that did not participate in the fur trade. In addition, they also contrast with the tool assemblages of early Late Archaic deer hunting groups from throughout Texas. The primary difference between the fur trading and other contemporaneous and preceding deer hunting groups is in the large number of scrapers in general, and end scrapers in particular.

Figure 12.5 presents a generalized reconstruction of trends in tool use and reduction strategies from the Late Archaic to the historic period in central and west-central Texas. Only a small number of isolated components exist from these periods, and few of these have been reported in detail and analyzed in a comparable manner. It is necessary to emphasize that these trends represent generalized *reconstruction* based on a limited number of residential camp assemblages and

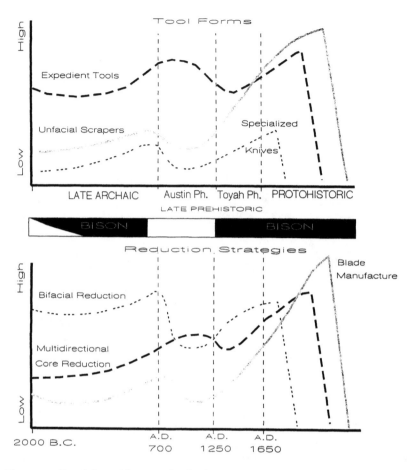

Figure 12.5. Trends in tool forms and reduction strategies in central and west-central Texas.

that variability in the composition of assemblages from other site types and even within the camp sites reviewed does exist.

Nonetheless, based on the patchy information available, it appears that the use of expedient tools increased throughout the sequence, peaking in the historic period. In general, the use of specialized bifacial cutting tools and end scrapers was low at the initiation of the Late Archaic but increased steadily throughout the period, peaking near its end. Thereafter, the use of these specialized tools appears to have decreased in the early late prehistoric Austin phase, only to be followed by a second increase into the historic period. The use of specialized cutting tools dropped rapidly as metal knives were replacing them, while the use of end scrapers continued to rise.

Biface manufacture flakes dominate debitage assemblages from the early portion of the Late Archaic period yet, as noted above, specialized bifacial knives are lacking in these assemblages. Although manufacture-failed bifaces are common in early Late Archaic assemblages, they are the products of making medium to large projectile points from nodules and large flake blanks. The proportion of biface manufacture debitage increases during the later portion of the Late Archaic as specialized bifacial knives are added to assemblages and both large (Marshall, Marcos, Castroville) and small (Ensor, Ellis, Frio, Fairland) projectile points continue to be bifacially made. The manufacture of these smaller projectile point types allows for a greater reliance on medium-sized flake blanks and brings about an increase in core reduction. The further decrease in point sizes with the advent of the bow and arrow allows an even greater reliance on core reduction for point blank manufacture. This trend is further magnified by the decrease in specialized knife manufacture—during the Austin phase—that led to a decrease in the availability of flakes of suitable size for expedient tools. The increase in specialized bifacial knife manufacture in the later part of the late prehistoric increased the proportion of biface manufacture debitage in these assemblages. However, the replacement of these large bifacial tools by Euroamerican metal variants significantly reduced both the actual and archaeological visibility of biface reduction in historic assemblages. Blade and blade-like flake manufacture, using unidirectional and opposed bidirectional core reduction paralleled the use of end scrapers through time.

These trends indicate that variability in biface and core reduction debitage seems to have originated from two sources: actual differences in the manufacture of formal bifacial and expedient tools through time, and differences in the archaeological visibility of the two reduction strategies. The differences in the archaeological visibility of the two reduction strategies were, in turn, conditioned by variability in artifact categories being manufactured and debitage recovery techniques.

SUMMARY AND CONCLUSION

In this paper, I argue that formal hafted tools used in cutting and scraping activities have significant advantages compared to their expedient counterparts. These advantages, consisting primarily of greater leverage during use and reduced hand strain, provide significant advantages to the tool user, particularly in the performance of lengthy and strenuous tasks. Therefore, the relative proportions of expedient versus formal and standardized tool forms, and in particular specialized cutting and scraping tools, in prehistoric assemblages should reflect the intensity of processing requirements associated with hunted resources. I also suggested that the use of bifacial reduction strategies does not necessarily contrast with the practice of multidirectional core reduction because each reduction strategy can provide blanks for both tool forms. Although variability in the use of the two reduction strategies does exist through time, in part, it seems to be related to the size of the tools being manufactured versus the size of the blanks employed.

These interpretations are in strong contrast to the general perspective that tool form is primarily conditioned by mobility. To support the processing requirement alternative, I, too, rely on a number of examples of highly mobile faunal procurement strategies. The procurement of bison and deer from the Late Archaic to the historic period was surely and by necessity a mobile undertaking. Therefore, since most instances of formal knives and end scrapers cited above occur in association with bison and deer hunting, one may conclude that these examples do not contradict the explanations offered by Parry and Kelly's (1987) model. However, the procurement of these species would have involved some degree of mobility throughout prehistory and therefore we should have high proportions of formal specialized cutting and scraping tools throughout prehistory. Yet, as I suggested, significant changes can be noted in the proportion of formal to expedient tools particularly from the Late Archaic to the historic period. In this paper, I suggest that these changes in tool forms reflect responses to differences in resource processing requirements rather than mobility.

The thrust of these arguments is similar to that advanced by Hard et al. (1996) regarding changes in ground stone tool morphology (i.e., increased mano grinding surface area) accompanying increased maize dependence in the American Southwest. These arguments also echo Hayden and Gargett's (1988) explanation for the occurrence of tool specialization during the European Upper Paleolithic and Mesolithic periods. Based on design theory and industrial manufacturing principles, they argue that as the intensity of production tasks increases there is an increasing likelihood that tool specialization will take place (Hayden and Gargett 1988:14–17).

Using this processing-intensity perspective, it is possible to suggest that the proximate cause of the diachronic trends noted by Parry and Kelly (1987) and others may have been something other than increased sedentism. Instead, the pattern may reflect a decreased reliance on the procurement of large quantities of hunted resources over a short time. That is, the gradual decrease in formal tools in some archaeological assemblages, and the concomitant changes in reduction strategies, may reflect a shift to the procurement of smaller quantities of hunted resources that could be processed with expedient tools. Similarly, the correlation with the onset of agriculture noted by Parry and Kelly (1987), and also emphasized by Abbott et al. (1998), may be a significant factor but only to the degree that agricultural production, without trade and interregional exchange ties, may have reduced the need to produce large surpluses of meat. Therefore, hunting patterns may have shifted away from the procurement of large quantities of surplus to smaller quantities of meat on a steady basis. In contrast, assemblages containing moderate to large proportions of formal tools may reflect the procurement of large quantities of resources either over an extended or within a limited period. Using the same interpretive framework, the assemblages of hunter-gatherers living in highly seasonal environments should be characterized by high proportions of formal tools in response to increased processing requirements associated with bulk resource procurement. Therefore, such tool assemblages should be both highly reliable, as predicted by Bleed (1986) and Bamforth and Bleed (1997), as well as formal in manufacture and specialized in function (Hayden and Gargett 1988) to increase their effectiveness.

ACKNOWLEDGMENTS

I want to express my gratitude to Thomas R. Hester, Michael B. Collins, Timothy R. Perttula, Mike Quigg, Chris Lintz, and Robert J. Hard for allowing me to test these ideas on them, and for the reference materials they have provided or pointed me towards. I would also like to express my appreciation to George Odell and Michael Shott for their careful reviews of the paper and the insightful comments they provided. Similar gratitude is owed to an anonymous reviewer whose comments also have benefited the paper. Finally, I would like to thank Bill Andrefsky for inviting me to participate in the 1999 SAA symposium and for encouraging me to hammer a seemingly square peg into a round hole.

References Cited

Abbott, A. L., R. D. Leonard, and G. T. Jones
1998   Explaining the Change from Biface to Flake Technology: A Selectionist Applica-
        tion. In *Darwinian Archaeologies*, edited by H. Donald, G. Maschner, and
        S. Shennan, pp. 33–42. Plenum Press, New York.

Ackerman, R. E.
1996a   Ilnuk Site. In *American Beginnings: The Prehistory and Paleoecology of Beringia*,
        edited by F. H. West, pp. 464–469. University of Chicago Press, Chicago, Illinois.
1996b   Lime Hills, Cave 1. In *American Beginnings: The Prehistory and Paleoecology of
        Beringia*, edited by F. H. West, pp. 470–478. University of Chicago Press,
        Chicago, Illinois.

Adams, T., G. Bronitsky, and T. Cinadr
1974   Excavation Report, Room 246. Ms. on file, Arizona State Museum, Tucson.

Ahler, S. A.
1976   Mass Analysis of Flaking Debris. Ms. in possession of author.
1989a   Experimental Knapping with KRF and Midcontinent Cherts: Overview and Ap-
        plication. In *Experiments in Lithic Technology*, edited by D. S. Amick and R. P.
        Mauldin, pp. 199–234. BAR International Series 528. British Archaeological Re-
        ports, Oxford, UK.
1989b   Mass Analysis of Flaking Debris: Studying the Forest Rather Than the Trees. In
        Alternative Approaches to Lithic Analysis, edited by D. O. Henry and G. H. Odell,
        pp. 85–118. Archaeological Papers of the American Anthropological Association
        No. 1.

Ahler, S. A., and J. VanNess
1985   Temporal Change in Knife River Flint Reduction Strategies. In *Lithic Resource
        Procurement: Proceedings from the Second Conference on Prehistoric Chert Ex-
        ploitation*, edited by S. C. Vehik, pp. 183–198. Center for Archaeological Investi-
        gations, Occasional Papers 4. Southern Illinois University, Carbondale.

Ahr, S. W.
1998   Ramifications of Late Holocene Hide Processing Geographies along the Lower
        Medina River, Texas. Unpublished Master's Thesis, Texas A&M University, Col-
        lege Station.

Aldenderfer, M. S.
1989   The Archaic Period in the South-Central Andes. *Journal of World Prehistory*
        3:117–158.
1998   *Montane Foragers: Asana and the South-Central Andean Archaic.* University of
        Iowa, Iowa City.

Alexander, D.
1992   A Reconstruction of Prehistoric Land Use in the Mid-Fraser River Area Based on

Ethnographic Data. In *A Complex Culture of the British Columbia Plateau,* edited by Brian Hayden, pp. 47–98. University of British Columbia Press, Vancouver.

Allen, G. L. Jr., P. Allen, J. Cochran, L. F. Duffield, R. E. Forrester Jr., E. D. Helm, I. R. Lobdell, D. Lubell, R. E. Padgett, and R. L. Tapscott

1967   Stone Tools. *In* The Gilbert Site: A Norteño Focus Site in Northeastern Texas, edited by E. B. Jelks. *Bulletin of the Texas Archeological Society* 37:191–211.

Amick, D. S., and R. P. Mauldin

1989   Comments on Sullivan and Rozen's "Debitage Analysis and Archaeological Interpretation." *American Antiquity* 54:166–168.

1997   Effects of Raw Material on Flake Breakage Patterns. *Lithic Technology* 22:18–32.

Amick, D. S., and R. P. Mauldin (editors)

1989   *Experiments in Lithic Technology.* BAR International Series 528. British Archaeological Reports, Oxford, UK.

Amick, D. S., R. P. Mauldin, and S. A. Tomka

1988   An Evaluation of Debitage Produced by Experimental Bifacial Core Reduction of a Georgetown Chert Nodule. *Lithic Technology* 17:26–36.

Ammerman, A. J.

1979   A Study of Obsidian Exchange Networks in Calabria. *World Archaeology* 19:95–110.

Ammerman, A. J., and W. Andrefsky Jr.

1982   Reduction Sequences and the Exchange of Obsidian in Neolithic Calabria. In *Contexts for Prehistoric Exchange,* edited by J. Ericson and T. Earle, pp. 149–172. Academic Press, New York.

Anderson, D. D.

1970   Microblade Traditions in Northwestern Alaska. *Arctic Anthropology* 7:2–16.

1984   Prehistory of North Alaska. In *Handbook of North American Indians,* vol. 5, *Arctic,* edited by D. Damas, pp. 81–93. Smithsonian Institution, Washington, D.C.

Andrefsky Jr., W.

1986   A Consideration of Blade and Flake Curvature. *Lithic Technology* 15:48–54.

1987   Diffusion and Innovation from the Perspective of Wedge Shaped Cores in Alaska and Japan. In *The Organization of Core Technology,* edited by J. K. Johnson and C. A. Morrow, pp. 13–44. Westview Press, Boulder, Colorado.

1991   Inferring Trends in Prehistoric Settlement Behavior from Lithic Production Technology in the Southern Plains. *North American Archaeologist* 12:129–144.

1994a   Raw-Material Availability and the Organization of Technology. *American Antiquity* 59:21–34.

1994b   The Geological Occurrence of Lithic Material and Stone Tool Production Strategies. *Geoarchaeology* 9:345–362.

1995   Cascade Phase Lithic Technology: An Example for the Lower Snake River. *North American Archaeologist* 16:95–115.

1998   *Lithics: Macroscopic Approaches to Analysis.* Cambridge University Press, Cambridge, UK.

Andrefsky Jr., W., E. G. Wilmerding, and S. R. Samuels

1994   *Archaeological Testing at Three Sites along the North Umpqua Drainage, Douglas County, Oregon.* Center for Northwest Anthropology, Project Report No. 23. Washington State University, Pullman.

Arnold, J. E.

1987   Technology and Economy: Microblade Core Production from the Channel Islands. In *The Organization of Core Technology*, edited by J. K. Johnson and C. A. Morrow, pp. 207–238. Westview Press, Boulder, Colorado.

Austin, R. J.

1998 Technological Characterization of Lithic Waste-Flake Assemblages: Multivariate Analysis of Experimental and Archaeological Data. Unpublished ms. in possession of author.

Bamforth, D. B.

1986 Technological Efficiency and Tool Curation. *American Antiquity* 43:38–50.

Bamforth, D. B., and P. Bleed

1997 Technology, Flaked Stone Technology, and Risk. In *Rediscovering Darwin: Evolutionary Theory in Archaeological Explanation,* edited by C. M. Barton and G. A. Clark, pp. 109–140. Archaeological Papers of the American Anthropological Association No. 7. Arlington, Virginia.

Bar-Yosef, O., and S. L. Kuhn

1999 The Big Deal about Blades: Laminar Technologies and Human Evolution. *American Anthropologist* 101:322–338.

Baugh, S. T.

1986 Late Prehistoric Bison Distributions in Oklahoma. In *Current Trends in Southern Plains Archaeology,* edited by T. G. Baugh, pp. 31–114. Plains Anthropologist. Memoir 21, pt. 2.

Baumler, M. F., and C. E. Downum

1989 Between Micro and Macro: A Study in the Interpretation of Small-Sized Lithic Debitage. In *Experiments in Lithic Technology,* edited by D. S. Amick and R. P. Mauldin, pp. 101–116. BAR International Series 528. British Archaeological Reports, Oxford, UK.

Becher, M. E., and A. P. Sullivan III

1994 Kayenta Anasazi Ceramic Production. *Pottery Southwest* 21:1–4.

Beck, C., and G. T. Jones

1989 Bias and Archaeological Classification. *American Antiquity* 54:224–262.

Bell, R. E.

1984a The Plains Villagers: The Washita River. In *Prehistory of Oklahoma,* edited by R. E. Bell, pp. 307–324. Academic Press, New York.

1984b Protohistoric Wichita. In *Prehistory of Oklahoma,* edited by R. E. Bell, pp. 363–378. Academic Press, New York.

Bielwaski, E.

1988 Paleoeskimo Variability: The Early Arctic Small Tool Tradition in the Canadian Arctic. *American Antiquity* 53:52–74.

Binford, L. R.

1973 Interassemblage Variability: The Mousterian and the "Functional" Argument. In *The Explanations of Culture Change: Models in Prehistory,* edited by C. Renfrew, pp. 227–253. Duckworth, London.

1977 Forty-Seven Trips. In *Contributions to Anthropology: The Interior Peoples of Northern Alaska,* edited by E. S. Hall Jr., pp. 299–351. National Museum of Man Mercury Series, Archaeological Survey of Canada Paper No. 49. National Museums of Canada, Ottawa.

1978a *Nunamuit Ethnoarchaeology.* Academic Press, New York.

1978b Dimensional Analysis of Behavior and Site Structure: Learning From an Eskimo Hunting Stand. *American Antiquity* 43(3):330–361.

1979   Organization and Formation Processes: Looking at Curated Technologies. *Journal of Anthropological Research* 35:255–273.

1980   Willow Smoke and Dog's Tails: Hunter-Gatherer Settlement Systems and Archaeological Site Formation. *American Antiquity* 45:4–20.

1981   *Bones: Ancient Men and Modern Myths.* Academic Press, New York.

1983   *In Pursuit of the Past.* Thames and Hudson, London.

Binford, L. R., and M. L. Papworth

1963   The Eastport Site, Antrim County, Michigan. In *Miscellaneous Studies in Typology and Classification,* edited by A. M. White, L. R. Binford, and M. L. Papworth, pp. 71–123. Anthropological Papers No. 19. Museum of Anthropology, University of Michigan, Ann Arbor.

Bird, J.

1943   Excavations in Northern Chile. *Anthropological Papers of the American Museum of Natural History* 38(4):171–318.

Black, S. L.

1986   *The Clemente and Herminia Hinojosa Site, 41JW8: A Toyah Horizon Campsite in Southern Texas.* Center for Archeological Research, Special Report 18. The University of Texas at San Antonio.

1989   South Texas Plains. In *From the Gulf to the Rio Grande: Human Adaptation in Central, South and Lower Pecos Texas,* by T. R. Hester, S. L. Black, D. G. Steele, B. W. Olive, A. A. Fox, K. Reinhard, and L. C. Bement, pp. 39–62. Research Series No. 33. Arkansas Archeological Survey, Fayetteville.

Bleed, P.

1986   The Optimal Design of Hunting Weapons: Maintainability and Reliability. *American Antiquity* 51:737–747.

1996   Risk and Cost in Japanese Microcore Technology. *Lithic Technology* 21:95–107.

Boldurian, A. T.

1991   Folsom Mobility and Organization of Lithic Technology: A View from Blackwater Draw, New Mexico. *Plains Anthropologist* 36:281–296.

Bousman, C. B.

1993   Hunter-Gatherer Adaptations, Economic Risk, and Tool Design. *Lithic Technology* 18:59–86.

Bradbury, A. P.

1995   *A National Register Evaluation of Twelve Sites in Adair, Cumberland and Metcalfe Counties, Kentucky.* Contract Publication Series 95-69. Cultural Resource Analysts, Inc., Lexington.

1996   Chipped Stone Flake Debris: Beyond the Examination of Lithic Reduction Activities. Paper presented at the 1996 Kentucky Academy of Sciences Meeting, Frankfort, Kentucky.

1998   The Examination of Lithic Artifacts from an Early Archaic Assemblage: Strengthening Inferences through Multiple Lines of Evidence. *Midcontinental Journal of Archaeology* 23:263–288.

Bradbury, A. P., and P. J. Carr

1995   Flake Typologies and Alternative Approaches: An Experimental Assessment. *Lithic Technology* 20:100–115.

1999   Examining Stage and Continuum Models of Flake Debris Analysis: An Experimental Approach. *Journal of Archaeological Science* 26:105–116.

Bradbury, A. P., and J. D. Franklin

2000   Material Variability, Package Size and Mass Analysis. *Lithic Technology* 25:42–58.

Bradley, B. A.
1978   Hard Hammer—Soft Hammer: An Alternative Explanation. *Flintknapper's Exchange* 1(2):8–10.

Brooks, R. L.
1989   Village Farming Societies. In *From Clovis to Comanchero: Archeological Overview of the Southern Great Plains,* by J. L. Hofman, R. L. Brooks, J. S. Hays, D. W. Owsley, R. L. Jantz, M. K. Marks, and M. H. Manheim, pp. 71–90. Research Series 35. Arkansas Archeological Survey, Fayetteville.

Brose, D. S.
1975   Functional Analysis of Stone Tools: A Cautionary Note on the Role of Animal Fats. *American Antiquity* 40:86–94.

Bunzel, R. L.
1932a   *Introduction to Zuñi Ceremonialism.* 47th Annual Report of the Bureau of American Ethnology. U.S. Government Printing Office, Washington, D.C.

1932b   *Zuñi Katsinas: An Analytical Study.* 47th Annual Report of the Bureau of American Ethnology. U.S. Government Printing Office, Washington, D.C.

Cahen, D., L. H. Keeley, and F. L. Van Noten
1979   Stone Tools, Toolkits, and Human Behavior in Prehistory. *Current Anthropology* 20:661–683.

Callahan, E.
1979   The Basics of Biface Knapping in the Eastern Fluted Point Tradition: A Manual for Flintknappers and Lithic Analysts. *Archaeology of Eastern North America* 7:1–180.

1994   A Mammoth Undertaking. *Bulletin of Primitive Technology* 1(7):23–39.

Cantwell, A.-M.
1980   New Data for Old Hypotheses: A Re-Examination of the Theories of Fowke, Holmes, and Cushing. *Lithic Technology* 9:66–67.

Carmines, E. G., and R. A. Zeller
1979   *Reliability and Validity Assessment.* Sage Publications, Beverly Hills, California.

Carr, P. J.
1994   Technological Organization and Prehistoric Hunter-Gatherer Mobility: Examination of the Hayes Site. In *The Organization of North American Prehistoric Chipped Stone Tool Technologies,* edited by P. J. Carr, pp. 35–44. Archaeological Series 7. International Monographs in Prehistory, Ann Arbor, Michigan.

1995   Hunter-Gatherers, Mobility, and Technological Organization: The Early Archaic of East Tennessee. Ph.D. dissertation, Department of Anthropology, University of Tennessee, Knoxville.

Carr, P. J. (editor)
1994   *The Organization of North American Prehistoric Chipped Stone Tool Technologies.* Archaeological Series 7. International Monographs in Prehistory, Ann Arbor, Michigan.

Cassedy, D. F.
1986   Toward a More Comparative Measure of Lithic Reduction Activity. *Journal of Middle Atlantic Archaeology* 2:23–35.

Chance, N. A.
1990   *The Iñupiat and Arctic Alaska: An Ethnography of Development.* Holt, Rinehart, and Winston, Fort Worth, Texas.

Ciolek-Torrello, R. S.
1978   A Statistical Analysis of Activity Organization at Grasshopper Pueblo, Arizona.

Unpublished Ph.D. dissertation, Department of Anthropology, University of Arizona.

1985   A Typology of Room Function at Grasshopper Pueblo, Arizona. *Journal of Field Archaeology* 12:41–63.

Clark, D. W., and A. M. Clark

1993   *Batza Tena: Trail to Obsidian.* Mercury Series Paper No. 147. Anthropological Survey of Canada, Hull, Quebec.

Clark, J. E.

1987   Politics, Prismatic Blades, and Mesoamerican Civilization. In *The Organization of Core Technology,* edited by J. K. Johnson and C. A. Morrow, pp. 259–284. Westview Press, Boulder, Colorado.

1990   Fifteen Fallacies in Lithic Workshop Interpretation: An Experimental and Ethnoarchaeological Perspective. In *Etnoarqueologia: Coloquio Bosch-Gimpera,* edited by Y. Sugiura Y. and M. Carmen Serra P., pp. 497–512. Universidad Nacional Autonoma de Mexico, Mexico City.

Collins, M. B.

1968   The Andrews Lake Locality: New Archeological Data from the Southern Llano Estacado, Texas. Unpublished Master's thesis, Department of Anthropology, The University of Texas, Austin.

1975   Lithic Technology as a Means of Processual Inference. In *Lithic Technology: Making and Using Stone Tools,* edited by E. H. Swanson, pp. 15–34. Aldine, Chicago, Illinois.

1995   Forty Years of Archeology in Central Texas. *Bulletin of the Texas Archeological Society* 66:361–400.

1999   *Clovis Blade Technology.* University of Texas Press, Austin.

Connor, E. F., and D. Simberloff

1986   Competition, Scientific Method, and Null Models in Ecology. *American Scientist* 74:155–162.

Cook, R. A.

1995   Long-Term Upland Wild-Resource Subsistence Technology: Evidence from Fire-Cracked-Rock Piles in the Upper Basin, Kaibab National Forest, Northern Arizona. Master's thesis, Department of Anthropology, University of Cincinnati, Ohio.

Cotterell, B., and J. Kamminga

1979   The Mechanics of Flaking. In *Lithic Use-Wear Analysis,* edited by B. Hayden, pp. 97–112. Academic Press, New York.

1987   The Formation of Flakes. *American Antiquity* 52:675–708.

1990   *Mechanics of Pre-Industrial Technology.* Cambridge University Press, Cambridge, UK.

Cowan, F. L.

1999   Making Sense of Flake Scatters: Lithic Technological Strategies and Mobility. *American Antiquity* 64:593–607.

Crabtree, D. E.

1967   Notes on Experiments in Flintknapping: 3, The Flintknapper's Raw Materials. *Tebiwa* 10:8–24.

1968   Mesoamerican Polyhedral Cores and Prismatic Blades. *American Antiquity* 33:446–478.

1972   *An Introduction to Flintworking.* Occasional Papers of the Idaho State Museum
        No. 28. Pocatello, Idaho.

Creel, D.
1990   *Excavations at 41TG91, Tom Green County, Texas.* Publications in Archaeology
        No. 38. Texas State Department of Highways and Public Transportation, Austin.
1991   Bison Hides in Late Prehistoric Exchange in the Southern Plains. *American An-
        tiquity* 56(1):40–49.

Cross, J. R.
1983   Twigs, Branches, Trees, and Forests: Problems of Scale in Lithic Analysis. In
        Archaeological Hammers and Theories, edited by J. A. Moore and A. S. Keene,
        pp. 87–106. Academic Press, New York.

Cushing, F. H.
1970   *My Adventures at Zuñi.* America West Publishing Company, Palo Alto, Califor-
        nia.

Darling, A.
1998   Mass Inhumations and the Execution of Witches in the American Southwest.
        American Anthropologist 100:732–752.

Daugherty, R. D., J. J. Flenniken, and J. M. Welch
1987   *A Data Recovery Study of Judd Peak Rockshelter (45-LE-222) in Lewis County,
        Washington.* Studies in Cultural Resource Management No. 8. USDA Forest
        Service, Pacific Northwest Region, Portland, Oregon.

Del Bene, T. A.
1982   *The Anangula Lithic Technological System: An Appraisal of Eastern Aleutian Tech-
        nology circa 8250–8750 B.P.* Ph.D. Dissertation, University of Connecticut. Uni-
        versity Microfilms, Ann Arbor, Michigan.
1992   Chipped Stone Technology of the Anangula Core and Blade Site, Eastern
        Aleutian Islands. *Anthropological Papers of the University of Alaska* 24:51–72.

Deutchman, H., V. Nienue, and S. Powell
1975   Room Report, Room 246. Ms. on file, Arizona State Museum, Tucson.

Dibble, H. L.
1997   Platform Variability and Flake Morphology: A Comparison of Experimental and
        Archeological Data and Implications for Interpreting Prehistoric Lithic Techno-
        logical Strategies. *Lithic Technology* 22:150–170.

Dibble, H. L., and A. Pelcin
1995   The Effect of Hammer Mass and Velocity on Flake Mass. *Journal of Archaeologi-
        cal Science* 22:429–439.

Dibble, H. L., and J. C. Whittaker
1981   New Experimental Evidence on the Relation between Percussion Flaking Flake
        Variation. *Journal of Archaeological Science* 8:283–296.

Dillehay, T. D.
1974   Late Quaternary Bison Population Changes on the Southern Plains. *Plains
        Anthropologist* 19(65):180–196.

Dobres, M.-A., and C. R. Hoffman
1999   *The Social Dynamics of Technology: Practice, Politics, and World Views.* Smithson-
        ian Institution Press, Washington, D.C.

Donnan, C. B., and M. E. Moseley
1968   The Utilization of Flakes for Cleaning Fish. *American Antiquity* 33:502–503.

Dozier, E. P.

1965   Southwestern Social Units and Archaeology. *American Antiquity* 31:38–47.

Draper, J. A., and G. A. Lothson

1990   *Test Excavations at 10NP143 and 10NP292, Lower Clearwater River, West-Central Idaho.* Center for Northwest Anthropology, Project Report No. 12. Washington State University, Pullman.

Duffield, L. F., and E. B. Jelks

1961   *The Pearson Site: A Historic Indian Site in Iron Bridge Reservoir, Rains County, Texas.* Archaeology Series No. 4. Department of Anthropology. The University of Texas, Austin.

Dumond, D. E.

1977   *The Eskimos and Aleuts.* Thames, London.

1984   Prehistory of the Bering Sea Region. In *Handbook of North American Indians,* vol. 5, *Arctic,* edited by D. Damas, pp. 94–105. Smithsonian Institution, Washington, D.C.

Dunnell, R. C.

1971   *Systematics in Prehistory.* Free Press, New York.

1982   Science, Social Science, and Common Sense: The Agonizing Dilemma of Modern Archaeology. *Journal of Anthropological Research* 38:1–25.

1986   Five Decades of American Archaeology. In *American Archaeology Past and Future,* edited by D. J. Meltzer, D. D. Fowler, and J. A. Sabloff, pp. 23–76. Smithsonian Institution Press, Washington, D.C.

Eerkens, J.

1998   Reliable and Maintainable Technologies: Artifact Standardization and the Early to Later Mesolithic Transition in Northern England. *Lithic Technology* 23:42–53.

Eggan, F.

1950   *Social Organization of the Western Pueblos.* University of Chicago Press, Chicago, Illinois.

Elliott, J., and R. Anderson

1974   A Butchering Experiment with Flaked Obsidian Tools. *Archaeology of Montana* 15(1):1–10.

Ensor, H. B., and E. Roemer Jr.

1989   Comments on Sullivan and Rozen's Debitage Analysis and Archaeological Interpretation. *American Antiquity* 54(1):175–178.

Euler, R. C.

1969   *The Archaeology of the Canyon Country.* U.S. Geological Society Professional Paper No. 670:8–20. Government Printing Office, Washington, D.C.

Finnell, T. L.

1966   Geologic Map of the Chediski Peak Quadrangle, Navajo County, Arizona. United States Geological Survey, Washington, D.C.

Fish, P. R.

1981   Beyond Tools: Middle Paleolithic Debitage Analysis and Cultural Inference. *Journal of Anthropological Research* 37:374–386.

Fisher, J. W., and H. C. Strickland

1991   Dwellings and Fireplaces: Keys to the Efe Pygmy Campsite Structure. In *Ethnoarchaeological Approaches to Mobile Campsites,* edited by C. S. Gamble and W. A. Boismier, pp. 215–236. International Monographs in Prehistory, Ethnoarchaeological Series 1, Ann Arbor, Michigan.

Fitting, J. F.

1967   *The Camp of the Careful Indian: An Upper Great Lakes Chipping Station.* Papers
        of the Michigan Academy of Science, Arts, and Letters 52: 237–242.

Fladmark, K. R.

1982   Microdebitage Analysis: Initial Considerations. *Journal of Archaeological Science*
        9:205–220.

Flenniken, J. J.

1981   *Replicative Systems Analysis: A Model Applied to the Vein Quartz Artifacts from the
        Hoko River Site.* Washington State University, Laboratory of Anthropology, Re-
        ports of Investigations No. 59. Pullman, Washington.

1984   The Past, Present, and Future of Flintknapping. *Annual Review of Anthropology*
        13:187–203. Annual Reviews, Inc., Palo Alto.

1987a   The Paleolithic Dyuktai Pressure Blade Technique of Siberia. *Arctic Anthropology*
        24:117–132.

1987b   *The Lithic Technology of the East Lake Site, Newberry Crater, Oregon.* Contract
        Publication. Lithic Analysts, Inc., Pullman, Washington.

Frederick, C. D., M. D. Glascock, H. Neff, and C. M. Stevenson

1994   *Evaluation of Chert Patination as a Dating Technique: A Case Study from Fort
        Hood, Texas.* United States Army Fort Hood, Archeological Resource Manage-
        ment Series, Research Report No. 32. Mariah and Associates, Austin.

Frederick, C. D., and C. Ringstaff

1994   Lithic Resources at Fort Hood: Further Investigations. In *Archeological Investiga-
        tions on 571 Prehistoric Sites at Fort Hood, Bell and Coryell Counties, Texas.* United
        States Army Fort Hood, Archeological Resource Management Series, Research
        Report No. 31. Mariah and Associates, Austin.

Frison, G. C.

1968   A Functional Analysis of Certain Chipped Stone Tools. *American Antiquity*
        33:149–155.

1978   *Prehistoric Hunters of the High Plains.* Academic Press, New York.

Frison, G. C., and B. A. Bradley

1980   *Folsom Tools and Technology at the Hanson Site, Wyoming.* University of New
        Mexico Press, Albuquerque.

Gallagher, J. P.

1977   Contemporary Stone Tools in Ethiopia: Implications for Archaeology. *Journal of
        Field Archaeology* 4:407–414.

Geib, P. R.

1992   Technological Inferences Based on Debitage Condition Categories. Ms. in pos-
        session of author.

Giddings, J. L.

1964   *The Archaeology of Cape Denbigh.* Brown University Press, Providence, Rhode
        Island.

1967   *Ancient Men of the Arctic.* Knopf, New York.

Giddings, J. L., and D. D. Anderson

1986   *Beach Ridge Archaeology of Cape Krusenstern: Eskimo and Pre-Eskimo Settlements
        around Kotzebue Sound, Alaska.* Publications in Archaeology No. 20, National
        Park Service, Department of the Interior, Washington, D.C.

Gilreath, A.

1984   Stages of Bifacial Manufacture: Learning from Experiments. Paper presented at the 49th Annual Meeting of the Society for American Archaeology, Portland, Oregon.

Goodard, P. E.

1904   Life and Culture of the Hupa. *University of California Publications in American Archaeology and Ethnology* 1(1):1–88.

Goodyear, A. C.

1979   *A Hypothesis for the Use of Cryptocrystalline Raw Materials among Paleoindian Groups of North America.* Research Manuscript Series 156. South Carolina Institute of Archaeology and Anthropology, University of South Carolina, Columbia.

1993   Tool Kit Entropy and Bipolar Reduction: A Study of Interassemblage Lithic Variability among Paleo-Indian Sites in the Northeastern United States. *North American Archaeologist* 14:1–23.

Gould, R. A.

1969   *Yiwara: Foragers of the Australian Desert.* Charles Scribner's Sons, New York.

Grace, R.

1996   Use-Wear Analysis: The State of the Art. *Archaeometry* 38:209–229.

Graves, M., S. Holbrook, and W. A. Longacre

1982   Aggregation and Abandonment at Grasshopper Pueblo: Evolutionary Trends in the Late Prehistory of East-Central Arizona. In *Multidisciplinary Research at Grasshopper Pueblo,* edited by W. A. Longacre, S. Holbrook, and M. Graves, pp. 110–122. Anthropological Papers of the University of Arizona No. 40. Tucson.

Grayson, D. K.

1986   Eoliths, Archaeological Ambiguity, and the Generation of "Middle-Range" Research. In *American Archaeology Past and Future,* edited by D. J. Meltzer, D. D. Fowler, and J. A. Sabloff, pp. 77–133. Smithsonian Institution Press, Washington, D.C.

Green, F. E.

1963   The Clovis Blades: An Important Addition to the Llano Complex. *American Antiquity* 29:145–165.

Green, L. M., and T. R. Hester

1973   [1975] The Finis Frost Site: A Toyah Phase Occupation in San Saba County, Central Texas. *Bulletin of the Texas Archeological Society* 44:69–88.

Griffin, J. W.

1974   *Investigations of Russel Cave.* Publications in Archeology 13. U.S. Department of Interior, National Park Service, Russel Cave National Monument, Alabama.

Gryba, E.

1988   A Stone Age Pressure Method of Folsom Fluting. *Plains Anthropologist* 33:53–66.

Guernsey, S. J., and A. V. Kidder

1921   *Basket-maker Caves of Northeastern Arizona.* Papers of the Peabody Museum of Archaeology and Ethnology, Vol. 8, No. 2. Harvard University, Cambridge.

Gunn, J.

1975   Idiosyncratic Behavior in Chipping Style: Some Hypotheses and Preliminary Analysis. In *Lithic Technology: Making and Using Stone Tools,* edited by E. Swanson, pp. 35–61. Mouton, The Hague.

1977   Idiosyncratic Chipping Style as a Demographic Indicator: A Proposed Application to the South Hills Region of Idaho and Utah. In *The Individual in Prehistory,* edited by J. Hill and J. Gunn, pp. 166–204. Academic Press, New York.

Habicht-Mauche, J. A., A. A. Levendosky, and M. J. Schoeninger

1994   Antelope Creek Phase Subsistence: The Bone Chemistry Evidence. In *Skeletal Biology in the Great Plains Migration, Warfare, Health, and Subsistence*, edited by D. W. Owsley, and R. L. Jantz, pp. 291–304. Smithsonian Institution Press, Washington, D.C.

Hall, E. S., Jr.

1975   An Archaeological Survey in Interior Northwest Alaska. *Anthropological Papers of the University of Alaska* 17:13–29.

Hall, G. D.

1981   *Allens Creek: A Study in the Cultural Prehistory of the Lower Brazos River Valley, Texas.* Texas Archeological Survey, Research Report No. 61. The University of Texas, Austin.

Hanson, J. R.

1986   Adjustment and Adaptation on the Northern Plains: The Case of Equestrianism among the Hidatsa. *Plains Anthropologist* 31(112):93–107.

Hard, R. J., R. P. Mauldin, and G. R. Raymond

1996   Mano Size, Stable Carbon Isotope Ratios, and Macrobotanical Remains as Multiple Lines of Evidence of Maize Dependence in the American Southwest. *Journal of Archaeological Method and Theory* 3:253–318.

Harris, R. K., I. M. Harris, J. C. Blaine, and J. L. Blaine

1965   A Preliminary Archeological and Documentary Study of the Womack Site, Lamar County, Texas. *Bulletin of the Texas Archeological Society* 36:287–363.

Hawley, F.

1950   Big Kivas, Little Kivas, and Moiety Houses in Historical Reconstruction. *Southwestern Journal of Anthropology* 6(3):286–302.

Hayashi, K.

1968   The Fukui Microblade Technology and Its Relationships in Northeast Asia and North America. *Arctic Anthropology* 5:128–190.

Hayden, B.

1989   From Chopper to Celt: The Evolution of Resharpening Techniques. In *Time, Energy, and Stone Tools*, edited by R. Torrence, pp. 7–16. Cambridge University Press, Cambridge, UK.

1997   *The Pithouses of Keatley Creek.* Harcourt Brace College Publishers, Fort Worth.

Hayden, B., N. Franco, and J. Spafford

1996   Evaluating Lithic Strategies and Design Criteria. In *Stone Tools: Theoretical Insights into Human Prehistory*, edited by G. H. Odell, pp. 9–50. Plenum Press, New York.

Hayden, B., and R. Gargett

1988   Rooms, Roofs, Rims, and Resources: The Anatomy of Interior Housepits. Paper presented at the annual meeting of the Canadian Archaeological Association, Whistler, British Columbia.

Hayden, B., and W. K. Hutchings

1989   Whither the Billet Flake. In *Experiments in Lithic Technology*, edited by D. S. Amick and R. P. Mauldin, pp. 235–258. BAR International Series 528. British Archaeological Reports, Oxford, UK.

Hayes, A. C., J. N. Young, and A. H. Warren

1981   *Excavations of Mound 7, Gran Quivira National Monument, New Mexico.*

National Park Service Publications in Archeology 16. U.S. Department of the Interior, Washington, D.C.

Henn, W.
1978   *Archaeology on the Alaska Peninsula: The Ugashik Drainage, 1973–1975.* Anthropological Papers of the University of Oregon No. 14.

Henry, D. O., C. V. Haynes, and B. Bradley
1976   Quantitative Variations in Flaked Stone Debitage. *Plains Anthropologist* 21:57–61.

Hester, T. R.
1977   *Archaeological Research at the Hinojosa Site (41JW8), Jim Wells County, Southern Texas.* Center for Archaeological Research. Archaeological Survey Report 42. The University of Texas at San Antonio.
1994   The Archaeological Investigations of the Colha Project, 1983 and 1984. In *Continuing Archaeology at Colha, Belize,* edited by T. R. Hester, H. J. Shaffer, and J. D. Eaton, pp. 1–9. Texas Archaeological Research Laboratory, The University of Texas, Austin.
1995   The Prehistory of South Texas. *Bulletin of the Texas Archeological Society* 66:427–460.

Hester, T. R., and B. D. Barber
1990   A Large Biface from Atascosa County, with Comments on the Function of Such Artifacts in Prehistoric South Texas. *La Tierra* 17(2):24.

Hester, T. R., and L. M. Green
1972   Functional Analysis of Large Bifaces from San Saba County, Texas. *The Texas Journal of Science* 24(3):343–350.

Hester, T. R., and H. J. Shafer
1975   An Initial Study of Blade Technology on the Central and Southern Texas Coast. *Plains Anthropologist* 20(69):175–185.

Hester, T. R., H. J. Shafer, J. D. Eaton, R. E. W. Adams, and G. Ligabue
1983   Colha's Stone Tool Industry. *Archaeology* 36:45–52.

Hester, T. R., and R. L. Spence, C. Busby, and J. Bard
1976   Butchering a Deer with Obsidian Tools. *Contributions of the University of California Archaeological Research Facility* 33:45–56.

Highley, L.
1986   *Archaeological Investigations at 41LK201, Choke Canyon Reservoir, Southern Texas.* Center for Archaeological Research, Choke Canyon Series 11. The University of Texas at San Antonio.

Hill, J. N.
1970   *Broken K Pueblo: Prehistoric Social Organization in the American Southwest.* Anthropological Papers of the University of Arizona No. 18. University of Arizona Press, Tucson.

Hiscock, P.
1994   Technological Responses to Risk in Holocene Australia. *Journal of World Prehistory* 8:267–292.

Hofman, J. L.
1984a   The Plains Villagers: The Custer Phase. In *Prehistory of Oklahoma,* edited by R. E. Bell, pp. 287–306. Academic Press, New York.
1984b   The Western Protohistoric: A Summary of the Edwards and Wheeler Complexes.

In *Prehistory of Oklahoma*, edited by R. E. Bell, pp. 347–362. Academic Press, New York.

1992   Recognition and Interpretation of Folsom Technological Variability in the Southern Plains. In *Ice Age Hunters of the Rockies,* edited by D. Stanford and J. Day, pp. 193–224. University Press of Colorado, Niwot, Colorado.

Hofman, J. L., and C. A. Morrow

1985   Chipped Stone Technologies at Twenfafel: A Multicomponent Site in Southern Illinois. In *Lithic Resource Procurement: Proceedings from the Second Conference on Prehistoric Chert Exploitation,* edited by S. C. Vehik, pp. 165–182. Center for Archaeological Investigations Occasional Paper 4. Southern Illinois University, Carbondale.

Holbrook, S. J.

1982   The Prehistoric Local Environment of Grasshopper Pueblo, Arizona. *Journal of Field Archaeology* 9:207–215.

Holmes, W. H.

1894   Natural History of Flaked Stone Implements. In *The Archaeology of William Henry Holmes,* edited by D. J. Meltzer and R. C. Dunnell (1992), pp. 120–139. Smithsonian Institution Press, Washington, D.C.

1897   Manufacture of Flaked Stone Implements. In *The Archaeology of William Henry Holmes,* edited by D. J. Meltzer and R. C. Dunnell (1992), pp. 29–79. Smithsonian Institution Press, Washington, D.C.

Honea, K.

1965   A Morphology of Scrapers and Their Methods of Production. *Southwestern Lore* 31:25–40.

1983   *Lithic Technology: An International Annotated Bibliography, 1725–1980.* Center for Archaeological Research, Lithic Technology Special Publication No. 2. University of Texas, San Antonio.

Hutchings, W. K.

1996   The Namu Obsidian Industry. In *Early Human Occupation in British Columbia,* edited by R. Carlson and L. Dalla Bona, pp. 167–176. University of British Columbia Press, Vancouver.

Ingbar, E. E.

1994   Lithic Material Selection and Technological Organization. In *The Organization of North American Chipped Stone Technologies,* edited by P. J. Carr, pp. 45–56. International Monographs in Prehistory, Ann Arbor, Michigan.

Ingbar, E. E., M. Larson, and B. Bradley

1989   A Nontypological Approach to Debitage Analysis. In *Experiments in Lithic Technology,* edited by D. S. Amick and R. P. Mauldin, pp. 117–136. BAR International Series 528. British Archaeological Reports, Oxford, UK.

Irving, W. N.

1964   Punyk Point and the Arctic Small Tool Tradition. Ph.D. dissertation, University of Wisconsin, Madison.

Isaac, B. L.

1987   Introduction. *Research in Economic Anthropology* 9:2–21.

Jackson, L. J., and P. T. Thacker

1992   Harold J. Cook and Jesse D. Figgins: A New Perspective on the Folsom Discovery.

In *Rediscovering Our Past: Essays on the History of Archaeology,* edited by J. E. Reyman, pp. 217–240. Aldershot, Avebury, UK.

Jelinek, A. J.

1966   Some Distinctive Flakes and Flake Tools from the Llano Estacado. *Papers of the Michigan Academy of Science, Arts, and Letters* 51: 399–405.

1977   A Preliminary Study of Flakes from the Tabun Cave, Mount Carmel. *Eretz-Israel* 13:87–96.

Jelinek, A. J., B. A. Bradley, and B. B. Huckell

1971   The Production of Secondary Multiple Flakes. *American Antiquity* 36:198–200.

Jelks, E. B.

1962   *The Kyle Site: A Stratified Central Texas Aspect Site in Hill County, Texas.* Archeology Series 5. Department of Anthropology, The University of Texas, Austin.

Jelks, E. B. (editor)

1967   The Gilbert Site: A Norteño Focus Site in Northeastern Texas. *Bulletin of the Texas Archeological Society* 37:1–248.

Jeske, R. J.

1989   Economies in Raw Material Use by Prehistoric Hunter-Gatherers. In *Time, Energy, and Stone Tools,* edited by R. Torrence, pp. 34–45. Cambridge University Press, Cambridge, UK.

1992   Energetic Efficiency and Lithic Technology: An Upper Mississippian Example. *American Antiquity* 57:467–481.

1996   Review of: The Organization of North American Prehistoric Stone Tool Technologies, edited by P. J. Carr. *American Antiquity* 61:175–176.

Jeske, R., and R. Lurie

1993   The Archaeological Visibility of Bipolar Technology: An Example from the Koster Site. *Midcontinental Journal of Archaeology* 18:131–160.

Jobson, R. W.

1986   Stone Tool Morphology and Rabbit Butchering. *Lithic Technology* 15:9–20.

Jochim, M. A.

1989   Optimization and Stone Tool Studies: Problems and Approaches. In *Time, Energy, and Stone Tools,* edited by R. Torrence, pp. 106–111. Cambridge University Press, Cambridge, UK.

Johnson, J. K.

1981   *Lithic Procurement and Utilization Trajectories: Analysis, Yellow Creek Nuclear Power Plant Site, Tishomingo County, Mississippi,* vol. 2. Publications in Anthropology 28. Tennessee Valley Authority, Knoxville.

1987a   Cahokia Core Technology in Mississippi: The View from the South. In *The Organization of Core Technology,* edited by J. K. Johnson and C. A. Morrow, pp. 187–206. Westview Press, Boulder, Colorado.

1987b   The Utility of Production Trajectory Modeling as a Framework for Regional Analysis. Paper presented at the Summer Institute of Lithic Analysis, University of Tulsa, Oklahoma.

1989   The Utility of Production Trajectory Modeling as a Framework for Regional Analysis. In *Alternative Approaches to Lithic Analysis,* edited by D. O. Henry and G. H. Odell, pp. 119–138. Archaeological Papers of the American Anthropological Association No. 1.

1996   Lithic Analysis and Questions of Cultural Complexity: The Maya. In *Stone Tools:*

Theoretical Insights into Human Prehistory, edited by G. H. Odell, pp. 159–179. Plenum Press, New York.

1997 Stone Tools, Politics, and the Eighteenth Century Chickasaw in Northeast Mississippi. *American Antiquity* 62:215–230.

Johnson, J. K,. and C. A. Raspet

1980 Delta Debitage. *Mississippi Archaeology* 15(1):3–11.

Johnson, L. L.

1978 A History of Flint-knapping Experimentation. *Current Anthropology* 19:337–372.

1994 *The Life and Times of Toyah Culture Folk: The Buckhollow Encampment Site 41KM16, Kimble County, Texas.* Office of the State Archeologist Report 38. Texas Department of Transportation and Texas Historical Commission, Austin.

Jones, P. R.

1980 Experimental Butchery with Modern Stone Tools and Its Relevance for Paleolithic Archaeology. *World Archaeology* 12:153–165.

Kaldahl, E. J.

2000 Late Prehistoric Technological and Social Reorganization along the Mogollon Rim, Arizona. Unpublished Ph.D. dissertation, Department of Anthropology, University of Arizona, Tucson.

Kalin, J.

1981 Stem Point Manufacture and Debitage Recovery. *Archaeology of Eastern North America* 9:134–175.

Katz, P. R.

1976 *A Technological Analysis of the Kansas City Hopewell Chipped Stone Industry.* Ph.D. dissertation, University of Kansas, Lawrence. University Microfilms, Ann Arbor, Michigan.

Keefer, D. K., S. D. deFrance, M. E. Moseley, J. B. Richardson III, D. R. Satterlee, and A. Day-Lewis

1998 Early Maritime Economy and El Niño Events at Quebrada Tacahuay, Peru. *Science* 281:1833–1835.

Keeley, L. H.

1982 Hafting and Retooling: Effects on the Archaeological Record. *American Antiquity* 47:798–809.

Kelley, J. H., and M. P. Hanen

1988 *Archaeology and the Methodology of Science.* University of New Mexico Press, Albuquerque.

Kelly, R. L.

1988 The Three Sides of a Biface. *American Antiquity* 53:717–734.

1992 Mobility/Sedentism: Concepts, Archaeological Measures, and Effects. *Annual Review of Anthropology* 21:43–66.

Kelly, R. L., and L. C. Todd

1988 Coming into the Country: Early Paleoindian Hunting and Mobility. *American Antiquity* 53:231–244.

Kerr, J. P., and S. D. Creasman.

1995 *Phase III Investigations at the Martin Justice Site (15PI92) Pike County, Kentucky.* Contract Publication Series 95-24. Cultural Resource Analysts, Inc. Lexington, Kentucky.

Kidder, A. V.

1932 *The Artifacts of Pecos.* Yale University Press, New Haven, Connecticut.

Knecht, Heidi (editor)
1997   *Projectile Technology.* Plenum Press, New York.
Kobayashi, T.
1970   Microblade Industries in the Japanese Archipelago. *Arctic Anthropology* 7:38–58.
Koldehoff, B.
1987   The Cahokia Flake Tool Industry: Socioeconomic Implications for Late Prehis-
        tory in the Central Mississippi Valley. In *The Organization of Core Technology,*
        edited by J. Johnson and C. Morrow, pp. 151–185. Westview Press, Boulder,
        Colorado.
Kuhn, S. L.
1994   A Formal Approach to the Design and Assembly of Mobile Toolkits. *American
        Antiquity* 59:426–442.
Kuijt, I., W. C. Prentiss, and D. J. Pokotylo
1995   Bipolar Reduction: An Experimental Study of Debitage Variability. *Lithic Tech-
        nology* 20:116–127.
Kunz, M. L.
1977   The Mosquito Lake Site (PSM-049). In *Pipeline Archaeology,* edited by J. P. Cook,
        pp. 747–982. Fairbanks, Alaska.
Kvamme, K. L.
1998   Spatial Structure in Mass Debitage Scatters. In *Surface Archaeology,* edited by
        A. P. Sullivan III, pp. 127–141. University of New Mexico Press, Albuquerque.
Labadie, J. H.
1988   *Archaeological Excavations at the Shrew Site, 41WN73, Wilson County, Southern
        Texas.* Contract Reports in Archaeology 2. Texas State Department of Highways
        and Public Transportation, Austin.
Lamberg-Karlovsky, C. C.
1970   Operations Problems in Archeology. In *Current Directions in Anthropology,* ed-
        ited by A. Fischer, pp. 111–114. American Anthropological Association, Washing-
        ton, D.C.
Lange, C. H.
1968   *Cochiti: A New Mexico Pueblo, Past and Present.* Southern Illinois University
        Press, Carbondale.
Larsen, H.
1968   Trail Creek: Final Report on the Excavation of Two Caves on Seward Peninsula,
        Alaska. *Acta Arctica* 15.
Larson, M., and M. Kornfeld
1997   Chipped Stone Nodules: Theory, Method, and Examples. *Lithic Technology*
        22:4–18.
Lavallée, D., M. Julien, P. Béarez, P. Usselmann, M. Gontugne, and A. Bolaños
1999   Pescadores-Recolectores Arcaicos del Extremo Sur Peruano. Excavaciones en la
        Quebrada del los Burros (Tacan, Perú). Primeros Resultados 1995–1997. *Bulletin
        de L'Institut Français d'Etudes Andines* 28(1):13–52.
LeBlanc, R.
1992   Wedges, Pieces Esquillees, Bipolar Cores, and Other Things: An Alternative to
        Shott's View of Bipolar Industries. *North American Archaeologist* 13:1–14.
Lepofsky, D., K. D. Kusmer, B. Hayden, and K. Lertzman
1996   Reconstructing Prehistoric Socioeconomies from Paleoethnobotanical and

Zooarchaeological Data: An Example from the British Columbia Plateau. *Journal of Ethnobiology* 16:31–62.

Lintz, C.

1984   *Architecture and Community Variability of the Antelope Creek Phase of Texas Panhandle.* Oklahoma Archaeological Survey. Studies in Oklahoma's Past No 14. Norman.

1990   *Landergin Mesa: The 1984 Phase II Field Results.* Report Prepared for the Texas Historical Commission, Austin.

n.d.   The Roper Site: 41Hc–6, a Prehistoric Subhomestead Site in Hutchinson County, Texas. Ms. in possession of author.

Llagostera, A.

1979a   9,700 Years of Maritime Subsistence on the Pacific: An Analysis by Means of Bioindicators in the North of Chile. *American Antiquity* 44:309–324.

1979b   Tres Dimensiones en la Conquista Prehistorica del Mar, un Aporte Para el Estudio de las Formaciones Pescadoras de la Coasta Sur Andina. *Actas del VIII Congreso de Arqueologia Chilena,* pp. 217–245.

1989   Caza y Pesca Marítima. In *Culturas de Chile, Prehistoria,* edited by J. Hidalgo, V. Schiappacasse, H. Niemeyer, C. Aldunate, and I. Solomano, pp. 57–79. Editorial Andrés Bello, Santiago, Chile.

Longacre, W. A., S. J. Holbrook, and M. W. Graves

1982   *Multidisciplinary Research at Grasshopper Pueblo, Arizona.* Anthropology Papers No. 40. University of Arizona Press, Tucson.

Longacre, W. A., and J. J. Reid

1974   The University of Arizona Archaeological Field School at Grasshopper: Eleven Years of Multidisciplinary Research and Teaching. *The Kiva* 40(1–2):3–38.

Lorrain, D.

1967   Animal Remains. In The Gilbert Site: A Norteño Focus Site in Northeastern Texas, edited by E. B. Jelks. *Bulletin of the Texas Archeological Society* 37:225–243.

Lyman, R. L., M. J. O'Brien, and R. C. Dunnell (compilers)

1997   *The Rise and Fall of Culture History.* Plenum Press, New York.

MacDonald, D. H.

1994   Lithic Technological Organization at the Hunting Camp Spring Site (35WA96), Blue Mountains, Oregon. Unpublished Master's thesis, Department of Anthropology, Washington State University, Pullman.

MacDonald, G. F.

1968   *Debert: A Paleoindian Site in Central Nova Scotia.* Anthropological Papers 16. National Museums of Canada, Ottawa.

Magne, M. P.

1983   Review of: Whitlam, R. (1980) Archaeological Investigations at Cache Creek (EeRh 3). *Canadian Journal of Archaeology* 6:229–233.

1985   *Lithics and Livelihood: Stone Tool Technologies of Central and Southern Interior British Columbia.* Mercury Series Archaeological Survey of Canada Paper No. 133. National Museum of Man, Ottawa.

1989   Lithic Reduction Stages and Assemblage Formation Processes. In *Experiments in Lithic Technology,* edited by D. S. Amick and R. P. Mauldin, pp. 15–32. BAR International Series 528. British Archaeological Reports, Oxford, UK.

1996   Comparative Analysis of Microblade Cores from Haida Gwai. In *Early Human*

Occupation in British Columbia, edited by R. L. Carlson and L. Dalla Bona, pp. 151–158. University of British Columbia Press, Vancouver.

2000	Evidence and Implications of In-Situ Development of Microblade Technology in Gwaii Haanas. Paper presented at the 33rd Annual Meetings of the Canadian Archaeological Association, Ottawa.

Magne, M. P., and D. Pokotylo

1981	A Pilot Study in Bifacial Lithic Reduction Sequences. *Lithic Technology* 10(2, 3):34–47.

Malyk-Selivanova, N.

1998	Determination of Geological Sources for Prehistoric Chert Artifacts, Northwestern Alaska. Ph.D. dissertation, Rutgers University, New Brunswick, New Jersey.

Martin, P. S., W. A. Longacre, and J. N. Hill

1967	Chapters in the Prehistory of Eastern Arizona, III. *Fieldiana: Anthropology* 57.

Mason, O. K., and C. Gerlach

1995	Chukchi Hot Spots, Paleo-Polynyas, and Caribou Crashes: Climatic and Ecological Dimensions of North Alaska Prehistory. *Arctic Anthropology* 32(1):101–130.

Mauldin, R. P.

1993	Lithics. In *The Chihuahua Lake Basin to the Chihuahua Desert: Archaeological Studies along the Arizona Interconnection Project Transmission Line Corridor,* edited by J. S. Bruder, pp. 5.29–5.97. Zuni Archaeology Program Report No. 347. Zuni Archaeology Program, Pueblo of Zuni, New Mexico.

Mauldin, R. P., and D. S. Amick

1989	Investigating Patterning in Debitage from Experimental Bifacial Core Reduction. In *Experiments in Lithic Technology,* edited by D. S. Amick and R. P. Mauldin, pp. 67–88. BAR International Series 528. British Archaeological Reports, Oxford, UK.

Meltzer, D. J.

1985	North American Archaeology and Archaeologists, 1879–1934. *American Antiquity* 50:249–260.

Meltzer, D. J., and R. C. Dunnell

1992	Introduction. In *The Archaeology of William Henry Holmes,* edited by D. J. Meltzer and R.C. Dunnell, pp.vii–1. Smithsonian Institution Press, Washington, D.C.

Metcalf, G.

1970	Some Wooden Scraper Handles from the Great Plains and the Southwest. *Plains Anthropologist* 15(47):46–53.

Mink, P. B.

1999	A GIS Analysis of Factors Affecting Archaeological Site Placement in the Upper Basin, Kaibab National Forest, Northern Arizona. Master's thesis, Department of Anthropology, University of Cincinnati, Ohio.

Mitchell, J. L., C. K. Chandler, and T. C. Kelly

1984	The Rudy Haiduk Site (41KA23): A Late Archaic Burial in Karnes County, Texas. *La Tierra* 11(2):12–39.

Mobley, C. M.

1991	*The Campus Site: A Prehistoric Camp at Fairbanks, Alaska.* University of Alaska Press, Fairbanks.

Morlan, R. E.

1970 Wedge-Shaped Core Technology in Northern North America. *Arctic Anthropology* 7:17–37.

Morrison, J. G., and W. Andrefsky Jr.

1996 *Archaeological Testing at the Leaning Oak Site (35JA349) along the North Fork of Big Butte Creek, Jackson County, Oregon.* Center for Northwest Anthropology, Project Report No. 31. Washington State University, Pullman.

Morrow, C. A.

1984 A Biface Production Model for Gravel-Based Chipped Stone Industries. *Lithic Technology* 13:20–28.

Morrow, J. E.

1996 The Organization of Early Paleoindian Lithic Technology in the Confluence Region of the Mississippi, Illinois, and Missouri Rivers. Ph.D. dissertation, Department of Anthropology, Washington University, St. Louis.

Morrow, T. A.

1996 Bigger is Better: Comments on Kuhn's Formal Approach to Mobile Tool Kits. *American Antiquity* 61:581–590.

1997 A Chip off the Old Block: Alternative Approaches to Debitage Analysis. *Lithic Technology* 22:51–69.

Mull, C. G., and K. E. Adams

1985 Introduction. In *Guidebook 7, Dalton Highway, Yukon River to Prudhoe Bay Alaska: Bedrock Geology of the Eastern Koyukuk Basin, Central Brooks Range, and Eastcentral Arctic Slope,* vol. 1, edited by C. G. Mull and K. E. Adams, pp. 1–16. Division of Geological and Geophysical Services, Fairbanks, Alaska.

Mull, C. G., and E. E. Harris

1985 Road Log from Chandalar Shelf (Mile 237.1) to Prudhoe Bay (Mile 414). In *Guidebook 7, Dalton Highway, Yukon River to PrudhoeBay Alaska: Bedrock Geology of the Eastern Koyukuk Basin, Central Brooks Range, and Eastcentral Arctic Slope,* vol. 1, edited by C. G. Mull and K. E. Adams, pp. 101–132. Division of Geological and Geophysical Services, Fairbanks, Alaska.

Muñoz, I.

1982 Las Sociedades Costeras en el Litoral de Arica durante el Período Arcaico Tardí o y sus Vinculaciones con la Costa Peruana. *Chungará* 9:124–151.

Muñoz, I., B. Arriaza, and A. Aufderheide (editors)

1993 *Acha-2 y los Orígenes del Poblamiento Humano en Arica.* Universidad de Tarapacá, Arica, Chile.

Murdoch, J.

1892 *Ethnological Results of the Point Barrow Expedition.* Smithsonian Institution Press, Washington, D.C.

Nagy, M.

1994 A Critical Review of the Pre-Dorset–Dorset Tradition. In *Threads of Arctic Prehistory: Papers in Honor of William E. Taylor, Jr.,* edited by D. Morrison and J. L. Pilon, pp. 1–14. Archaeological Survey of Canada, Mercury Series Paper 149. Canadian Museum of Civilization, Hull, Quebec.

Nance, J. D.

1987 Reliability, Validity, and Quantitative Methods in Archaeology. In *Quantitative Methods in Archaeology,* edited by M. Aldenderfer, pp. 244–293. Sage Publications, Beverly Hills, California.

Nance, J. D., and B. F. Ball

1986 No Surprises? The Reliability and Validity of Test Pit Sampling. *American Antiquity* 51(3):457–483.

Nash, S. E.

1996 Is Curation Useful or Heuristic? In *Stone Tools: Theoretical Insights into Human Prehistory,* edited by G. H. Odell, pp. 81–99. Plenum Press, New York.

Nassaney, M. S.

1996 The Role of Chipped Stone in the Political Economy of Social Ranking. In *Stone Tools: Theoretical Insights into Human Prehistory,* edited by G. H. Odell, pp. 181–224. Plenum Press, New York.

Nelson, E. E.

1899 *The Eskimo about Bering Strait.* Smithsonian Institution Press, Washington, D.C.

Nelson, M. C.

1991 The Study of Technological Organization. In *Archaeological Method and Theory,* vol. 3, edited by M. B. Schiffer, pp. 57–100. University of Arizona Press, Tucson.

Neumann, T. M., and E. Johnson

1979 Patrow Site Lithic Analysis. *Midcontinental Journal of Archaeology* 4:79–111.

Newcomer, M. H.

1971 Some Quantitative Experiments in Handaxe Manufacture. *World Archaeology* 3:84–93.

Niessen, K., and M. Dittemore

1974 Ethnographic Data and Wear Pattern Analysis: A Study of Socketed Eskimo Scrapers. *Tebiwa* 17:67–87.

Nuñez, L.

1983 Paleoindian and Archaic Cultural Periods in the Arid and Semiarid Regions of Northern Chile. In *Advances in World Archeology,* vol. 2, edited by F. Wendorf and A. Close, pp. 161–203. Academic Press, New York.

1989a Hacia la Producción de Alimentos y la Vida Sedentaria. In *Culturas de Chile, Prehistoria,* edited by J. Hidalgo, V. Schiappacasse, H. Niemeyer, C. Aldunate, and I. Solomano, pp. 81–105. Editorial Andrés Bello, Santiago, Chile.

1989b Los Primeros Pobladores. In *Culturas de Chile, Prehistoria,* edited by J. Hidalgo, V. Schiappacasse, H. Niemeyer, C. Aldunate, and I. Solomano, pp. 13–31. Editorial Andrés Bello, Santiago, Chile.

Nuñez, L., J. Varela, and R. Casamiquela

1983 *Ocupación Paleoindio en Quereo (IV región): Reconstrución Multidisciplinaria en el Terretorio Semiá Rido de Chile.* Universidad del Norte, Antofagasta, Chile.

Odell, G. H.

1980 Butchering with Stone Tools: Some Experimental Results. *Lithic Technology* 9:39–48.

1985 Archaic Lithic Assemblages from the Stratified Napoleon Hollow Site in Illinois. *Wisconsin Archaeologist* 66:327–358.

1989 Experiments in Lithic Reduction. In *Experiments in Lithic Technology,* edited by D. S. Amick and R. P. Mauldin, pp. 163–198. BAR International Series 528. British Archaeological Reports, Oxford, UK.

1994a The Role of Stone Bladelets in Middle Woodland Society. *American Antiquity* 59:102–120.

1994b Assessing Hunter-Gatherer Mobility in the Illinois Valley: Exploring Ambiguous Results. In *The Organization of North American Chipped Stone Tool Technologies,* edited by P. J. Carr, pp. 70–86. International Monographs in Prehistory Archaeological Series 7. Ann Arbor, Michigan.

1996 *Stone Tools and Mobility in the Lower Illinois Valley.* International Monographs in Prehistory Archaeological Series 10. Ann Arbor, Michigan.

Odell, G. H., and F. Cowan

1986 Experiments with Spears and Arrows on Animal Targets. *Journal of Field Archaeology* 13:195–212.

Ohel, M. Y.

1987 The Acheulian Handaxe: A Maintainable Multifunctional Tool. *Lithic Technology* 16:54–55.

Olsen, J. W.

1980 A Zooarchaeological Analysis of Vertebrate Faunal Remains from the Grasshopper Pueblo, Arizona. Unpublished Ph.D. dissertation, Department of Anthropology, University of California, Berkeley.

Olsen, S. L.

1979 A Study of Bone Artifacts from Grasshopper Pueblo, AZ P:14:1. *Kiva* 44(4):341–373.

Owen, L. R.

1988 *Blade and Microblade Technology: Selected Assemblages from the North American Arctic and the Upper Paleolithic of Southwest Germany.* BAR International Series 441. British Archaeological Reports, Oxford, UK.

Ozbun, T. L.

1987 A Technological Analysis of the Lithic Assemblage from the Buttonhole Rockshelter/Quarry Site, Northeastern New Mexico. Master's thesis, Washington State University, Pullman.

Parry, W. J.

1987 Technological Change: Temporal and Functional Variability in Chipped Stone Debitage. In *Prehistoric Stone Technology on Northern Black Mesa, Arizona,* edited by W. J. Parry and A. L. Christenson, pp. 199–256. Center for Archaeological Investigations, Occasional Paper No. 12. Southern Illinois University, Carbondale.

1994 Prismatic Blade Technologies in North America. In *The Organization of North American Prehistoric Chipped Stone Tool Technologies,* edited by P. J. Carr, pp. 87–98. International Monographs in Prehistory, Ann Arbor, Michigan.

Parry, W. J., and R. L. Kelly

1987 Expedient Core Technology and Sedentism. In *The Organization of Core Technology,* edited by J. K. Johnson and C. A. Morrow, pp. 285–304. Westview Press, Boulder, Colorado.

Parsons, E. C. (editor)

1925a *A Pueblo Indian Journal, 1920–1921.* The Collegiate Press, George Banta Publishing Company, Menasha, Wisconsin.

Parsons, E. C.

1925b *The Pueblo of Jemez.* Yale University Press, New Haven, Connecticut.

Patterson, J. T.

1936 The Corner-Tang Flint Artifacts of Texas. *The University of Texas Bulletin,* No. 3618, and *Anthropological Papers of The University of Texas* 1(4):1–54.

1937 Supplementary Notes on the Corner-Tang Artifact. *The University of Texas Bulletin,* No. 3734, and *Anthropological Papers of The University of Texas* 1(5):31–39.

Patterson, L. W.

1975   Lithic Wear Patterns in Deer Butchering. *Texas Archeology* 19(2):10–11.

1982   Replication and Classification of Large Size Lithic Debitage. *Lithic Technology*
        11:50–58.

1990   Characteristics of Bifacial-Reduction Flake-Size Distribution. *American Antiq-
        uity* 55:550–558.

1992   Current Data on Early Use of the Bow and Arrow in Southern North America.
        La Tierra 19(4):6–15.

1997   Comments on Shott's Bifacial Reduction Debitage Analysis. *Lithic Technology*
        22:184–188.

Patterson, P. E.

1977   A Lithic Reduction Sequence: A Test Case in the North Fork Reservoir Area,
        Williamson County, Texas. *Bulletin of the Texas Archaeological Society* 48:53–82.

Pearce, W. M.

1936   A Survey of the Sand-Hill Camp Sites of Lamb and Bailey Counties. *Bulletin of
        the Texas Archeological and Paleontological Society* 8:184–186.

Pecora, A. M., J. P. Kerr, and S. D. Creasman

1995   Lithic Analysis of the Martin Justice Site Assemblage. In *Phase III Investigations
        at the Martin Justice Site (15PI92) Pike County, Kentucky*. Contract Publication
        Series 95-24. Cultural Resource Analysts, Inc. Lexington, Kentucky.

Pelcin, A.

1997a   The Formation of Flakes: The Role of Platform Thickness and Exterior Platform
        Angle in the Production of Flake Initiations and Terminations. *Journal of Ar-
        chaeological Science* 24:1107–1113.

1997b   The Effect of Indentor Type on Flake Attributes: Evidence from a Controlled
        Experiment. *Journal of Archaeological Science* 24:613–621.

Perttula, T. K.

1994   French and Spanish Colonial Trade Policies and the Fur Trade among the Cad-
        doan Indians of the Trans-Mississippi South. In *The Fur Trade Revisited*, edited
        by J. S. H. Brown, W. J. Eccles, and D. P. Heldman, pp. 71–91. Michigan State Uni-
        versity Press, East Lansing.

Pope, S. T.

1974   Hunting with Ishi, the Last Yana Indian. Reprint. *Journal of California Anthropol-
        ogy* 1(2):151–173. Originally published 1923, in Pope's *Hunting with the Bow and
        Arrow*. J. H. Barry, San Francisco, California.

Poteet, S.

1938   The Occurrence and Distribution of Beveled Knives. *Bulletin of the Texas Arche-
        ological and Paleontological Society* 10:245–262.

Powell, J. W.

1895a   *The Exploration of the Colorado River and its Canyons*. Dover Publications, Inc.,
        New York.

1895b   Stone Art in America. *American Anthropologist* [o.s] 8:1–7.

Prentiss, W. C.

1993   Hunter-Gatherer Economics and the Formation of a Housepit Floor Lithic As-
        semblage. Ph.D. dissertation, Department of Archaeology, Simon Fraser Univer-
        sity, Burnaby, British Columbia.

1998   The Reliability and Validity of a Lithic Debitage Typology: Implications for
        Archeological Interpretation. *American Antiquity* 63:635–650.

2000   The Formation of Lithic Debitage and Flake Tool Assemblages in a Canadian

Plateau Winter Housepit Village: Ethnographic and Archaeological Perspectives. In *The Ancient Past of Keatley Creek*, vol. 1, *Taphonomy*, edited by Brian Hayden, pp. 213–230. Archaeology Press, Burnaby, British Columbia.

Prentiss, W. C., and E. J. Romanski

1989 Experimental Evaluation of Sullivan and Rozen's Debitage Typology. In *Experiments in Lithic Technology*, edited by D. S. Amick and R. P. Mauldin, pp. 89–100. BAR International Series 528. British Archaeological Reports, Oxford, UK.

Prentiss, W. C., E. J. Romanski, and M. L. Douthit

1988 Hunter-Gatherer Land Use and Lithic Procurement in the Central Big Horn Basin, Wyoming. *The Wyoming Archaeologist* 31(12):33–53.

Prewitt, E. R.

1981 Cultural Chronology in Central Texas. *Bulletin of the Texas Archeological Society* 52:65–89.

1982 *Archeological Investigations at the San Gabriel Reservoir District, Central Texas*, vol. 4. Archeology Program, Institute of Applied Sciences, North Texas State University, Denton.

1985 From Circleville to Toyah: Comments on Central Texas Chronology. *Bulletin of the Texas Archeological Society* 54:201–238.

Purtill, M. P.

1995 Analysis and Interpretation of Chipped-Stone Tool Assemblages from the Upper Basin, Kaibab National Forest, Northern Arizona. Master's thesis, Department of Anthropology, University of Cincinnati, Ohio.

Pyne, S. J.

1982 *Dutton's Point: An Intellectual History of the Grand Canyon.* Monograph No. 5. Grand Canyon Natural Association, Grand Canyon, Arizona.

Quigg, J. M., and J. Peck

1995 *The Rush Site (41TG346) A Stratified Late Prehistoric Locale in Tom Green County, Texas.* Technical Report No. 816C. Mariah and Associates, Inc., Austin.

Raab, L. M., R. F. Cande, and D. W. Stahle

1979 Debitage Graphs and Archaic Settlement Patterns in the Arkansas Ozarks. *Midcontinental Journal of Archaeology* 4:167–182.

Rasmussen, K. A.

1998 Exploring the Origin of Coastal Sedentism in the South-Central Andes. Unpublished Ph.D. dissertation, Department of Anthropology, University of California, Santa Barbara.

Ravines, R.

1972 Secuencia y Cambios en los Artifactos Liticos del Sur del Peru. *Revista del Museo Nacional (Lima)* 38:133–184.

Redman, K.

1998 An Experiment-Based Evaluation of the Debitage Attributes Associated with "Hard" and "Soft" Hammer Percussion. Master's thesis, Department of Anthropology, Washington State University, Pullman.

Reid, J. J.

1989 A Grasshopper Perspective on the Mogollon of the Arizona Mountains. In *Dynamics of Southwest Prehistory*, edited by L. S. Cordell and G. J. Gumerman, pp. 65–97. Smithsonian Institution Press, Washington, D.C.

Reid, J., and S. Whittlesey

1982 Households at Grasshopper Pueblo. *American Behavioral Scientist* 25(6):687–703.

1997   *The Archaeology of Ancient Arizona.* University of Arizona Press, Tucson.
Ricklis, R. A.
1994   Toyah Components: Evidence for Occupation in the Project Area during the Latter Part of the Late Prehistoric Period. In *Archaic and Late Prehistoric Human Ecology in the Middle Onion Creek Valley, Hays County, Texas,* vol. 1, *Archeological Components,* edited by R. A. Ricklis and M. B. Collins, pp. 207–316. Studies in Archeology 19. Texas Archeological Research Laboratory, University of Texas, Austin.
Root, M. J.
1992   *The Knife River Flint Quarries: The Organization of Stone Tool Production.* Ph.D. dissertation, Washington State University. University Microfilms, Ann Arbor, Michigan.
1997   Production for Exchange at the Knife River Flint Quarries, North Dakota. *Lithic Technology* 22:33–50.
Roth, B. J., and H. L. Dibble
1998   Production and Transport of Blanks and Tools at the French Middle Paleolithic Site of Combe-Capelle Bas. *American Antiquity* 63:47–62.
Rozen, K. C.
1981   Patterned Associations among Lithic Technology, Site Content, and Time: Results of the TEP St. Johns Project Lithic Analysis. In *Prehistory of the St. Johns Area, East-Central Arizona: The TEP St. Johns Project,* edited by D. A. Westfall, pp. 157–232. Arizona State Museum Archaeological Series No. 153. University of Arizona, Tucson.
Rozen, K. C., and A. P. Sullivan III
1989a   The Nature of Lithic Reduction and Lithic Analysis: Stage Typologies Revisited. *American Antiquity* 54:179–184.
1989b   Measurement, Method, and Meaning in Lithic Analysis: Problems with Amick and Mauldin's Middle-Range Approach. *American Antiquity* 54:169–175.
Rundel, P. W., M. O. Dillon, B. Palma, H. A. Mooney, S. L. Gulmon, and J. R. Ehleringer
1991   The Phytogeography and Ecology of the Coastal Atacama and Peruvian Deserts. *Aliso* 13(1):1–49.
Salmon, W. C.
1973   Confirmation. *Scientific American* 228: 75–83.
1984   *Logic.* 3d edition. Prentice-Hall, Englewood Cliffs, New Jersey.
1992   Explanation in Archaeology: An Update. In *Metaarchaeology: Reflections by Archaeologists and Philosophers,* edited by L. Embree, pp. 243–253. Kluwer Academic Publishers, Dordrecht, Netherlands.
Sanders, P. H.
1992   *Archaeological Investigations along the Pend Oreille River: Site 45PO149.* Center for Northwest Anthropology, Project Report No. 18. Washington State University, Pullman.
Sandweiss, D. H.
1992   *The Archaeology of Chincha Fishermen: Specialization and Status in Inka Peru.* Bulletin of Carnegie Museum of Natural History No. 29.
Sandweiss, D. H., J. B. Richardson III, E. J. Reitz, J. T. Hsu, and R. A. Feldman
1989   Early Maritime Adaptations in the Andes: Preliminary Studies at the Ring Site, Peru. In *Ecology, Settlement, and History in the Osmore Drainage, Peru,* edited by D. Rice, C. Stanish, and P. Scar, pp. 35–84. BAR International Series 545. British Archaeological Reports, Oxford, UK.

Sandweiss, D. H., H. McInnis, R. L. Burger, A. Cano, B. Ojeda, R. Paredes,
M. D. C. Sandweiss, and M. D. Glascock
1998   Quebrada Jaguay: Early South American Maritime Adaptations. *Science*
        281:1830–1832.

Saner Jr., B., and S. A. Tomka
1998   Unifacial Corner-Tang Artifact Report: An Investigation of an Unusual and
        Rarely Reported Lithic Tool. *La Tierra* 25(3):24–36.

Sappington, R. L.
1991   *Archaeological Investigations at the Clearwater Fish Hatchery Site (10CW4), North
        Fork of the Clearwater River, North Central Idaho.* University of Idaho Anthropo-
        logical Reports No. 91. University of Idaho, Moscow.

Sassaman, K. E.
1994a   Changing Strategies of Biface Production in the South Carolina Coastal Plain. In
        The Organization of North American Prehistoric Chipped Stone Tool Technologies,
        edited by P. J. Carr, pp. 99–117. International Monographs in Prehistory Archae-
        ological Series 7. Ann Arbor, Michigan.
1994b   Production for Exchange in the Mid-Holocene Southeast: A Savannah River
        Example. *Lithic Technology* 19(1):42–51.

Schiappacasse, V., and H. Niemeyer (editors)
1984   *Description y Analysis Interpretativo de un Sitio Arcaico Temprano en la Quebrada
        de Camarones.* Museo Nacional de Historia Natural, Universidad de Tarapacá
        Publicacion Ocasional No. 41. Arica, Chile.

Schiffer, M.
1983   Toward the Identification of Formation Processes. *American Antiquity*
        48(4):675–706.
1985   Is There a "Pompeii" Premise in Archaeology? *Journal of Anthropological
        Research* 41(1):18–41.
1988   The Structure of Archaeological Theory. *American Antiquity* 53:461–485.

Schoenberg, K. M.
1985   *The Archaeology of Kurupa Lake.* National Park Service, Research/Resources
        Management Report AR-10. Anchorage, Alaska.

Schumacher, P.
1951   Stone-Flaking of the Klamath River Yurok. In *The California Indians: A Source
        Book,* edited by R. F. Heiser and M. A. Whipple, pp. 305–307. University of Cali-
        fornia Press, Berkeley.

Shaller, R., C. Lintz, and D. W. Owsley
1997   Description and Analysis of the Keith Site Burial, 41RD52, Randall County,
        Texas. *The Steward* 4:15–29.

Shea, J. J.
1992   Lithic Microwear Analysis in Archaeology. *Evolutionary Anthropology*
        1(4):143–150.

Sheets, P. D., and G. R. Muto
1972   Pressure Blades and Total Cutting Edge: An Experiment in Lithic Technology.
        Science 175:632–634.

Shelley, P. H.
1990   Variation in Lithic Assemblages: An Experiment. *Journal of Field Archaeology*
        17:187–193.
1993   A Geoarchaeological Approach to the Analysis of Secondary Lithic Deposits.
        Geoarchaeology 8:59–72.

Shott, M. J.

1986   Technological Organization and Settlement Mobility: An Ethnographic Exami-
           nation. *Journal of Anthropological Research* 42:15–51.

1989   Bipolar Industries: Ethnographic Evidence and Archaeological Implications.
           North American Archaeologist 10:1–24.

1993   *The Leavitt Site: A Parkhill Phase Paleo-Indian Occupation in Central Michigan.*
           University of Michigan Museum of Anthropology, Memoirs No. 25. Ann Arbor,
           Michigan.

1994   Size and Form in the Analysis of Flake Debris: Review and Recent Approaches.
           Journal of Archaeological Method and Theory 1:69–110.

1996a   Stage Versus Continuum in the Debris Assemblage from Production of a Fluted
           Biface. *Lithic Technology* 21:6–22.

1996b   An Exegesis of the Curation Concept. *Journal of Anthropological Research*
           52:259–280.

1997   Lithic Reduction at 13HA365, a Middle Woodland Occupation in Hardin
           County. *Journal of the Iowa Archaeological Society* 44:109–120.

Siegel, P. E.

1984   Functional Variability Within an Assemblage of Endscrapers. *Lithic Technology*
           13(2):35–51.

Sievert, A. K.

1992   *Maya Ceremonial Specialization: Lithic Tools from the Sacred Cenote at Chichen
           Itza, Yucatan.* Prehistory Press, Madison, Wisconsin.

Skelton, D. W.

1977   *Archeological Investigations at the Fayette Power Project Fayette County, Texas.* Re-
           search Report No. 60. Texas Archeological Survey. University of Texas, Austin.

Solecki, R. S.

1950   A Preliminary Report of an Archaeological Reconnaissance of the Kukpowruk
           and Kokolik Rivers in Northwest Alaska. *American Antiquity* 16:66–69.

1996   Prismatic Core Sites on the Kukpowruk and Kugururuk Rivers. In *American
           Beginnings: The Prehistory and Paleoecology of Beringia,* edited by F. H. West,
           pp. 513–524. University of Chicago Press, Chicago, Illinois.

Sollberger, J. B., and L. W. Patterson

1976   Prismatic Blade Replication. *American Antiquity* 41:517–531.

Spafford, J. G.

1991   Artifact Distributions on Housepit Floors and Social Organization in Housepits
           at Keatley Creek. Master's thesis, Department of Archaeology, Simon Fraser Uni-
           versity, Burnaby, British Columbia.

Spielmann, K. A., M. J. Schoeninger, and K. Moore

1990   Plains-Pueblo Interdependence and Human Diet at Pecos Pueblo, New Mexico.
           American Antiquity 55:745–765.

Stafford, B.

1980   Prehistoric Manufacture and Utilization of Lithics from Corduroy Creek. In
           Studies in the Prehistory of the Forestdale Region, Arizona, edited by C. R. Stafford
           and G. E. Rice, pp. 251–297. Anthropological Field Studies No. 1. Arizona State
           University, Tempe.

Stahle, D. W., and J. E. Dunn

1982   An Analysis and Application of the Size Distribution of Waste Flakes from the
           Manufacture of Bifacial Tools. *World Archaeology* 14:84–97.

1984 *An Experimental Analysis of the Size Distribution of Waste Flakes from Bifacial Reduction.* Technical Paper No. 2. Arkansas Archaeological Survey, Fayetteville.

Stanford, D. J.
1979 Bison Kill by Ice Age Hunters. *National Geographic* 155(1):114–121.

Stanford, D. J., and F. Broilo
1981 Frank's Folsom Campsite. *The Artifact* 19:1–11.

Steffen, A., E. J. Skinner, and P. W. Ainsworth
1998 A View to the Core: Technological Units and Debitage Analysis. In *Unit Issues in Archaeology,* edited by A. F. Ramenofsky and A. Steffen, pp. 131–146. The University of Utah Press, Salt Lake City.

Stegner, W.
1954 *Beyond the Hundredth Meridian: John Wesley Powell and the Second Opening of the West.* Penguin Books, New York.

Stephen, A. M.
1936 *Hopi Journal of Alexander M. Stephen.* Columbia University Press, New York.

Stephenson, R. L.
1970 Archeological Investigations in the Whitney Reservoir Area, Central Texas. *Bulletin of the Texas Archeological Society* 41:37–286.

Stevenson, M. C.
1904 *The Zuñi Indians: Their Mythology, Esoteric Fraternities, and Ceremonies.* Twenty- third Annual Report of the Bureau of American Ethnology. U.S. Government Printing Office, Washington, D.C.

Studer, F. V.
1934 Texas Panhandle Culture Ruin No. 55. *Bulletin of the Texas Archeological and Paleontological Society* 6:80–96.

Suhm, D. A.
1957 Excavations at the Smith Rockshelter, Travis County, Texas. *The Texas Journal of Science* 9(1):26–58.

Sullivan III, A. P.
1986 *Prehistory of the Upper Basin.* Arizona State Museum Archaeological Series No. 167. University of Arizona, Tucson.

1987 Probing the Sources of Variability: A Regional Case Study near Homolovi Ruins, Arizona. *North American Archaeologist* 8(1):41–71.

1992 Pinyon Nuts and Other Wild Resources in Western Anasazi Subsistence Economies. In *Long-Term Subsistence Change in Prehistoric North America,* edited by D. R. Croes, R. A. Hawkins, and B. L. Isaac, pp. 195–240. JAI Press, Greenwich, Connecticut.

1995 Artifact Scatters and Subsistence Organization. *Journal of Field Archaeology* 22:49–64.

1996 Risk, Anthropogenic Environments, and Western Anasazi Subsistence. In *Evolving Complexity and Environmental Risk in the Prehistoric Southwest,* edited by J. A. Tainter and B. B. Tainter, pp. 145–167. Addison-Wesley, Reading, Massachusetts.

1997 Theoretical Implications of Regional Variation in Prehistoric Puebloan Subsistence and Settlement at Grand Canyon. Paper presented at the 62nd Annual Meeting of the Society for American Archaeology, Nashville, Tennessee.

Sullivan III, A. P. (editor)
1998 *Surface Archaeology.* University of New Mexico Press, Albuquerque.

Sullivan III, A. P., R. A. Cook, and M. P. Purtill

2001   Formation Histories of Unprecedented Archaeological Phenomena: Lessons
        from Grand Canyon's Fire-Cracked-Rock Piles. In *Archaeological Investigations
        of Once-Hot Rocks: Archaeological, Ethnographic, Experimental, and Theoretical
        Perspectives,* edited by A. V. Thoms and J. Leach. BAR International Series.
        British Archaeological Reports, Oxford, UK. In press.

Sullivan III, A. P., and K. C. Rozen

1985   Debitage Analysis and Archaeological Interpretation. *American Antiquity*
        50:755–779.

Swanton, J. R.

1942   *Source Material on the History and Ethnology of the Caddo Indians.* Bureau of
        American Ethnology, Bulletin No. 132. Washington, D.C.

Teltser, P. A.

1991   Generalized Core Technology and Tool Use: A Mississippian Example. *Journal of
        Field Archaeology* 18:363–375.

Thacker, P. T.

1996   Hunter-Gatherer Lithic Economy and Settlement Systems: Understanding
        Regional Assemblage Variability in the Upper Paleolithic of Portuguese
        Estremadura. In *Stone Tools: Theoretical Insights into Human Prehistory,*
        edited by G. H. Odell, pp. 101–124. Plenum Press, New York.

Thomas, D. H.

1970   Archaeology's Operational Imperative: Great Basin Projectile Points as a Test
        Case. University of California, Department of Anthropology. *Archaeological
        Survey, Annual Report* 12:28–60.

1976   *Figuring Anthropology.* Holt, Rinehart and Winston, New York.

1986   Contemporary Hunter-Gatherer Archaeology in America. In *American Archae-
        ology Past and Present,* edited by D. J. Meltzer, D. D. Fowler, and J. A. Sabloff,
        pp. 237–256. Smithsonian Institution Press, Washington, D.C.

Titmus, G.

1985   Some Aspects of Stone Tool Notching. In *Stone Tool Analysis: Essays in Honor of
        Don E. Crabtree,* edited by M. G. Plew and M. G. Pavesic, pp. 243–264. University
        of New Mexico Press, Albuquerque.

Tomka, S. A.

1989   Differentiating Lithic Reduction Techniques: An Experimental Approach. In
        Experiments in Lithic Technology, edited by D. S. Amick and R. P. Mauldin,
        pp. 137–162. BAR International Series 528. British Archaeological Reports,
        Oxford, UK.

Torrence, R.

1983   Time Budgeting and Hunter-Gatherer Technology. In *Hunter-Gatherer Economy
        in Prehistory,* edited by G. N. Bailey, pp. 11–22. Cambridge University Press,
        Cambridge, UK.

1989a   *Time, Energy, and Stone Tools.* Cambridge University Press, Cambridge, UK.

1989b   Tools as Optimal Solutions. In *Time, Energy, and Stone Tools,* edited by R.
        Torrence, pp. 1–6. Cambridge University Press, Cambridge, UK.

1994   Strategies for Moving on in Lithic Studies. In *The Organization of North
        American Chipped Stone Tool Technologies,* edited by P. J. Carr, pp. 123–131.
        International Monographs in Prehistory Archaeological Series 7, Ann Arbor,
        Michigan.

Tsirk, A.
1979   Regarding Fracture Initiations. In *Lithic Use-Wear Analysis,* edited by B. Hayden, pp. 89–96. Academic Press, New York.

Turner, E. S., and T. R. Hester
1993   *A Field Guide to Stone Artifacts of Texas Indians.* 2d edition. Texas Monthly Field Guide Series, Gulf Publishing Co., Houston.

Von Krogh, G. H.
1977   Preliminary Report on Three Archaeological Sites in the Central Brooks Range, Alaska. In *Sagavanirktok Early Man Project,* edited by H. L. Alexander. Department of Anthropology, Simon Fraser University, Occasional Publications No. 4. Vancouver, British Columbia.

Voorrips, A.
1982   Manbrino's Helmet: A Framework for Structuring Archaeological Data. In *Essays in Archaeological Typology,* edited by R. Whallon and J. A. Brown, pp. 93–126. Center for American Archaeology Press, Evanston, Illinois.

Wahrhaftig, C.
1965   *Physiographic Divisions of Alaska.* United States Geological Survey Professional Paper 482. Washington, D.C.

Walker, P. L.
1978   Butchering and Stone Tool Function. *American Antiquity* 43:710–715.

Walker, P. L., and J. C. Long
1977   An Experimental Study of the Morphological Characteristics of Tool Marks. *American Antiquity* 42:605–616.

Walker, W. H.
1995   Ceremonial Trash? In *Expanding Archaeology,* edited by J. M. Skibo, W. H. Walker, and A. E. Nielsen, pp. 67–79. University of Utah Press, Salt Lake City.

Wandsnider, L.
1998   Regional Scale Processes and Archaeological Landscape Units. In *Unit Issues in Archaeology,* edited by A. F. Ramenofsky and A. Steffen, pp. 87–102. University of Utah Press, Salt Lake City.

Waters, M.
1992   *Principles of Geoarchaeology.* University of Arizona, Tucson.

Watson, C. E.
1959   Climate of Alaska. In *Climates of the States, U.S. Weather Bureau, Climatography U.S.,* pp. 60–69. Washington, D.C.

Wedel, W. R.
1970   Antler Tine Scraper Handles in the Central Plains. *Plains Anthropologist* 15(47):36–45.

White, L. A.
1932   *The Acoma Indians.* 47th Annual Report of the Bureau of American Ethnology. U.S. Government Printing Office, Washington, D.C.

Whitlam, R.
1980   *Archaeological Investigations at Cache Creek (EeRh 3).* Occasional Papers of the Heritage Conservation Branch No. 5, Victoria.

Whittaker, J. C.
1984   *Arrowheads and Artisans: Stone Tool Manufacture and Individual Variation at Grasshopper Pueblo.* Ph.D. dissertation, University of Arizona. University Microfilms, Ann Arbor, Michigan.

1987a   Individual Variation as an Approach to Economic Organization: Projectile
         Points at Grasshopper Pueblo, Arizona. *Journal of Field Archaeology* 14:465–480.
1987b   Making Arrowpoints in a Prehistoric Pueblo. *Lithic Technology* 16:1–12.
1994   *Flintknapping: Making and Understanding Stone Tools*. University of Texas Press,
         Austin.

Whittaker, J. C., and M. Stafford
1999   Replicas, Fakes, and Art: The Twentieth Century Stone Age and Its Effects on
         Archaeology. *American Antiquity* 64:203–214.

Wilke, P. J., J. J. Flenniken, and T. L. Ozbun
1991   Clovis Technology at the Anzick Site, Montana. *Journal of California and Great
         Basin Anthropology* 13:242–272.

Wilmsen, E. S., and F. H. H. Roberts
1978   *Lindenmeier, 1934–1974, Concluding Report on Investigations*. Smithsonian Con-
         tributions to Anthropology No. 24. Washington, D.C.

Wise, K.
1990   Late Archaic Period Maritime Subsistence Strategies in the South-Central An-
         des. Unpublished Ph.D. dissertation, Department of Anthropology, Northwest-
         ern University, Champagne-Urbana, Illinois.
1997   The Late Archaic Period Occupation at Carrizal, Peru. *Contributions in Science*
         467:1–16. Los Angeles County Museum of Natural History.

Wise, K., N. R. Clark, and S. R. Williams
1994   A Late Archaic Period Burial from the South-Central Andean Coast. *Latin Amer-
         ican Antiquity* 5:212–227.

Wyatt, D.
1970   Microblade Attribute Patterning: A Statistical Examination. *Arctic Anthropology*
         7:97–105.

Yerkes, R.W.
1987   *Prehistoric Life on the Mississippi Flood-Plain: Stone Tool Use, Settlement Organi-
         zation, and Subsistence Practices at the Labras Lake Site, Illinois*. University of
         Chicago Press, Illinois.

Yerkes, R. W., and P. N. Kardulias
1993   Recent Developments in the Analysis of Lithic Artifacts. *Journal of Archaeological
         Research* 1:89–119.

Young, D. E., and R. Bonnichsen
1984   *Understanding Stone Tools: A Cognitive Approach*. University of Maine, Orono.

Young, L. C.
1994   Lithics and Adaptive Diversity: An Examination of Limited-Activity Sites in
         Northeast Arizona. *Journal of Anthropological Research* 50:141–154.

Zedeño, M. N.
1994   *Sourcing Prehistoric Ceramics at Chodistaas Pueblo, Arizona: The Circulation of
         People and Pots in the Grasshopper Region*. Anthropological Papers No. 58. Uni-
         versity of Arizona Press, Tucson.

Zingg, T.
1935   Beitrage zur Schatteranaylse. *Schweizerische Mineralogische und Petrographische
         Mitteilungen* 15:39–140.

Contributors

William Andrefsky Jr.
Department of Anthropology
Washington State University
Pullman, Washington

Andrew P. Bradbury
Cultural Resource Analysts, Inc.
Lexington, Kentucky

Philip J. Carr
Department of Sociology and Anthropology
University of South Alabama
Mobile, Alabama

Jay K. Johnson
Department of Sociology and Anthropology
University of Mississippi
Oxford, Mississippi

Eric J. Kaldahl
Department of Anthropology
University of Arizona
Tucson, Arizona

Martin P. R. Magne
Western Canada Service Centre
Parks Canada
Calgary, Alberta

Albert M. Pecora
Department of Anthropology
Ohio State University
Columbus, Ohio

William C. Prentiss
Department of Anthropology
University of Montana
Missoula, Montana

Jeffrey Rasic
Department of Anthropology
Washington State University
Pullman, Washington

Phillip H. Shelley
Department of Anthropology
Eastern New Mexico University
Portales, New Mexico

April K. Sievert
Department of Sociology and Anthropology
Shippensburg University
Shippensburg, Pennsylvania

Alan P. Sullivan III
Department of Anthropology
University of Cincinnati
Cincinnati, Ohio

Steve A. Tomka
Center for Archaeological Research
San Antonio, Texas

Kristen E. Wenzel
Mercyhurst Archaeological Institute
Erie, Pennsylvania

John Whittaker
Department of Anthropology
Grinnell College
Grinnell, Iowa

Karen Wise
Los Angeles County Museum of Natural History
Los Angeles, California

Index

Acoma Pueblo, 58

Adams, K. E., 116

aggregate analysis, of debitage, 3–6, 9, 12, 13

Ahler, S. A., 3, 4, 5, 6, 7, 15, 24, 128, 132, 174, 195

Alaska: and Arctic Small Tool Tradition, 106–23; and blade cores in mobile tool-kits, 61–78. *See also* Arctic

Aldenderfer, 103

Alyeska Pipeline Project, 108

American Antiquity (journal), 18

American Paleo-Arctic Tradition, 66

Amick, D. S., 2, 5, 8, 11, 19, 21, 23, 172, 196

Ammerman, A. J., 3, 5, 8

Anaktuvuk Pass (Alaska), 150

analytical core unit (ACU), 142, 143–45, 146

analytic theory, and lithic analysis, 128, 129

Anangula site (Alaska), 121

Anderson, D. D., 63, 64, 108, 110

Anderson, R., 211

andesite, 100. *See also* raw materials

Andrefsky, W., Jr., 3, 6, 8, 9, 10, 11, 13, 16, 18, 19, 22, 26, 62, 63, 76, 86, 107, 113, 115, 134, 194, 195

Antelope Creek phase (Texas), 214

antler tools, 39–41, 123. *See also* bone tools

application load typologies, 6

archaeological context, of midden at Grasshopper Pueblo (Arizona), 33–36

Archaic period: and fishing village site on Andean coast, 82–83, 84, 98, 102, 103, 104, 105; and Martin Justice site (Kentucky), 184

Arctic: and lithic raw materials, 106–23; and seasonal variations in resource availability, 78

Arizona: and Bailey Ruin site, 54; and Hay Hollow Valley and Silver Creek sites, 51; and Upper Basin Archaeological Research Project, *198*, *199*, *200*. *See also* Grasshopper Pueblo

assemblage population, and attribute analysis, 11–12

Atigun River Valley (Alaska), 108

attribute analysis, of debitage, 9–12, 13, 195

Austin, R. J., 147

Austin phase (Texas), 220, 221

Bailey Ruin (Arizona), 54

Bamforth, D. B., 87, 176, 223

basalt, 100, 166. *See also* raw materials

Baugh, S. T., 217

Baumler, M. F., 8, 147, 172

Becher, M. E., 202

behavioral interpretations, and typological analysis, 6, 8

Bell, R. E., 214

Bielwaski, E., 107

bifaces: and coastal technology in Peru, *96*; and core technologies in Alaska, 70, 72, 74–78; definition of, 63; distribution of in Grasshopper Pueblo (Arizona) middens, 35, 41–46, 55–56, 57, 60; flake debris analysis and production of, 137–38; and knives, 217–19; mobility and reduction strategies, 208; reduction of and reliability analysis, 150

Binford, L. R., 63, 64, 66, 77, 126, 150, 173, 174, 175, 176, 181, 184

bipolar technique, and Kilometer 4 site on Andean coast, 91–92

Bird, J., 83

bison, 212, 215, 217, 219, 222. *See also* hunting

Black, S. L., 215, 216